Imagining Asia in the Americas

Asian American Studies Today

This series publishes scholarship on cutting-edge themes and issues, including broadly based histories of both long-standing and more recent immigrant populations; focused investigations of ethnic enclaves and understudied subgroups; and examinations of relationships among various cultural, regional, and socioeconomic communities. Of particular interest are subject areas in need of further critical inquiry, including transnationalism, globalization, homeland polity, and other pertinent topics.

Series Editor: Huping Ling, Truman State University

Stephanie Hinnershitz, *Race, Religion, and Civil Rights: Asian Students on the West Coast, 1900–1968*

Jennifer Ann Ho, *Racial Ambiguity in Asian American Culture*

Haiming Liu, *From Canton Restaurant to Panda Express: A History of Chinese Food in the United States*

Jun Okada, *Making Asian American Film and Video: History, Institutions, Movements*

Kim Park Nelson, *Invisible Asians: Korean American Adoptees, Asian American Experiences, and Racial Exceptionalism*

Zelideth María Rivas and Debbie Lee-DiStefano, eds., *Imagining Asia in the Americas*

David S. Roh, Betsy Huang, and Greta A. Niu, eds., *Techno-Orientalism: Imagining Asia in Speculative Fiction, History, and Media*

Imagining Asia in the Americas

EDITED BY
ZELIDETH MARÍA RIVAS
AND DEBBIE LEE-DISTEFANO

RUTGERS UNIVERSITY PRESS
NEW BRUNSWICK, NEW JERSEY, AND LONDON

Library of Congress Cataloging-in-Publication Data
Names: Rivas, Zelideth María, 1979– | Lee-DiStefano, Debbie.
Title: Imagining Asia in the Americas /
edited by Zelideth María Rivas and Debbie Lee-DiStefano.
Description: New Brunswick, New Jersey : Rutgers University Press, 2016. | Series: Asian American studies today | Includes bibliographical references and index.
Identifiers: LCCN 2015047307| ISBN 9780813585215 (hardcover : alkaline paper) | ISBN 9780813585208 (paperback : alkaline paper) | ISBN 9780813585222 (ePub) | ISBN 9780813585239 (Web PDF)
Subjects: LCSH: Asia—Relations—America. | America—Relations—Asia. | Asia—Foreign public opinion, American. | Asia—Foreign public opinion, Caribbean. | Asia—Foreign public opinion, Latin American. | Public opinion—America. | Asians—America—Social conditions. | Immigrants—America—Social conditions. | Transnationalism—Social aspects—America. | Community life—America.
Classification: LCC DS33.4.A45 I47 2016 | DDC 303.48/25097—dc23
LC record available at http://lccn.loc.gov/2015047307

A British Cataloging-in-Publication record for this book is available from the British Library.

Visit our website: http://rutgerspress.rutgers.edu

Manufactured in the United States of America

CONTENTS

ACKNOWLEDGMENTS

On November 4, 2011, we sat at a pho restaurant after a conference with Roshni Rustomji-Kerns and Alejandro Lee, lamenting the fact that our panels on Asians in Latin America were sparsely attended. Instead of feeling discouraged, we thought how wonderful it would be to host our own conference that highlighted the intersections of Asian, Latin American, and Asian American Studies. In 2012, under Debbie's guidance, Southeast Missouri State University hosted the first symposium of Asians in the Americas with Karen Tei Yamashita as the keynote speaker. The symposium continued the next year in 2013 at Pepperdine University with David Simonowitz as the organizer and Ann Kaneko as the keynote speaker. In 2014, the symposium grew larger, coming to Rutgers University through Kathleen López featuring Curtis Chin, Konrad Aderer, Lisa Yun, and Gaiutra Bahadur. Finally, in 2015, the symposium was held at La Salle University through the organization of Luisa Ossa with a guest lecture by Melanie Herzog. These symposia would not have been possible without the co-organizers Alejandro Lee, Rick H. Lee, Mey-Yen Moriuchi, Hsiao-Ping Hu Biehl, and Tara Carr-Lemke. This volume emerged from these four symposia.

The editors would like to thank all the participants in these four symposia for contributing to the volume through thoughtful questions and comments after each presentation: Alejandro Lee, Junyoung Verónica Kim, Roshni Rustomji-Kerns, Ann Kaneko, León Chang Shik, Saskia Hertlein, Philip Anthony Ramirez, David Simonowitz, Juan Ishikawa, Chisu Teresa Ko, Jennifer Bengston, Martín Valadez, Anne-Marie Lee-Loy, Justina Hwang, Jungwon Park, Koichi Hagimoto, Anjoli Roy, Colin Root, Danielle Seid, Hailing Guan, Guneeta Bhalla, Kathleen López, Swati Rana, Sandra So Hee Chi Kim, James Ong, George Carlsen, Alan Tollefson, Benjamín Narváez, Julia Katz, Tao Leigh Goffe, Yeon-Soo Kim, Roanne Kantor, Anita Baksh, Kavitha Ramsamy, K. Kale Yu, Apoorva Jadhav, Sayu Bhojwani, Ana Paulina Lee, Augusto Espiritu, Maria Tham, Eric Hung, Fredy González, Elliott Young, Erika Lee, Allison E. White, Malathi M. Iyengar, Jessica M. Falcone, Nicholas Birns, Ana Maria Candela, Rosanne Sia, Lisa Yun, Andre K. Deckrow, Hsiao-Ping Hu Biehl, Jiahong Wang, Christina Lee, Mey-Yen Moriuchi, Dennis Carr, Lesley Shipley, Luisa Ossa, and Elena Valdez.

Lastly, this volume would not have been possible without the support and contributions of many people. Dania Abreu-Torres, Michelle Nasser, Bridget Christine Arce, and Kathleen López read proposal drafts. Zack Rakes tirelessly worked on the volume's bibliography. Charles DiStefano helped format figures. Marshall University College of Liberal Arts Dean Robert Bookwalter and Southeast Missouri State University Dean Francisco Barrios and Chair of the Department of Global Cultures and Languages Dr. Toni Alexander generously provided funding for permissions. And, finally, we would like to thank our families who supported us through symposia planning, hosting, and travel, all of which made this edited volume possible.

Imagining Asia in the Americas

Introduction

DEBBIE LEE-DISTEFANO

In 1999, Roshni Rustomji-Kerns, along with her coeditors Rajini Srikanth and Leny Mendoza Strobel, published an anthology that would interpolate onto the academic world a seemingly incongruent topic: Asians in the Americas. Indeed, the anthology *Encounters: People of Asian Descent in the Americas* brought not a collection of scholarly essays professing to delve into the many facets of what it means to be Asian in the Americas; instead it brought the lives, stories, poems, voices, and memories of citizens of this hemisphere from every Asiatic background and ethnic combination imaginable. It offered the world a glimpse into the complexities that migration, immigration, nation-state, citizenry, diaspora, transnational and geopolitical policies play in the day-to-day lives of people of Asian descent who have connections to this American hemisphere.

Roshni, by her own admission in the anthology, was looking to answer questions particularly regarding "how different people from Asia in different areas of the Americas (from different classes, genders, generations, length of residence in the Americas, place of birth, and similar factors) define Asia for themselves and for the communities they live in, and how they describe their connections or lack of connections to Asia, and recognize their own roles and the role of Asia in the Americas."[1] She was striving to uncover the "negotiating and renegotiating of relationships, spaces, and places."[2] This anthology differed from previous research because it brought to the academic forefront the lives of everyday people who were experiencing what it meant to be Asian in the Americas. Roshni points to the necessity to hear such experiences by stating that the "multiple, often fluid and overlapping locations that appear . . . involve families, communities, countries, and the imagination."[3] The anthology achieved what the traditional scholarly approach could not: it humanized the subjects and gave voice to the everyday people whose everyday lives are affected by the fact that they are of Asian descent and reside somewhere in the Americas. The emotion presented to the reader is palpable, the questions of identity very real and poignant. The reader is removed from the realm of theory and possibilities and placed squarely in front of the reality of subjects who are simply striving to understand their place in this hemisphere.

There are many questions one must attempt to answer when engaging with this topic, the first of which is: Who is Asian in the Americas and what does that mean exactly? These seemingly simple, straightforward questions bring to the forefront some concerns that speak to the historical challenges one faces when traditional bodies of knowledge are confronted with reality, particularly in regards to the definitions of America and Asia and how those terms have been historically juxtaposed and united. To begin, the inclusion of the entire hemisphere or "America" as a single entity is oftentimes seen as problematic. The desire to separate the United States from every other context is based on many factors that have imbued in them centuries of United States' dominance in the hemisphere as well as the boundaries of nation, language, and culture; these factors, while purported to be inherent, are indeed manmade constructs that are remnants of colonial and neocolonial dominance. The idea of Asia is equally problematic given that Asia is not an enclosed space with a singular cultural identity. It holds within its somewhat fluid borders a multiplicity of ethnicities, languages, cultures, and histories that also bear the mark of thousands of years of colonial intrusion.

To be sure, Asian immigration, not counting the original migration across the Bering Strait millennia ago, has been a constant since the time of Columbus, which is where the point of juncture begins and we employ the term *America* coined by Américo Vespucci. Indeed, the Manila-Acapulco Galleon Trade (1565–1815) initiated contact and exchanges between Asia and Latin America that would be constant into the modern day. And yet, there are issues that arise when *Asian* and *American* are employed together. The referent seems to refer historically to the US context, whereas in reality, Asian immigrants settled throughout the entire hemisphere, primarily in the Caribbean and South America, long before there was a significant Asian presence in the United States. However, the terms are perceived as referring to the US English-speaking context, separating it from the English-, Spanish-, or Portuguese-speaking experiences south of the United States. A further complication is that the field of Latin American studies has also overlooked the Asian presence. Traditionally the Latin American ethnic landscape has been comprised of Africans, Amerindians, and Europeans. Their histories have dominated when questions arise regarding ethnicity and its role in the inclusion or exclusion of groups in national processes, nationhood, and citizenry. Indeed, people of varying Asian descents have remained a footnote in the annals of history, regardless of the fact they have been prominent citizens (writers, painters, presidents, philosophers, etc.) and have contributed greatly to the shaping of the ethnic, cultural, and political trajectories in the Americas.

Many scholars both before and after *Encounters* have dedicated their academic careers to bringing to light the hidden or eclipsed past of Asians of varying descents in the Americas. Evelyn Hu-DeHart, Lane Ryo Hirabayashi, Gary Okihiro, Jeffrey Lesser, Kathleen López, and Ignacio López-Calvo are but a few who have sought to undo this exclusion.[4] Their numerous monographs and articles openly interrogate the histories, cultures, literatures, and national discourses of countries from both Americas. Hu-DeHart's groundbreaking research regarding the Chinese coolie trade interjected into Latin American studies the Chinese element, noting with great care and precision the history and contributions of the Chinese who, like their counterparts in the United States, were a driving force behind the development of their communities. Lesser's research had the same effect by bringing in the Japanese element, particularly in the case of Brazil. Ignacio López-Calvo's most recent publications explore the literary representations of identity of Peruvians of Chinese and Japanese descent. Numerous scholars have continued the project that scholars such as these started so many years ago. The field expands as scholars begin to theoretically engage the terminology and the systems of power that lie at the heart of these erasures.

In order to adjust the histories so that they are more inclusive, it is necessary to look beyond the traditional methods that separate the continents and approach them as a single entity in exchange for a comparative approach that allows for individual histories to exist alongside a more comprehensive look at the systems that keep people of Asian descent on the peripheries and in the shadows of national inclusion. One need only to remember Benedict Anderson's pivotal text *Imagined Communities* to realize that imagined communities are abundant in both the center and the margin.[5] While the individual communities envision themselves in the greater context of belonging to their respective nations, the power of hegemony removes this option from them. Asian immigrants, regardless of their longevity, permanence, or contributions, are often placed in the category of perpetual foreigner. This removal is twofold when their histories are erased or eclipsed because they are not from the United States.

An approach that focuses on comparisons and intersections of experiences acknowledges that the process of exclusion is the same in the contexts of both North and South America. One can learn from and advance the understanding of these processes by looking at the experiences of Asians in the Americas, from Alaska to Patagonia. Indeed, many scholars in diaspora studies agree that this approach would be very worthwhile. Sukanya Banerjee in the collection *New Routes in Diaspora Studies* proposes a very similar approach by stating, "It is imperative that we braid together a study of diaspora that remains sensitive to the multiplicity of global histories and movements, with an examination of the evolving incarnations of *diaspora* and awareness of the concerns and filters that must attend its study."[6] Banerjee also contends that this will require the inclusion of several disciplines: "And a significant part of the scholarly responsibility in 'routing' diasporas lies in the entwining—routing together—of different disciplinary approaches in ways that yield new possibilities of analysis while remaining sensitive . . . to diaspora as experience, practice, analytical category, and metaphor."[7] Finally, Banerjee cautions the scholar by warning that focusing on the diasporic experience as a singular isolated entity with particular dynamics can trap the investigation: "By identifying complex configurations and hybrid networks as elements of a particular diaspora, we run the risk of reifying the relationship between those elements and their purported 'home' or 'point of origin.'"[8] This comparative approach lessens the rigidity that has been created by the separations discussed earlier and provides a space for meaningful dialogue regarding experiences across cultural/linguistic/national borders.

The experiences of diaspora and that of the transnational, while not always viewed as the same, are quite similar. Both involve migration and entry into a receiving country/culture that is most probably quite dissimilar to their own. However, academic definitions and approaches tend to be slow in adjusting to the complex structures that are being created in our ever-increasing global society. May Friedman and Silvia Schultermandl express this same concern in *Growing Up Transnational: Identity and Kinship in a Global Era*. They state that the "contemporary globalization has rendered a presumption of fixity an antiquated and outmoded line of enquiry."[9] Migration in the twenty-first century bears little resemblance to that a century ago. Questions of time and space have changed drastically when one considers that the various waves of migration emerge from differing temporal and geographic points of intersection. As Kim Butler states:

> Diversity within diasporas is often posited geo-historically, because dispersed communities have resettled and followed distinct, yet interlinked trajectories. In other words, we think of the constituent segments of a diaspora as location A, B, C, and so on. While this is an appropriate mapping approach for certain research questions, it does not capture the complexity of overlapping waves of diaspora arrivals or remigrations that bring branches of the diaspora together in one location.[10]

This complex nature requires that we add a comparative element to our research when we are discussing the experiences of the transnational, primarily when engaging in questions of identity, nation, citizenship, alienation, and marginalization. It is no longer a question of point A to point B but rather a plethora of journeys that cross and intertwine never before considered fixed borders, ethnic identities, and national affiliations, linking them together in ever-increasingly interesting combinations. By comparing experiences one can begin to examine the systems that work against the transnationals and diasporic subjects as they negotiate ideas of national inclusion and strive to see themselves represented in their new home. Seyla Benhabib and Judith Resnick in the introduction to *Migrations and Mobilities: Citizenship, Borders and Gender* remark:

> [W]e must also look at the center/margin, those with access to the state and legal rights and protections and those who don't. We also have what they call commuters, those who go back and forth, building ties to more than one place. Migrations are about immigrants and emigrants. Citizenship is a legal, a cultural, and an economic relationship, official recognition of a relationship between the individual and the state.[11]

It is this very relationship that begs for a comparative approach. The multiplicity of connections that are common these days render many approaches difficult or impossible. Groupings by any dichotomies become problematic because they exclude mention of the experiences of other groupings. How can Japanese Americans from the United States and their experiences with the state and inclusion in the national framework differ from Chinese Americans from the United States or Peru or Cuba? How can those of South Asians in the Bahamas be that different from those of Lebanese Americans in the United States? In short, if the goal is to explore, expose, and expel processes that exclude people of Asian descent from full participation and enfranchisement in their respective American communities, a comparative approach is better suited and more effective. It reveals the systemic nature of hegemony, regardless of border, language, and culture, and the abuse it has caused and continues to perpetrate on Asians in this hemisphere. The encounters, to use Roshni's term, are what matters and where we learn the realities that have been created by age-old processes that hark back to colonialism. The encounters between subject and system are where meaning can be unraveled and reconstituted to represent the totality of the society in which these subjects reside. The idea is not to forget individual histories nor stop researching them; it is a call to see the totality of a whole constituted by these many parts, a puzzle that we painstakingly put together.

Let us fast forward to 2012. Debbie Lee-DiStefano, with financial support from Southeast Missouri State University, hosted the first Asians in the Americas Symposium. The goal of the symposium was to encourage this comparative approach, to bring together scholars whose primary research was any aspect of Asians in the Americas; the plenary topics ranged from socio-historical perspectives to literary analyses to theoretical queries regarding how this field was similar to and different from other academic topics regarding the idea of Asia and America. The symposium's resounding success engendered three future symposia, hosted by David Simonowitz at Pepperdine University in 2013, Kathleen López at Rutgers University in 2014, and Luisa Ossa at LaSalle University in 2015. Each year brought more plenary speakers and expanded the discussion regarding the complexities of how Asia and America are a synergetic duo that has created transnational migration and subsequent generations whose identities are oftentimes caught in limbo.

The essays in this collection are representative of the ideas brought forward at the symposia. The papers are grouped by topic, accompanied by introductions in which Kathleen López makes expert observations regarding the historical, artistic, and social significance of each topic. She guides the collection through what we call the "post *Encounters*" phase. She demonstrates how the phrase "Asians in the Americas" takes on new dimensions as each author's approach reveals yet another aspect of the condition of what it means to be Asian and American. The reader will realize that perhaps the definition that s/he started with will be challenged on occasion. Western discourse and learning models have dictated to us certain bodies of knowledge that this collection will challenge. This collection is not expected to be a complete body of literature regarding the Asian American experience. Rather, it serves as an academic testament to the many people whose identities, realities, literatures, and histories have not been given a voice; the hope is that this collection serves as an impetus to continue the discussion. Decades after the publication of *Encounters* we are still encountering and still moving forward, uncovering, unearthing the past with the hopes of establishing an equal presence for Asians in the Americas.

NOTES

1. Roshni Rustomji-Kerns, Rajini Srikanth, and Leny Mendoza Strobel, eds., *Encounters: People of Asian Descent in the Americas* (Lanham, Md.: Rowman & Littlefield, 1999), xvi–xvii.
2. Ibid., 7.
3. Ibid.
4. For examples, see Evelyn Hu-DeHart, *Across the Pacific: Asian Americans and Globalization* (Philadelphia: Temple University Press, 1999); Lane Ryo Hirabayashi, Akemi Kikumura-Yano, and James A. Hirabayashi, eds., *New Worlds, New Lives: Globalization and People of Japanese Descent in the Americas and from Latin America in Japan* (Stanford, Calif.: Stanford University Press, 2002); Lane Ryo Hirabayashi, *The Politics of Fieldwork: Research in an American Concentration Camp* (Tucson: University of Arizona Press, 1999); Gary Y. Okihiro, *Common Ground: Reimagining American History* (Princeton: Princeton University Press, 2001); Gary Y Ohikiro, *Cane Fires: The Anti-Japanese Movement in Hawaii, 1865–1945* (Philadelphia: Temple University Press, 1991); Gary Y. Okihiro, *Pineapple Culture: A History of the Tropical and Temperate Zones* (Berkeley: University of California Press, 2009); Jeffrey Lesser, *Negotiating National Identity: Immigrants, Minorities, and the Struggle for Ethnicity in Brazil* (Durham, N.C.: Duke University Press, 1999); Jeffrey

Lesser, *A Discontented Diaspora: Japanese Brazilians and the Meanings of Ethnic Militancy, 1960–1980* (Durham, N.C.: Duke University Press, 2007); Jeffrey Lesser, ed., *Searching for Home Abroad: Japanese Brazilians and Transnationalism* (Durham, N.C.: Duke University Press, 2003); Kathleen López, *Chinese Cubans: A Transnational History* (Chapel Hill: University of North Carolina Press, 2013); Ignacio López-Calvo, ed., *Peripheral Transmodernities: South-to-South Intercultural Dialogues between the Luso-Hispanic World and 'The Orient'* (Newcastle upon Tyne: Cambridge Scholars Pub., 2012); Ignacio López-Calvo, ed., *Alternative Orientalisms in Latin America and Beyond* (Newcastle: Cambridge Scholars Pub., 2007); Ignacio López-Calvo, *Imagining the Chinese in Cuban Literature and Culture* (Gainesville: University Press of Florida, 2008); and Ignacio López-Calvo, *The Affinity of the Eye: Writing Nikkei in Peru* (Tucson: University of Arizona Press, 2013).

5. Benedict Anderson, *Imagined Communities: Reflections on the Origin and Spread of Nationalism* (New York: Verso, 1991).
6. Sukanya Bannerjee, Aims McGuinness, and Steven C. McKay, eds., *New Routes for Diaspora Studies* (Bloomington: Indiana University Press, 2012), 3.
7. Ibid.
8. Ibid., 9.
9. May Friedman and Silvia Schultermandl, ed. *Growing Up Transnational: Identity and Kinship in a Global Era* (Toronto: University of Toronto Press, 2011).
10. Kim Butler, "Multilayered Politics in the African Diaspora: The Metadiaspora and the Minidiaspora Realities," in *Opportunity Structures in Diaspora Relations: Comparisons in Contemporary Multilevel Politics of Diaspora and Transnational Identity*, ed. Gloria Totoricagüena (Reno, Nev.: Center for Basque Studies, 2007), 22.
11. Seyla Benhabib and Judith Resnick, "Introduction: Citizenship and Migration Theory Engendered," in *Migrations and Mobilities: Citizenship, Borders, and Gender*, ed. Seyla Benhabib and Judith Resnick (New York: New York University Press, 2009), 2.

PART I

Encounters

Moving Past *Encounters: People of Asian Descent in the Americas*

KATHLEEN LÓPEZ

The contributors to the anthology *Encounters* (1999) charted new territory through their exploration of Asians in the hemisphere coming into contact and conflict with, intertwining with, and leaving an imprint upon multicultural and multiethnic societies. A generation later, in-depth ethnographic case studies from Cuba, Mexico, and Argentina move beyond an exploration of encounters to theorize what the presence of Asians in the Americas means for the construction of individual and collective identities and developments in global economies and geopolitical alignment. They offer new methodologies and approaches to archival sources and invite us to move beyond national narratives based on race, ethnicity, and culture that portray Asians as insular and beyond inclusion.

While we know much about the economic and political aspects of the nineteenth-century system of Indian and Chinese indentured labor in the British, Spanish, French, and Dutch colonies, less visible are the experiences of Asians as they moved off plantations and intermixed with local populations. Reflecting on the experiences of people of African descent alongside people of Asian descent captures important points of contact and conflict within overlapping diasporic frames. Like African slaves, Asian indentured laborers protested the labor regime through resistance and rebellion, the legal system, interracial alliances, religious practices, and ethnic associations. In Cuba, where Chinese indentured labor was firmly entrenched within a plantation society based on African slavery, the paper trail diminishes as coolies and slaves moved out of bondage and off plantations. The historical archive of the Spanish colonial state often leads to silences regarding the interior lives of the formerly enslaved.

Martin A. Tsang confronts these silences head-on to examine Afro-Asian interactions in the social and spiritual realms in Cuba from the colonial period to the present day. He turns to performance and oral tradition to uncover a distinct Afro-Chinese religious practice within the Lukumi religion, which is usually categorized as "Afro-Cuban"—a designation of syncretism that subsumes and obscures a Chinese influence dating back to the nineteenth century. Although often small-scale and hidden from official view, these kinds of interracial interactions cumulatively shaped the development of Chinese communities and families in Cuba and their incorporation into a multiracial Cuban nation. Tsang's discussion with a Chinese Cuban priestess reveals that while the Chinese presence is silenced and sidelined in scholarship and official narratives, the practitioners of Lukumi take it for granted.

For some countries in the hemisphere the arrival of immigrants from Asia is a relatively new postwar phenomenon. Although Koreans were recruited to work on henequen plantations in Mexico's Yucatan Peninsula in 1905, larger numbers have been immigrating to South America since the 1980s, with a notable presence in Brazil and Argentina. Non-European immigrants in the region have generally been considered temporary and fleeting migrant streams without a permanent imprint on society. Asians in particular have been cast as the eternal "other" and remain largely outside discussions of process of *mestizaje* and Creolization in Latin America and the Caribbean. In Argentina, for example, the demographic makeup of the nation has changed over the past century through state-promoted white European immigration. The resulting myth of a white Argentina denies its indigenous and African past as well as the full participation of Asians in the present. Junyoung Verónica Kim's discussions with Koreans in Argentina highlight marginalization and negative stereotypes of Koreans as exploiters, acutely experienced by Argentinian-born people of Korean descent—citizens who may have little or no connection to South Korea or the garment industry.

Present-day geopolitics of the Americas affirms it as a contact site of globalization and intermixing of populations and raises new questions about the Asian presence. In particular, the People's Republic of China has dramatically entered the economic and diplomatic stage. Adrian H. Hearn turns the research lens on two different Chinese communities in Latin America to examine the tensions produced by the increase in Chinese entrepreneurship. In Mexico, with a longstanding Chinese minority population, the increase in Chinese manufactured imports has generated negative news media and actions toward Chinese businesses, considered a threat to national economic interests. The Chinese community in Cuba drastically declined after the 1959 socialist revolution and lost its economic vitality. Today, however, mixed descendants are experiencing a renewed interest from the Cuban government in promoting tourism within a state-controlled economy and from the Chinese government in staking a diplomatic and economic claim. Yet, as Hearn observes, in both places the Chinese and their descendants are viewed with suspicion by locals and officials.

We are reminded that from the nineteenth century onward, politically and economically inspired popular uprisings periodically turned against the Chinese, resulting in the massacres of Chinese in Peru's Cañete Valley in 1881, at Rock Springs, Wyoming, in 1885, and in Torreón, Mexico, in 1911. Anti-Chinese movements developed throughout the region, and by the 1930s, a period of global depression and populist policies, most Latin American and Caribbean nations imposed "nationalization of labor" laws to protect native-born workers. Mexico went as far as to deport Chinese merchants (and their Mexican wives) from the northern regions in which they were concentrated. What impact do developments in Asian economies and partnerships with Asian nations have on diasporic communities in the Americas today? Will Asians be accorded a positive minority role in the development of the nation, as they sometimes were in the case of Japanese in Brazil? Or will there be a reemergence of yellow peril discourse and related violence? Looking to the past, we know that these two responses are always intertwined and intersectional. While Kim and Hearn observe a reemergence of anti-Asian discourse, their studies also point to potential alternative outcomes based on productive relationships, the support of entrepreneurial activities, and genuine dialogue about community and national interests.

Related to these present-day geopolitical issues are the complexities of migrants' relationship to homeland and diaspora. Chinese indentured laborers in Latin America and the Caribbean were all but forgotten by the Qing government until international investigations exposed the atrocities of the coolie trade to Cuba and Peru. Today, however, the Chinese government takes an active role in the promotion of Chinese communities and culture overseas as one prong of a "soft power" strategy in the region, even with countries that officially recognize Taiwan. In contrast, Kim's interlocutors attest to a double marginalization as diasporic subjects who are considered a less important component of the Korean diaspora than their counterparts in the United States. This uneven treatment has fostered the development of a unique Korean Argentine identity. Their embrace of the nation is not grounded in a white European foundation, but in a more fluid and flexible one based on heterogeneity.

Above all, these essays demonstrate that alongside and in conjunction with dominant national narratives, Asians in the Americas have always been imagining communities. Theirs may be transnational and diasporic, but also localized and intertwined in a rhizomatic form with other communities.

1

Yellow Blindness in a Black-and-White Ethnoscape

Chinese Influence and Heritage in Afro-Cuban Religiosity

MARTIN A. TSANG

The conceptualization of Chinese identity in Cuba has been historically recounted in terms of an ossified and immutable discourse, and unsurprisingly, embedded within a thoroughly Orientalizing narrative. Asian, specifically Chinese subjects, whether by birth or migration, are envisioned in terms of adulterating the status quo, rather than being embraced as an integral facet of Cuban society, an impact that continues to have a foothold in the postcolonial context. Such Orientalist depictions and ascriptions of Latin American citizens, Debra Lee-DiStefano explains, mark such citizens as representations of Asia rather than the Americas.[1] In this essay, I present an ethnographic snapshot of how Afro-Cuban religions create space for Cubans, especially those of Chinese and Afro-Chinese descent, to construct personhood and communities that are based on kinship ties and ethnic heritage.

The Chinese in Cuba are similarly significant by their historical absence in literatures concerning identity making and community formation processes. I present an ethnographic snapshot that demonstrates some of the ways that Afro-Cuban religion creates space that allows Cubans to construct personhood and community as premised on kinship and ethnic heritage. These spaces challenge the ascription of Cuban bodies as simply the product of transculturation, a set of processes first laid out in Fernando Ortiz's impactful *Cuban Counterpoint: Tobacco and Sugar* (1947).[2] Transculturation describes a process of "mutual cultural fashioning" premised on blending and interaction illustrated through the *ajiaco*, a Cuban stew that blends African, European, indigenous, and Asian ingredients, the Caribbean equivalent of the melting pot analogy employed farther north.[3] Like the ajiaco, Cuban culture is an amalgam of representations and influences of its constituent parts; however, there is no precise recipe nor are the transculturative methods of mixing and making made transparent. Transculturation soon became the dominant turn in culture theory in Cuba and other parts of the Caribbean, replacing the hypothesis of movement and attainment of cultures, ostensibly from areas of high culture to those deemed lacking, indicated by the cluster of terms, such as "cultural change," "acculturation," "diffusion," and "migration, or cultural osmosis."[4] Transculturation sought to distinguish Cuba and its citizens as emerging from coloniality, as well as anchoring the nation firmly within the Atlantic rather than the Mediterranean. However, Asia and, in particular, the large number of Chinese present on the island barely feature in this constructive enterprise. In response, by focusing on what I call *sinalidad*, or Chineseness (as a counterpoint to Cubanness, *la cubanidad*), we can ascertain a deeper understanding of the legacy, presence, and role of persons of Chinese descent—both religiously and biologically, within Cuba's Lukumí religion.

Lukumí is the emic name given to the worship of *orisha*, deities brought to Cuba by enslaved and free persons from West Africa, including the Oyo, Egba, Ijesha, and Ondo, who are collectively known today as Yoruba. The orisha are known and worshiped alongside other deities, and recorded through African Christian missions operating in the area in neighboring Benin (ex-Dahomey) and Togo, as well as in Sierra Leone among Yoruba settlers. Lukumí is also known by the widely used but pejorative *Santería*, and in Spanish, as *la regla de Osha*, the rule or Osha (a contraction of orisha). The Lukumí religion contains a rich material culture and an extensive range of practices that facilitate the communication and interaction of multiple deities in the lives of adherents. Initiation, trance possession, celebrations, sacrifice, and divination are some of the articulations of worship Lukumí religiosity is renowned for, and the consecration of deities and the construction of elaborate household shrines are tangible examples of the importance that the orisha play in quotidian Cuban life. Cognate religions are found throughout the Americas; in Trinidad an analogous religion to Lukumí is known as Shango, in Brazil as Candomblé Nagô and Ketu, and Haitian Vodou includes a great deal of Nago orisha themes and practices. Accurate demographics and statistical data on the numbers of Cuban Lukumí practitioners do not exist given the antireligious stance of the state experienced on the island since the Cuban Revolution of 1959. Yet, both personal experience and a long and rich history of scholarly inquiry in these religions indicate that Lukumí and other Afro-Cuban religions are tremendously important and have garnered a very significant following, both on the island and in the wider Cuban diaspora.[5]

The Chinese, who arrived as indentured workers from the mid-nineteenth century, and their subsequent Afro-Chinese descendants have greatly impacted Afro-Cuban religions in important ways. In the pages that follow, I set the stage by first illustrating Lukumí religious formation from the perspective of a Chinese-Cuban priestess. I then discuss the nature of existing, two-dimensional representations of the Chinese in Cuba and the particular and peculiar historical articulations of racial politics that have sought to blend the yellow into the black. It is a legacy that informs the ways in which racial mixing and hybridity in Cuba have discursively followed statist promotions of an idealized and unified identity. Of importance here are the intersections of transnationalism, diasporic experience, and culture contact that have produced new religious vernaculars and expressions. I posit, therefore, that both religion and Cuban identity making have followed biracial constructions, where other ethnic groups outside of the black/Afro-Cuban and white/European dyad have been obscured and elided to fit within these parameters. The Chinese, along with other Asian and indigenous Caribbean and Latin American ethnicities, have been blanketed within the "nonwhite" category to fall under the label of "Afro," in turn removing "Afro" from being a racial descriptor to one including political definitions. Moving from indeterminate lumping is achieved by offering insight into Cuban religious practice from a different register: an inclusive communal space for the precipitation and expression of Cuba's diverse ethnic, religious, and racial assemblages.

The Lukumí religion is an excellent case in point as it provides a space wherein Afro-Chinese and Chinese-Cuban practitioners, along with Chinese material culture, are integral to its practice on the island. I conclude by offering some comments on the use of the framework interdiasporic cross-fertilization instead of syncretism as a lens for understanding the complex and often messy ways that plural diasporas interact in terms of identity, culture, and religious exchange. This study aligns with the contributions assembled in the volume to go beyond the socioeconomic, social, and labor capital interventions that have been attributed to Asian migrations and rationalized their worth in the Americas.

Hidden in Plain Sight: Meet Charo, La China Obatalá

Rosario Chen ushers me into her house, telling me to call her Charo, and we both share a laugh; as truth be told, the only name that she is really known by is "La China Obatalá."[6] Charo arrived for our meeting at her daughter's house riding in the sidecar of her daughter's motorcycle at precisely the same time as I did. She stepped out onto the sidewalk with ease, and I noticed she was wearing a beautiful white-beaded bracelet associated with her guardian orisha, Obatalá. It was an especially cold start to 2012, and Charo was full of energy and warmth, and moved with an agility and grace that defied her seventy years of age. I easily pictured her giving people half, or even a quarter of her age, a good run for their money.

Within the space of a few minutes she had greeted her extended family assembled in her daughter's house, picked up the toys her grandchildren had scattered across the floor of her orisha room, and made a huge pot of Cuban coffee on the small stove that was powered by a propane cylinder. After pouring the sweet *café* into a dozen demitasse cups and distributing them, she sat down opposite me and tells me with great aplomb how nice it is to have some time to relax, for once.

We had agreed to meet on one of the few days off from "working the religion," which is the term she used to describe her professional participation in Lukumí rituals that were conducted for others. She was staying at her daughter's house for the holidays, one of the few quiet times in the calendar of Lukumí religious events when larger ceremonies such as priesthood initiations were delayed to the New Year if possible. Typically for Cuban families, the period of time from *Nochebuena* (December 24 or Christmas Eve, the most important day for celebrating Christmas in Cuba) to the New Year is spent with family, both biological and religious. Each Lukumí household performs rites of cleaning and refreshing their orisha and ancestor shrines, and some observe the custom of paying respects to the orisha, Oduduwá, on the first day of the year. Charo's daughter's house is located in the far north of Havana, where Charo has a sizable bedroom to herself and where her own orisha and the orisha of her daughter reside. When Charo is working the religion in the city, which is more often than not, she stays in an apartment by the Malecón, the famous Havana promenade and seawall, with a fellow priestess, with whom she has a close relationship.

I had made the journey by foot to her daughter's house. I had little choice given that it was New Year's Day and both *guaguas* (buses) and *carros de diez pesos* (shared taxis) were hard to come by, especially in this part of town. Being the start of a new year, and because I am an initiated Lukumí priest, Charo automatically laid down an *estera*, a straw mat, in front of her shrine to Obatalá and performed a libation by sprinkling water onto the floor from a half gourd while I prostrated and rang Obatalá's *agogo*, his silver metal bell. Charo intoned a *moyubá*, a Lukumí invocation, and then a short *oriki*, a praise poem for Obatalá, asking her guardian orisha to bless me this coming year with "*iré owó, iré omá, iré arikú babawá*," blessings of money/prosperity, of knowledge and wisdom, and that I may be blessed to live a long and full life. Charo then lit a candle in front of her *canastillero*, the cabinet containing her orisha, and we sat down for the interview. I began by asking her to tell me about herself:

[CHARO]: Well, my name is Charo, I'm *cubana* [laughs], and I was born in Lawton but grew up in central Havana. I was born in 1943. My mother, María Juarez, was from Tenerife and she came to Cuba as a young child. My father's name was Miguel Chen. He worked on the railways and was from Canton. I have one brother, who is a Babalawo [a (male) priest of the orisha Orunla, specialist in Ifá divination]. I married at twenty-three, had three daughters, and I was widowed at the age of thirty. . . . I worked and raised my daughters by myself. They are my pride and joy and I have six grandchildren, four girls and two boys who are all healthy, thanks to Obatalá.

Charo explains that she is in demand because of her religious lineage and because of her knowledge:

I grew up in this religion, I spent my time going from one ceremony to the next. . . . I became proficient in many areas of working *santo [saint, referring to the orishas or Lukumí deities]* so that when I am called, I just get on with it. Nobody needs to tell me what to do. For example, when I get to a santo, I check that everything has been prepared, the *coco [pieces of coconut used for divination]*, the table inside the *cuarto de santo* [used to hold all the items needed during the ritual], and the orisha—I check there is nothing missing. If there is something out of place, I fix it. You need to have a good eye for detail because it is the worst thing to be in the middle of an *ocha* [priesthood initiation ceremony] and find something is missing. It interrupts the sacred moment. I am mostly called to be the *oyubona* [the second initiatory godparent who assists with all of the practical details of the initiation and whose duty it is to take care of the initiate during the weeklong process—bathing, clothing, feeding him or her]. That way, they have a Cuban oyubona alongside their godparent that brought them to Cuba. They become part of my religious family and I become part of theirs.

[MARTIN]: I want to ask how being Chinese-Cuban influences or affects the religious work that you do.

[C]: It has never been an issue, for one. I have always had respect, for my knowledge and because of my elders. The Lukumí are really mixed, like all Cubans. When we *moyubá* [invocatory prayer performed before every Lukumí rite], you will hear the names of many *egun* [ancestors], both santeros [the colloquial term for a male orisha priest] and babalawos referred to who were Chinese-Cuban, *los Chinos Lukumíses*. There was "La China" Estevez, Luisa "La China" Silvestre *Oshun Miwa*, Adela Alonso "La China" *Odú Ala*, Raúl "El Chino" *Eshubi*, "El Chino" Tanke *Iroso Di*, and José "El Chino" Poey *Oche Yekun*, to name just a few. I am sure there are more if I thought about it. These were very important priests, the architects of the religion we practice today. . . . I don't think many people consider the extent of how much the religion rests on priests that were Chinese. I am very proud of my heritage and I see it as complementing my religious life very well.

For Charo and many other Lukumí priests, their Chinese and mixed religious and blood ancestors are testaments to the understudied and misunderstood facets of the processes of negotiation and production of Lukumí religion according to racial and ethnic demarcations. Time and again, the presence of persons, ideas, and practices of Chinese origins and descent in Lukumí religion was wholly taken for granted. Charo was in fact fairly bemused as to the ways that sinalidad (Chineseness) was hardly ever acknowledged outside of a general appreciation of discernible popularized elements such as porcelain, food, and medicine. In Charo's words:

> It is not as though we can easily hide our Chineseness, I am very proud of the fact that I have Chinese blood, and that it was the Chinese, along with Africans and white people who made this religion what it is today. I suppose that the Chineseness is just a bit harder to discuss, as it is just a fact that nobody really questions and gets pushed to the side. Although, it could be a case of nobody really having investigated it before; it is hidden but right in front of your eyes!

Writing against Transculturation

Gregor Benton cautions that transculturation is weak in its ability to help us understand religious encounters for two reasons: first by the lack of focus and contribution of the Chinese in the model, and second, for a lack of understanding of specifically Chinese cultural interaction in Cuba.[7] We therefore require a different model than offered by transculturation, one that is able to detect the subtleties of cross-racial input and religious causality, if we are to adequately observe and record Chinese and Afro-Chinese persons in the Afro-Cuban religiosity and the theoretical explications for them. These works were the baseline upon which ethnic labels became increasingly reified, sidestepping the issue of creolization and hybrid turns in ethnogenesis. Cuban culture and religiosity are produced and reproduced in transcultural models by the popular macro-level trope of the ajiaco, the Caribbean equivalent of a racial melting pot.

This new way of examining both religion and its adherents brings together discourses of cultural and religious change to bear on alternative formulations of community. The considerable migration of indentured Cantonese to Cuba from the nineteenth century and their impressive influence on Afro-Cuban, Lukumí religion, is evident in a plethora of material culture, oral narratives, and performativity. The ethnic and racial implications of these influences and the validity and reach of categorizing intersectional Lukumí religion simply as "Afro-Cuban" requires attention. In this regard, I work against the specific framework of transculturation that has dominated racial identity and classification in Cuba and reverberated to affect other nation-making ideologies, highlighting its many discursive limitations and explicating its geopolitical agenda.

The term *Afro-Cuban religion* is a catch-all designation that includes several distinct religions. Slaves brought from West Africa, namely from the environs of the Bight of Benin, carried with them religious beliefs that would later grow into perceptibly Afro-Cuban forms of African deity reverence. In particular, *la regla de Ocha* (the rule of Ochá) contains a complex array of deities called orisha, deities that mediate between a distant God, Olofin/Olorun/Olodumare, and the human world, as well as ancestors and elders who are venerated. The tabling of correspondences of West African deities to Catholic saints has greatly dominated discussions of syncretism in Afro-Cuban religion and has been a feature of both acculturation and transculturation schools of thought. Ethnographers and religious specialists have compiled in great detail the matching of orisha to one or more saints, not just in Cuba, but also in Brazil, Haiti, Trinidad and Tobago, and many other places where colonialism and slavery have shaped the socio-religious fields alongside arable fields and plantations. Andrew Apter points out the "slippage" that occurs when matching African gods to saints, which ignores centuries of interethnic warfare, migration, and monarchy.[8] Such a list of syncretic correspondences takes Africa as an immutable baseline and fails to appreciate that to claim a deity as solely belonging to the Yoruba as opposed to the Ewe Fon—two of the greatest intertwined empires in South West Africa—is foolhardy, and so too are their corresponding religious pantheons in the Caribbean. Popularly syncretized with Catholic imagery, the orisha transplanted in Cuba soon became the religion synonymous with Afro-Cuban religion; however, the diversity and plurality of Afro-Atlantic religions in Cuba is sizable. An important distinction made by practitioners and believers is the separate yet associated cult of the orisha Orunmila/Ifá, whose priests are babalawo, and whose métier is divination, and the proscription of remedies for healing and spiritual, corporal, emotional, and material progression. Syncretism is a troublesome construct that, by and large, has shaped the course of discourse on plural, mobile, and shifting religious fields and practices. One of the biggest contentions to engaging syncretism lies in its reliance on religious cores and peripheries, wherein syncretism itself may subjectively create, maintain, and overcome boundaries in its own heuristics.[9] In addition to Lukumí and Ifá, there are further Afro-Cuban religious practices that have different balances of ethno-racial compositions. Given the lack of reliable statistics on the popularity of Afro-Cuban religions, the high visibility—through dress, adornment, semi-public celebrations, and so on—suggests that the constellation of Lukumí, Ifá, and other religions are germane to Cuban identity and social experiences. *Tambors*, or orisha celebrations that involve elaborate drumming and possession performances, happen daily in neighborhoods across the island, a burgeoning material economy and network of initiated priests have become known as tailors, cooks, and artisans in the service of the deities. Popular art and music are heavily laden with references to these religions, blurring the lines between secular aesthetics and religion. A cartoon series based on Afro-Cuban myths of the hare and the tortoise, created more than two decades ago, is regularly aired, resulting in successive generations of Cubans becoming familiar with Afro-Atlantic legends and growing up knowing the orisha names and Olofi, the Lukumí name for God, used in the show. In addition to Lukumí and Ifá, there are several other religions that can be named and each deserves further research on its own Asian and other ethnic compositions although these are, understandably, beyond the scope of this text. The Efik and Ékpè of the Niger Delta spawned Abakuá in Cuba, and similarly, the Bakongo/Bantu ethnic group gave rise to a system of ancestor (*mpungo*) and deity (*nkisi*) reverence, which is widely known as Palo, and further nuanced in various pathways that include Mayombe, Kimbisa, and Briyumba. Similarly, Dahomean religious traditions were transplanted to Cuba, especially in the Province of Matanzas, where a Dahomean-derived religious framework is known locally as Arará, the name deriving from the port of Arada in West Africa. The deities of the Arará are known as *foddúces*, a creolized form of the Fon gbè word for deity, *vodun*, overlapping with and corresponding to Lukumí orisha. Although many of these religious frameworks are highly concentrated in specific geographic locales, their worship has spread both globally and locally. Arará, for example is deeply connected to Matanzas, yet there are priests in the Havana and Regla regions, who along with Matanzero *fodunci* (Arará priests) equally draw and interact with people from abroad seeking initiation. The same individual similarly practices many of these religions with each person determining their involvement in any combination of the religions, often alongside Catholicism, spiritism, and growing local interest in South Asian, European, and Judaic mystic/esoteric concepts.

Chinese influence, albeit in different registers, has been ascertained in all of these Afro-Cuban religions. The term Afro-Cuba makes no Asian or indigenous connections apparent; instead Afro-European mixing has been unanimously promoted across the board of religious expressions. The orisha are discursively syncretized with Catholic saints and iconographies in a number of ways, which is evidenced in a few practices by some adherents, such as calling or referring to the orisha using Catholic saint names. Some worshipers may also have a saint statue within their house or as part of their orisha shrine; however, these images are in addition to, not a replacement of the consecrated orisha emblems that form part of the Lukumí ritual complex, itself containing no obvious or outward signs or references to Christian dogma or iconography. How much of this is a result of syncretism, or the dual worship of both Catholic and West African powers, is ambiguous and relational. Further, there are practitioners that seek to minimize Catholic, as well as spiritist and other "external" influences to what is perceived as a [re]turn to a purer or more African idealized form of worship stripped of these influences.[10] In Cuba, as in West Africa, Yorùbá approaches to religion have been hospitable to deities, knowledge, and practices whose adherents encounter them through cultural interaction with differing regional and global practices. Lydia Cabrera, a noted Cuban ethnographer, wrote extensively on Lukumí religion and she remains a significant source of ethnographic knowledge for both social scientists and practitioners.[11] Much of the literature on Afro-Cuban religion deals solely with the notion of syncretism between European and Christian elements with African-derived religious traditions. Stephan Palmié infuses this discourse with a sophisticated analysis of the ability to perceive syncretism as a viable means of converting objectifications of African cultural forms into a form of capital, an ability, following Pierre Bourdieu, that warrants social mobility.[12] This intellectual currency may then be important to this study in explaining the ways religious practices fit within the wider framework operating in Cuba, and as a possible means of gaining or retrieving legitimacy within this new setting.

Afro-Cuban religion continues to undergo transformations and reevaluations of its constitutive elements and genealogy, where European and Catholic, West African appropriation, and Chinese diasporic influences are calibrated according to the individual practitioner and the community of worshipers. Recent studies examine the adoption and promotion of neo-Yorùbá religious practices as a return to legitimacy and authenticity in religious practices.[13] Religious change and the search for purity is offset by the argument of, if it works, why change it?[14] Ritual items unknown in Africa such as cakes, tobacco, and molasses are now central components of African-derived religion in Cuba and many practitioners see their contemporary expulsion from Lukumí religious praxis as problematic. These discussions bring about debates on local integrity, legitimacy, ethics, recovery, translation, and decay in a Cuba whose avenues to communication, travel, and transnational dialogue are slowly but surely widening. And while there is no longer the need to hide West African deities behind Catholic saints, the Catholic feast days are still greatly and joyously observed by Lukumí practitioners, who use these dates to construct celebratory altars for the orisha, more often than not, with little to no overt Catholic iconography.[15]

The Shifting Borders of Mixing and Diasporic Change

There is a conundrum regarding the scale and approach in the study of the Chinese in Cuba. The parameters that delineate the broader concepts of America, the Caribbean, and Latin America frequently shift and blur surreptitiously. Claims that Cuba should be treated separately from other countries in the Caribbean further clouds the ability for comparative study and dialog. Often we have to grope to deduce the size and lens of ethnographic enquiry in these areas when no clear key is given. We are also faced with textual imaginations of the Americas and the Caribbean, which focus on specific discursive groups of people as if they live segregated from all other ethnicities/identities. The diverse peoples of Asia, for example, are all too often glossed and collectively referred to as *los chinos* who exist in an environment that is filled with "*los indios*," "*los negros*," and "*los blancos*" or "*los españoles*," yet hardly ever do these textually or discursively framed constituencies become united. Similarly, the diverse peoples that originate from Africa, who are especially renowned for their complex heterogeneity, are reduced to a monochromatic color term, "*negro*."[16] These schemas further categorize and delineate "native" populations in yet another separate niche of academic examination. Following five hundred years of colonial history, the people of the Americas were known as *los indios*, an enduring legacy on the part of Christopher Columbus, and are still regarded, conceptually, as different and hermetically sealed off from intellectual discussions of black, Asian, or European identities.

Cuba was not the only country in the Caribbean and Pacific basin to receive large numbers of Chinese contracted migrants during the nineteenth and twentieth centuries. There have been several instances of mass movements of people from Asia in the nineteenth century in particular, to various parts of the Caribbean and Latin America.[17] Unlike Cuba, the numerous Chinese coolies that arrived in Guyana, Trinidad and Tobago, Guadeloupe, Suriname, Peru, and Jamaica quickly found ways to abandon the cane fields for urban centers where they established themselves in small-scale, commercial ventures.[18] While indentured labor and colonial rule do provide some basis for comparison, there are important regional variations with regards to demographics, identity making, and transnational movements of Chinese in the Caribbean and Latin America.

The majority of existing work on Asians in Cuba focuses almost exclusively on the Chinese in Cuba. The economic and political historicities of the Chinese in relation to indentured labor on the island are well known. However, the smaller yet significant migrations of Asians and their subsequent community formations in various provinces in Cuba are given far less attention. These other influxes include a notable Japanese presence of economic migrants, *dekasegui*, which commenced in 1868 and, according to a census conducted in 1996 by the Japanese Embassy in Cuba and the Japanese Cuban Association, 1,300 Cubans of Japanese descent are living in Cuba.[19] Fewer numbers of Vietnamese and Filipinos arrived during the first half of the twentieth century as part of failed pilot schemes to entice new forms of contracted labor to the island.[20] Because race is socially constructed, and is indeed a very pervasive creation, its use here is a heuristic move to better grasp the schismogenesis of Cuba's population and associated racial politics. Race and ethnicity are *immensely* popular topics in Cuba, despite the government's best and prolonged efforts to eradicate race as a factor of Cuba's national(ist) identity; it is continually discussed, contested, ascribed, and encountered in Cuba in many socio-cultural dimensions.

The transculturative paradigms that flourished in Cuba in the twentieth century reified Afro and Euro contact to produce a semblance of accepted, publicly raced identity. The combination of the two led to the discursive construction of Afro-Cubanity, or *Afrocubanismo*, an accepted yet limited and limiting way of understanding and talking about Cuban ethnicity. Yet the presence of the Chinese and other minorities has been consistently lumped with the nonwhite category and ambiguously configured as "other" within the transculturative paradigm. I give a brief survey of the Chinese in Cuba from the nineteenth century to the present and enlist data collected from fieldwork in Cuba to help illustrate the ways in which Chinese-Cubans are central to the practice and negotiation of these African-derived, yet wholly Cuban religions. While there are limitations to the term "Afro-Cuban," it is very well embedded within all forms of sociocultural discourse and narrative on Cuba. Abandoning it or banishing it would be folly and wholly unproductive. I concede that in order to ameliorate the pitfalls we begin to recognize those bodies that are omitted by the term's utterance and move toward reframing the larger framework to adequately account for the cultural and religious expressions of diasporic people. The term "Afro-Cuban" is particularly unhelpful with reference to religious discourse as it elides the entire process of religious formation from many distinct and diverse African ethnic groups and conflates them into a singular, unified, yet unspecified mix. The "Cuban" can and has stood for "Iberian," and indeed many scholars, practitioners, and scholarly practitioners refer to Afro-Iberian religious practices with pride.[21]

The Chinese in Cuba from Indenture to Olorisha

Toward the midpoint of the nineteenth century, Cuba resourced alternative forms of inexpensive human labor to work alongside African slaves. The search for new sources of workers was implemented to keep up with the growing global demand for sugar. The feared imminent collapse of existing routes of expendable labor presented plantations with a potential deficit of workers to carry out the dangerous, often fatal work in the cane fields and refineries. Both plantation owners and the companies engaged in the slavery (often one and the same) wished to hedge against and mitigate against the possible future loss of labor power and thus sugar production should the African slave trade become difficult or illegal to maintain. Forays into alternative labor sources sought immigrants from the Yucatan and the Canary Islands and, in 1847, the first frigate carrying Chinese indentured labor docked at the port of Regla on the outskirts of Havana (see Figure 1.1). Accounting for

FIGURE 1.1 Plaque commemorating the 150th anniversary of the arrival of the first ship carrying indentured Chinese at the port of Regla, Havana. Photo by Martin A. Tsang.

attrition of Chinese laborers en route to Cuba, approximately 125,000 arrived in Cuba between 1847 and 1874, accruing enormous profits for investors and plantation owners as coolies proved to be cheaper than African slaves and relatively easier to procure.[22] The size and magnitude of Chinese migration to Cuba from the mid-nineteenth century was eclipsed only by migration to the United States.[23]

The Chinese indentured migrant worker demographic was overwhelmingly (99.97 percent) male and was also fairly ethnically homogenous, with the majority Hakka and originating from Guangdong Province.[24] Hakka is a term designating a minority Chinese ethnic group distinguished from the hegemonic Han through separate language and distinct sociocultural practices. The term Hakka signifies guest status in the homeland, and the word is translated to mean "guest families," referring to historical patterns of migrations from central to south China, a designation whose meaning is thus extended to Hakka movements overseas. The high male sex ratio of Chinese who stayed and settled in Cuba past their contractual periods tended to form consensual unions with Afro-Cuban women. From these relationships began the formation and introduction of religious communities that were premised on and inclusive of Chinese elements in worship. In contrast to the visible presence of Chinese-Cubans in Cuba from the late nineteenth century, their presence was not reflected in ideologies of Cuban identity making. Writings that posited reinforcement of Cuban identification and citizenry were discarded with the notion that the Chinese could contribute positively to these formations. These Afro-Sino hybridities have been omitted or ignored from the majority of ethnographic and phenomenological examinations of African-derived religions in Cuba.

In Cuba, the public remembrance of the Chinese both in physical memorials and festivities celebrates their arrival and is concerned primarily with their patriotic service to fighting for an independent Cuba, and their economic labor. Thus the contributions of the Chinese are historically collapsed to labor and service, and the Chinese are underrepresented in terms of their direct contributions to forming ideas of community and religiosity. Despite such service and attempts at positive collective memory, the Chinese indentured laborers, or coolies, were effectively treated as slaves, sharing the same social standing as their African counterparts, and becoming targets for racism and xenophobia. Evelyn Hu-DeHart presents several documented cases collected during the nineteenth and twentieth centuries detailing the nature and extent of sinophobia, antichinismo, or chinofobia as well as the wholesale elision of the Chinese from national discourses of identification.[25] Verena Martinez-Alier writes that the importation of Chinese coolies gave rise to fissures in the existing classificatory schemas of race. Their legal skin tone was a conundrum as many Chinese were in fact of a lighter skin color than most "white Cubans" and proved a majority problem for legal racial taxonomies.[26] The Chinese are thus relegated to a two-dimensional othered identity that has been strategically invoked within rigid parameters of political and ideological perspectives.

Mapping Asia and Religion in Cuba

Havana is the largest city by area in the Caribbean. It is the political capital, commercial center, and most metropolitan hub of Cuba with a recorded population of 2.1 million.[27] It was one of the major ports by which the Chinese arrived, and it is to Havana that many Chinese relocated from other more rural provinces, post indenture. From 1847, the start of coolie contract labor, Havana had a visible and lively Asian presence, which led to the development of the oldest Chinatown in the Caribbean. Today, El Barrio Chino de la Habana (Havana's Chinatown) spans approximately forty-five square blocks, comprised of a multi-use environment of living quarters and economic ventures, Chinese associations, and a high concentration of restaurants, both Chinese and creole. Havana, Matanzas, Cienfuegos, and Santiago de Cuba were the four principal locations for fieldwork that I conducted between 2010 and 2013. Together, Chinatown and greater Havana are a major tourist destination, and are also the sites for a highly visible presence of African and Afro-Cuban culture and religiosity.

The 1959 Cuban Revolution effectively curtailed new Chinese migration to Cuba and also witnessed a massive outflow of Chinese-Cubans to New York/New Jersey, Florida, and Spain and Canada. With only a handful of elderly Chinese-born Cubans living on the island, the majority of my interviewees and participants were Cubans born of Chinese and mixed Chinese-African and European heritages.

Afro-Cuban religious practitioners have a difficult and confusing relationship with the state which surfaces in terms of regulation, especially when tourists and foreign Lukumí practitioners enter into the equation. Much of the complication stems from the turmoil experienced through the post-Soviet transition whose impact is still felt in broader understandings of Cuban cultural and state structuration, as well as influencing personal socioeconomic constraints. Kevin Delgado informs us that post-Soviet economic austerity made for an environment that opened avenues for change and innovation in Lukumí, and he views these as fundamental practical tenets of the religion throughout its history.[28] While the poorly defined and precarious relationship that religious members have with the strictly secularizing state is not a new phenomenon, practitioners of Lukumí have received patronage by foreigners in ever increasing numbers since the 1990s. Individual foreign attention and personal "investment" in otherwise socially marginalized practices have aided in alleviating some of the repression felt by its practitioners from the state. However, amplified foreign interest in Lukumí in recent years has resulted in tightened controls to religious access, swift penalties for Cuban nationals flouting these rules, and also an increase in the commodification of Afro-Cuban religiosity for its consumption by tourists through official channels. There is a great risk of unwanted attention, fines, and allegations that can be made against Cubans practicing their religion with or for foreigners, and ceremonies such as initiations are conducted in Cuban homes. Foreigners often lodge in the same house during the course of the religious activities, potentially putting the owner at risk of fines, if discovered, for not having obtained licensing for such activities. On the one hand, foreigners and their interest in Afro-Cuban religion, dubbed *Santurismo*, and associated culture is a lucrative opportunity, creating much needed income and access to overseas commodities; on the other, it presents a risk of being viewed as an unregulated, capitalist venture, creating animosity and conflict within local circuits and spaces of religious and secular communities.

Chinese Syncretism and Influence in Afro-Cuban Religion

Recent work has helped to identify some of the most popular and widespread cases of religious syncretism between Lukumí orisha and deities from Chinese popular religion practiced in Mainland China, Hong Kong, and Taiwan. It is comprised of the "Three Teachings" referring to the three main religions practiced by the Chinese: Confucianism, Buddhism, and Taoism.[29] The multiplicity of religions, ceremonies, and pantheons of deities and texts overlap within religious practices of mainland Chinese communities. Gregor Benton informs us that there is a consensus in the hospitable and osmotic nature of these three institutionalized religions, and that "they cooperate in ritual, worship, and texts, and are marked by exchanges rather than discontinuities."[30] The study of Chinese religion and their admixture has focused to date, mostly on Chinese communities within China and Taiwan.[31]

Data gathered from field research suggests that Sanfancón is one of, if not the most widely recognized Chinese deity in Cuba and therefore it is in connection to this deity, rather than a more obscure one, that any syncretistic mention in existing literature has been detailed. Mark Meulenbeld states that the most popular god for the Chinese during the Qing Dynasty was Guan Yu, a historical figure turned deity from the era of the Three Kingdoms.[32] Also known as Guan Di (Emperor Guan), or Guan Gong (Lord Guan), his apotheosis is depicted in a fourteenth-century novel, *The Romance of the Three Kingdoms*. He is found in popular practices of Buddhism, Taoism, and Confucianism and he became known as Sanfancón in Cuba. Sanfancón, the Hispanicized name for this deity who has become popular in his own right, is worshiped as a deity by both Chinese and non-Chinese-Cubans. He is also syncretized by some as Shangó, a royal orisha that shares military and judicial characteristics with Sanfancón, and by others as Orunmila, the orisha of wisdom and divination calling on the Chinese deity's strategic and intellectual correspondences. The name "Sanfancón" is particular to Cuba and it can be argued that it refers to a specifically Cuban composition of the Chinese deity. Ignacio López-Calvo, who conducted interviews in Havana's Chinatown in 2006, points to alternative definitions of *san*, finding that some Chinese-Cubans do see its meaning as "saint" while others divorce it from its hagiographic connotations, and link it instead to its roots in the Cantonese word for "alive" by referring to Guan Yu's mytho-historical apotheosis.

Chinese-Cuban religious elements are also found in the Lukumí diaspora. In the United States, shrines devoted to the orisha prominently feature Chinese religious attributes, statuary, and materials seen in Miami, Chicago, New York, and elsewhere. Botánicas, the religious supply stores that members of orisha and other Afro-Atlantic religions frequent, sell images of Buddha, Guan Yin, and

FIGURE 1.2 Sanfancón altar in Casino Chung Wah in Havana's Chinatown. Photo by Martin A. Tsang.

Guan Yu, or Sanfancón, and have been documented in diverse places, including Washington, D.C.[33]

Perhaps the reason little scholarship has been produced on Chinese-Cubans lies in a pan-global, homogeneous assumption of Chinese diasporas: that the Chinese are present but separate outside of their homeland, and averse to engaging in and assimilating with the host cultures. The Chinese are deemed ideologically and culturally distinct and distant, stereotyped by José Martí as being "passive and exotic."[34] Cantonese male workers were not meant to stay in Cuba after their indenture contracts had ended, let alone form relationships with the *other* other: black and mixed-race women. Charo's narrative, discussed here, and many like hers are testament to the inclusion of Chinese-Cuban practitioners and the ways that community articulates the self, formed through religious, specifically initiatory bonds prove to be just as important as sanguineous ties, and in some respects supersede them.

The bridges, linkages, and dialogics that occur between individuals of separately treated ethnicities and groups of people are a means to overcome such false divides and to cope with the limitations imposed through the ongoing employment of these terms. I concur with Lisa Yun that our pressing challenge is to unsettle binaries that have consolidated and glossed a multiplicity of histories and representations.[35] Accordingly, the Atlantic and the Pacific are envisaged as discrete entities each governed by their own epistemological geographies. Our challenge is to break from these discrete entities and view the linkages that are present, effectively observing these epistemes as a coherent whole. Stuart Hall writes that representations, a slippery but useful notion, play a constitutive role, not just a reflexive one, wherein culture and ideology are formed and not just informed by representations of subjectivity, identity, and politics.[36] Hall states that representations about being black or Asian are enunciations, a cultural practice that centers on the subject, whence he or she speaks.[37]

We are better able to understand Caribbean identities if we seek these representations as being framed between two axes, one of similarity and continuity, and the other of difference and rupture. We can then make sense of the ways in which black and Chinese subjects and their representations have been formed, not only in Cuba, but also in other topographies. Insight into formation happens through an observation of continuity with the past and by noting the ruptures explained as being fashioned from a process of "peoples dragged into slavery, transportation, colonization, migration, of persons that came predominantly from Africa—and when that ended, the supply was temporarily refreshed by indentured labour from the Asian subcontinent."[38]

What the Chinese contributed to Cuban community formation, how they made their lives, how their identities have been forged and assigned, all operate within a discourse that vacillates between two poles. One pole evokes romanticized, ahistorical notions of an orientalist, atavistic fantasy of opiates, martial arts, and sensual pleasure, and—at the other extreme—as predisposed to submission and humility.[39]

How could it be that Afro-Cuban religiosity, which has such a highly visible and lauded Chinese presence and influence at its core, is resolutely ignored in the literature? Perhaps the reason for this invisibility lies within the theoretical limits of the reigning epistemological lenses used to examine the Caribbean and Latin America, their cultures and religious practices. Part of the answer may also lie in the dislocation of embodied race to religious community inclusion that can be gleaned from the above ethnographic vignette. Charo helps us to understand the parameters of race and religion as discourse in the Lukumí community, and potentially intimates that individual practitioner identities locate race (along with gender and sexuality) in an entirely different register. The Lukumí religious self is configured along the lines of racial inclusion, which elicits very little reflexive anxiety in terms of racial differences, a reaction that is antithetical to the various transculturative modes that otherwise mark the self, outside of the spiritual arena.

By focusing on diaspora, this first aids in understanding processes of adaptation and religious transformations. Second, Ninian Smart notes that the high incidence of diasporas in the modern world (both ascribed and self-identified) is framed as "multiethnic" and very much commonplace.[40] Third, diasporas themselves directly affect the development of religion in the homeland whose impact is evidenced in terms of transnational, economic, and commodity ties that account for increased wealth transmission, education, and ideological linkages.[41] Economic and related movements occur through close connections and agents that operate simultaneously in both the homeland and host community, enabling flows of goods, services, and knowledge. Diasporas need to be examined individually, rather than being compared to a perfect or ideal type, with a view to both their internal and external fields of operation. I am surveying here, not a singular diasporic experience of either the Chinese or African presence in Cuba, but the diasporic intersection in which these two cultures met and proceeded to form religious praxis that were neither only Chinese, nor solely African/Afro-Cuban. They were directly born from interdiasporic processes. Underscoring the difference of meaning in diaspora and its association with the cultural and religious contact of what can be shorthanded as Afro-Chinese, I draw attention here to the term *syncretism*, which requires interrogation and clarification in its use and application, stemming from its diverse range of meanings and wildly straddling the disciplines. Syncretism (like its close cognates creolization and hybridization), like Afro-Cuban, has embedded racialized meanings, where the discursive terrain becomes ever more precarious. In response to this, I call for the consideration of different diasporas and their interreligious processes through the careful investigation of what happens in the particular communities that unite practitioners and how they describe their religious practices, both upon reflection and by examination of the body of knowledge expressed and transmitted from person to person in a religious context. Charles Stewart points out that syncretic-ness may be an underwhelming religious fact, in that it is or has been a legitimate practice in every religion, acknowledged or not.[42] Differentials in power, Stewart notes, are often ascribed through the labeling of religions as syncretic, something that is often done to a religion from the outside, rather than being claimed as a tenet. I contend that Afro-Chinese religious influence in the Lukumí religion is an example of owning and celebrating the inter-diasporic ties and strength gained from the unexpected venture and religious intersection that occurred in Cuba from indenture to the present. Inter-diasporic cross-fertilization is a way of understanding intergroup contact and how it is mediated by and through religion and belief, requiring understanding of the material, philosophical, and cultural forms of religious members. Seemingly disparate and misunderstood elements and identities lose their foreignness and become familiar in every sense of the word. The lives and voices that grace these pages attest to an ongoing, cross-cultural discursive enterprise that reconciles and makes relevant the traces of ancestors, progenies, and deities into life-affirming engagements.

NOTES

1. Debra Lee-DiStefano, "Siu Kam Wen and the Subjectification of Chinese Peruvians in 'El tramo final,'" in *Orientalism and Identity in Latin America: Fashioning Self and Other from the (Post)Colonial Margin*, edited by Erik Camayd-Freixas (Tucson: University of Arizona Press, 2013), 188.
2. Fernando Ortiz and Harriet De Onis, *Cuban Counterpoint: Tobacco and Sugar* (New York: A.A. Knopf, 1947).
3. Kevin A. Yelvington, "The Invention of Africa in Latin America and the Caribbean: Political Discourse and Anthropological Praxis, 1920–1940," in *Afro-Atlantic Dialogues: Anthropology in the Diaspora*, edited by Kevin Yelvington (Oxford: James Currey, 2006), 51.
4. Jerry Hoeg, "Cultural Counterpoint: Antonio Benítez Rojo's Postmodern Transculturation," *Journal of Latin American Cultural Studies* 6, no. 1 (1997): 65.
5. Diasporic evidence of significant levels of Afro-Cuban religious practice can be gleaned by the presence of botánicas in many religious goods stores that form the center of formal and informal Lukumí economies and supply necessary material culture. See Carolyn Morrow Long, *Spiritual Merchants: Religion, Magic, and Commerce* (Knoxville: University of Tennessee Press, 2001); Joseph M. Murphy, "Objects That Speak Creole: Juxtapositions of Shrine Devotions at Botánicas in Washington, DC," *Material Religion: The Journal of Objects, Art and Belief* 6, no. 1 (2010): 86–108; and Joseph M. Murphy, *Botánicas: Sacred Spaces of Healing and Devotion in Urban America* (Jackson: University Press of Mississippi, 2015). A comprehensive survey or census of Lukumí practitioners in Cuba and the diaspora has yet to be conducted.
6. Interviews conducted between December 28, 2012, and January 1, 2013 in Havana, Cuba.
7. See G. Benton, "San Fancón and the Goddess of Mercy: Two Chinese Folk Gods in Cuban Transfiguration," *Cultural and Social History* 10, no. 1 (2013).
8. Andrew Apter, "Herskovits's Heritage: Rethinking Syncretism in the African Diaspora," *Diaspora: A Journal of Transnational Studies* 1, no. 3 (1991): 224.
9. G. Benavides, "Power, Intelligibility, and the Boundaries of Religions," *Historical Reflections* 27 (2001): 483.
10. See Peel for a thorough examination on the formation of the Yorùbá, and Palmié for a discussion of claims of legitimacy in Lukumí religion. J.D.Y. Peel, *Religious Encounter and the Making of the Yoruba* (Bloomington: Indiana University Press, 2000) and Stephan Palmié, *The Cooking of History: How Not to Study Afro-Cuban Religion* (Chicago: University of Chicago Press, 2013).
11. See Lydia Cabrera, *El Monte: Igbo, Finda, Ewe Orisha, Vititi Nfinda: Notas Sobre las Religiones, la Magia, las Supersticiones y el Folklore de los Negros Criollos y del Pueblo de Cuba* (Miami: Ediciones Universal, 1974).

12. Stephan Palmié, "Against Syncretism: 'Africanizing' and 'Cubanizing' Discourses in North American Òrìsà Worship," in *Counterworks: Managing the Diversity of Knowledge*, edited by R. Fardon (London: Routledge, 1995), 93.
13. See Christine Ayorinde, *Afro-Cuban Religiosity, Revolution, and National Identity* (Gainesville: University of Florida Press, 2004) and Palmié, *The Cooking of History*.
14. Ayorinde, *Afro-Cuban Religiosity*, 179.
15. Some of the most popular include: October 4, Saint Francis of Assisi for Orunla; October 24, Archangel Raphael's day for Erinle; December 4 for Shangó; and December 17, Saint Lazarus for Babalu Aye.
16. Norman E. Whitten and Rachel Corr, "Indigenous Constructions of 'Blackness,'" in *Histories of the Present: People and Power in Ecuador*, edited by Norman E. Whitten Jr. and Dorothea Scott Whitten (Urbana: University of Illinois Press, 2011), 46.
17. Sing-Wu Wang, *The Organization of Chinese Emigration 1848–88* (San Francisco: Chinese Materials Center Inc., 1978), xi.
18. Coolie in Spanish is *culí* (singular) and *culíes* (plural) and has been and is used derogatively in several islands of the Caribbean. Within the Cuban Chinese context, *culí* was used by my interlocutors to discuss Chinese indentured laborers devoid of negative or offensive connotations. It is used here to refer to Chinese indentured laborers in Cuba. The term coolie has several dimensions and derivations: Mandarin 苦力 [*kǔlì*] "bitterly hard" use of strength, and for East Asian indentured or hired laborer: *kuli*, from the original Hindustani. See Lynn Pan, *Sons of the Yellow Emperor: A History of the Chinese Diaspora* (Boston: Little, Brown, 1990). See Walton Look Lai and Tan Chee-Beng, *The Chinese in Latin America and the Caribbean* (Leiden, The Netherlands: Brill, 2010).
19. See Rolando Álvarez Estévez, *Presencia Japonesa en Cuba: Centenario del Inicia de las Relaciones entre Cuba y Japón* (Havana: Ediciones GEO/Fundación Fernando Ortiz, 2003). Christopher David Cheng, "Japanese Cubans: Past, Present and Future" (M.A. thesis, Monterey Institute of International Studies, 2006), 26.
20. See Baldomero Álvarez Ríos, *La Inmigración China en la Cuba Colonial: El Barrio Chino de La Habana* (Havana: Publicigraf, 1995).
21. My use of the root words Sino, Chinese, African, and Cuban is applied with a consciousness of each of their relevant pasts and parts that they play and how they have each been conjured in academic writings on race and academia to seemingly make a coherent whole. The use of conjunctions Afro-Chinese, Afro-Chino, Afro-Sino is to bring attention and particular focus to their joining, their spatial proximities, and racial ambiguity that a compound word can invoke. I posit that the hyphen, which I have found a valuable device in alerting attention to unknown diasporic unions, simultaneously separates and unites Afro and Sino, and hints at the tensions and associations in community making.
22. Kathleen López, *Chinese Cubans: A Transnational History* (Chapel Hill: University of North Carolina Press, 2013), 22.
23. Benton, "San Fancón and the Goddess of Mercy," 93.
24. Juan Luis Martín, *De dónde Vinieron los Chinos de Cuba: Los Jaca, los Joló, los Puntí y los Amoyanos, en la Vida Cubana* (Havana: Editorial Atalaya, 1939), 5.
25. Evelyn Hu-DeHart, "Indispensable Enemy or Convenient Scapegoat? A Critical Examination of Sinophobia in Latin America and the Caribbean, 1870s to 1930s," in *The Chinese in Latin America and the Caribbean*, edited by Walton Look Lai and Tan Chee-Beng (Leiden, The Netherlands: Brill, 2010), 67.

26. See Verena Martínez-Alier, *Marriage, Class, and Colour in Nineteenth-Century Cuba: A Study of Racial Attitudes and Sexual Values in a Slave Society*, 2nd ed. (London: Cambridge University Press, 1989).
27. 2009 Cuban Census.
28. Kevin M. Delgado, "Spiritual Capital: Foreign Patronage and the Trafficking of Santería," in *Cuba in the Special Period: Culture and Ideology in the 1990s*, edited by Ariana Hernández-Reguant (New York: Palgrave Macmillan, 2009), 53.
29. Mark Meulenbeld, "Chinese Religion in the Ming and Qing Dynasties," in *The Wiley-Blackwell Companion to Chinese Religions*, edited by Randall L. Nadeau (Chichester: Blackwell Publishing, 2012), 125.
30. Benton, "San Fancón and the Goddess of Mercy," 93.
31. See David K. Jordan, *Gods, Ghosts, and Ancestors: The Folk Religion of a Taiwanese Village* (Berkeley: University of California Press, 1972); Paul Steven Sangren, *History and Magical Power in a Chinese Community* (Stanford, Calif.: Stanford University Press, 1987); and V. Goossaert, "1898: The Beginning of the End for Chinese Religion?" *Journal of Asian Studies, Ann Arbor* 65, no. 2 (2006).
32. Meulenbeld, "Chinese Religion in the Ming and Qing Dynasties," 126.
33. See Murphy, "Objects That Speak Creole."
34. See López, *Chinese Cubans.*
35. Lisa Yun, *The Coolie Speaks Chinese Indentured Laborers and African Slaves in Cuba* (Philadelphia: Temple University Press, 2008), xxii.
36. Stuart Hall, "New Ethnicities," in *Colonial Discourse and Postcolonial Theory*, edited by Patrick Williams and Laura Chrisman (New York: Columbia University Press, 1994), 224.
37. See Stuart Hall, "Cultural Identity and Diaspora," *Framework: the Journal of Cinema and Media* 36 (1989).
38. Ibid., 227.
39. Lisa Yun, "An Afro-Chinese Caribbean: Cultural Cartographies of Contrariness in the Work of Antonio Chuffat Latour, Margaret Cezair-Thompson, and Patricia Powell," *Caribbean Quarterly* 50, no. 2 (2004).
40. See Ninian Smart, "The Importance of Diasporas," in *Migration, Diasporas, and Transnationalism*, edited by Steven Vertovec and Robin Cohen (Cheltenham: Edward Elgar, 1999).
41. Ibid., 421.
42. Charles Stewart, "Relocating Syncretism in Social Science Discourse," in *Syncretism and the Commerce of Symbols*, edited by Göran Ajimer (Göteborg, Sweden: Institute for Advanced Studies in Social Anthropology [IASSA], 1995), 23.

2

Disrupting the "White Myth"

Korean Immigration to Buenos Aires and National Imaginaries

JUNYOUNG VERÓNICA KIM

On August 29, 2002, I conducted an interview with Maximiliano Choi, a descendant of Korean immigrants in Buenos Aires. Choi, a university student whose parents arrived in Argentina in the 1970s, pointed out the precarious situation of Korean immigrants in the Argentine national imaginary:

> Aunque soy argentino—nací en la Argentina; tengo un pasaporte argentino—nunca me van a aceptar como un verdadero argentino por mi cara. Ellos (los argentinos blancos), me miran y ven un "coreano," un "chino."
>
> [Although I'm Argentine—I was born in Argentina; I have an Argentine passport—I will never be truly accepted as Argentine because of my face. They (white Argentines) look at me and see a "coreano," a "chino."][1]

This same discourse was repeated various times in my interviews with other Korean immigrants who were born in Argentina. These lived experiences attest to the gap between political citizenship and social belonging, as well as to the direct correlation between national identity and racial configuration. Although they are legal Argentine citizens, they are seen as the Other—a foreigner and an Oriental. In this chapter, I plan to examine the discursive mechanism centered around notions of race and culture that transform a certain national subject into the Other by exploring how notions of Korean racial and cultural othering are constructed in relation to a presumed white Argentine imaginary.

The studies of Cristina Iglesia and Julio Schvartzman, and of Susana Rotker, have underlined the fundamental role of what has been denominated the "white myth" in the historical construction of the Argentine nation.[2] The white myth—Argentina as a nation of the white race and European culture—not only served as the hegemonic foundation of Argentine national identity, but also justified the state's actions against its nonwhite populations: the campaigns against indigenous peoples, the progressive disappearance of the Afro-Argentine community in the nineteenth century, and the obliteration of Argentina's working-class *mestizo* population (the latter referred to by the pejorative term *cabecitas negras*, or dark-headed).[3] During the course of history and in the present context, these subjects have been rejected, silenced, and forgotten in order to impose the metropolitan conditions of national representation and racialization of which Argentina's national elites dreamed. However, as Rotker has pointed out, that which is obliterated from the dominant Argentine national identity forms a constitutive part of it. In this vein, I will examine how the white myth continues to dictate the experiences and the cultural representations of non-European immigrants in present-day Argentina and to critically analyze the contradictory relations between the material status of Korean immigrants and their symbolic position within the contemporary Argentine nation.[4] I plan to discuss the ways in which these subjects, in the beginning of the twenty-first century, are imagined within the hegemonic discourse of a nation that has been constructed around myths of Europeanness and whiteness.

This essay is organized around two related axes: first, the dominant Argentine society's othering of Argentine national subjects of Korean descent through the racialization of Korean immigrant labor; second, the experiences of Korean immigrants and their descendants that deconstruct such discursive narratives of Korean racial and cultural othering. The first part of the essay examines the Argentine print media's representation of labor practices in the garment industry, in which labor exploitation is attributed to Koreanness, thereby positing problems inherent in garment manufacturing as those caused by immigration and immigrant labor. The racialization of immigrant labor leads to a discussion, in the next section of the essay, of the new Argentine racism that attempts to distance the current Argentine national imaginary from the history of settler colonialism and racism by declaring a postracial or even antiracial stance. However, as I will show, instead of signaling the end of racism, the present historical moment ushers in a new form of racism whereby race is substituted by notions of culture. In considering the nexus of race–culture–economy that underlies the present dominant Argentine narrative of Korean otherness, the essay concludes that the lived experiences of Korean immigrants and their descendants complicate and question simplistic national/cultural/racial identifications and identities, thereby highlighting the porous and ever changing nature of cultural and national forms.

In her study on the new waves of migration in Japan and the United States, the sociologist Saskia Sassen calls attention to the fact that immigration is not the only process that is organized according to the sociopolitical and economic needs of nations. Rather "immigrant employment is patterned as well; immigrants rarely have the same occupational and industrial distribution as citizens in receiving countries."[5] Kyeyoung Park echoes this claim in her sociological study of Korean small businesses in New York City, when she writes: "There is nothing surprising about the kinds of businesses that Koreans operate in American cities. They are the businesses that immigrants in America have operated for hundreds of years—labor-intensive produce stands, convenience stores, and garment factories."[6] The latter—the garment industry—has become the chief form of employment of Korean immigrants in Argentina, where currently at least 70 percent of the Korean community is dedicated in one form or another to this enterprise.[7] The Korean garment industry began with Korean door-to-door salesmen who sold cheap clothing in the *villasmiseria* (ghettos) that they bought wholesale from Jewish-owned garment factories. Similar to the case of Korean small businesses in North American cities that Park examines, the garment industry in Argentina, largely centered in Buenos Aires, had from the onset been an immigrant enterprise mostly run by Jewish immigrants from Eastern Europe. Starting mainly in the 1960s and 1970s, Korean immigrants began to work under these Jewish businessmen as assistants learning the craft of garment manufacturing. As the children of these Jewish immigrants became incorporated into the larger mainstream Argentine society, they moved on to other professions, leaving a vacancy in the garment industry.

The impetus for the emergence of the Korean clothing business in Argentina was assisted by the rise of the garment industry in South Korea under Park Chung Hee's rule in the 1970s where cheap labor coupled with rapid industrialization caused clothing to be one of the major South Korean exports. Upon hearing that the garment industry was a lucrative enterprise in Argentina, immigrants who arrived in the 1970s onward brought with them Japanese-made sewing machines and Korean-manufactured cloth, facilitating the setting up of their small-scale family enterprise. Thus, by the 1980s, the garment industry seemed to transform almost overnight from being a predominantly Jewish business into a Korean one. This in turn notably transformed the racial makeup of certain neighborhoods in Buenos Aires, such as el Once, Flores, and Floresta where most of the retail and wholesale clothing stores, as well as the garment factories, are located.

When I returned to Buenos Aires in 2002, "Koreanness" was almost synonymous with the textile industry, such that when I told people I was Korean, they immediately asked me where my or my parents' clothing store was located.

When I responded by saying that neither my parents nor I owned a clothing store, they pursued the same logic by then asking at which clothing store I worked. Being Korean and not having any affiliation with the garment industry seemed to baffle many people. This commonsensical view that equates Koreans with the garment industry and "Koreanness" with a small business "capitalist mentality" is furthermore projected onto a racial schema that stereotypes the Korean as labor "exploiter."

Beginning in the late 1980s, the Argentine media has bombarded the public with numerous cases where Korean business owners have mistreated their Bolivian and Paraguayan workers, on top of having practiced tax evasion. Not only are the Koreans singled out as the sole culprits of capitalist exploitation, but moreover this super-exploitation is represented as a Korean attribute that stems from Korean culture. By analyzing these newspaper articles and their representation of Korean immigrants, I examine the mechanisms of representation that intervene in this discourse.

One headline in *La Nación*, a major Argentine newspaper, dated April 21, 1993, explicitly states "La esclavitud que llegó desde el Oriente se quedó en Flores Sur" (Slavery coming from the Orient has stayed in Southern Flores). Another article also capitalizes on this supposedly unique Korean phenomenon by again using the term "slavery." The headline for the article written in the August 20, 1995, edition of *Clarín* reads: "Los esclavos de fin de siglo" (The slaves of the end of the century). In one of its principal passages, the article affirms the existence of this supposed new social problem:

> Casi a dos siglos de la abolición de la esclavitud en la Argentina, periódicamente se conocen nuevos casos de explotación, que afectan particularmente a extranjeros indocumentados [. . .]. En 1992 se conoció el caso del coreano Ju Hyon Kim, que tenía seis "empleadas-esclavas" recluidas en su casa, aprovechando su condición de indocumentadas. En 1993, en el llamado Barrio Chino del barrio de Floresta, se detectaron similares irregularidades en varias fábricas y talleres [. . .] [los empleados estaban] en habitaciones infrahumanas, totalmente hacinados.
>
> [Even after almost two centuries of the abolition of slavery in Argentina, periodically we get to know new cases of exploitation, especially those that affect foreign undocumented workers. In 1992 we found out about the case of the Korean Ju Hyon Kim, who had six "employee-slaves" hidden away in his house, taking advantage of their condition of being without legal status. In 1993, in what is known as Chinatown in the neighborhood of Floresta, we detected similar irregularities in various factories and sweatshops . . . the employees were in subhuman living conditions, piled on top of each other.]

During the last two decades, numerous major newspaper articles of this type have appeared that deploy the same language and tone as the passage cited above to report these supposedly "objective" facts concerning Korean business dealings. For instance, in an article in *Clarín* published on February 22, 2000, the reporter writes: "'Cuando llegaron los inspectores, los dueños de los talleres intentaron esconder a los obreros-esclavos en un sótano, hasta que depusieron esa actitud,' dijo el funcionario que comandó el operativo denominado 'Coreatown'" ("When the inspectors arrived, the owners of the sweatshops tried to hide their worker-slaves in the basement, until we stopped it," says the official who commanded the operation named "Koreatown"). The ways in which these articles repeat similar narratives, as well as deploy the same language—slavery, Chinatown, Koreatown, etc.—suggest that the validity of the newspaper articles rely on an a priori social prosecution of Korean immigrants for keeping slaves. In other words, the newspaper articles show that before the fact, before any investigation or evidence is provided, it is already assumed that Koreans are labor exploiters. Moreover, the slippage between the term Chinatown and Koreatown to designate racialized spaces and ethnic enclaves, as well as police operations targeting Korean immigrants, highlight the Orientalist representation that views all peoples of Asian descent as the same. I would like to call attention to the ways in which similar modes of representation are repeated in various discourses concerning Korean immigrants.

In the Argentine media and the Argentine society at large, "Koreanness" is articulated mainly through labor, and specifically a certain kind of labor, exploited/sweatshop labor. As we have seen earlier, this is no surprise since the majority of Korean immigrants dedicate themselves to one particular industry. The garment industry, due to its very nature, entails intensive labor and necessitates the labor of human beings as opposed to industries that depend predominantly on machine labor.[8] This is not to imply that I wish to engage in a simplistic rebuttal that excuses exploitation on the part of Korean business owners or to make sweeping relativistic statements that say, "since *all* garment factory owners exploit their workers, it's okay." Rather what is notable in the Argentine case is how an inherent problem of capitalist society, especially endemic to garment manufacturing, becomes relegated to one single ethnic group and thereby to one race: a problem of class or labor relations becomes transformed into an interracial and transcultural problem that lies outside the Argentine nation insomuch as it concerns "Koreans" exploiting "undocumented foreign workers" (in this case, mainly Bolivian and Paraguayan immigrants).

It is noteworthy that the writers of these articles do not discuss ways to remedy the situation of these "worker-slaves." They highlight the representation of the exploited Bolivian immigrant workers without discussing the sociopolitical and economic factors that contribute to their exploitation. Additionally there is no mention of possible changes that might be made to address this problem. For instance, in their essay on the Korean and Bolivian immigrant communities in Buenos Aires, Mirta Bialogorski and Daniel Bargman argue that "the image of the exploited Bolivian is often manipulated by the media to justify a rejection of Koreans who are perceived as exploiters with no feeling of commitment to Argentina."[9] In the media, the "exploited Bolivian" is further exploited: they are silenced; their voice is usurped, as they remain the subaltern who cannot speak. As one Bolivian worker pointed out to me in one of my many informal interviews: "Hay argentinos que explotan bolivianos. Además también hay bolivianos que explotan a sus mismos compatriotas. Lo que es importante es que sigue existiendo explotación." (There are Argentines who exploit Bolivians. There are Bolivians who exploit their fellow countrymen. What is important is that exploitation continues to exist.) Yet in the dominant media, what is of interest is not the situation of Bolivian workers per se, but rather their subaltern position vis-à-vis the Korean employer. This re-victimization of the Bolivian worker is in turn utilized to portray the Korean immigrant as labor exploiter.

When interviewing Korean immigrants who own clothing stores and garment factories concerning the issue of tax evasion, they uniformly told me that it is a phenomenon of Argentine society: "The taxes are impossibly high, so that anyone who can, tries to avoid paying tax." Subsequently, I asked Argentine business owners the same question, and they admitted that this is the case, that even white Argentines do not generally pay tax or at least they deliberately misreport their earnings. However, the Korean immigrants claim the national tax bureau mainly investigates Korean businesses for tax fraud.[10] We can read this situation in the terms Bialogorski and Bargman underline in their essay: "the Other becomes the object on to which structural and contemporary conflicts are projected."[11] The economic and social problems underlying Argentine society are construed as a problem emanating from the Korean presence in the nation. The language that is used to describe the fundamental problem within the capitalist system—the exploitation of workers—further attempts to distance the problem from "us" Argentines by displacing it onto them, "the Koreans."

Furthermore, by calling Korean exploitation of Bolivians (this is how it is mainly represented in popular discourse) "slavery," this distances the problem from contemporary Argentine society. As the writer in the newspaper article that I have cited earlier—"Los esclavos de fin de siglo" (The slaves of the end of the century)—emphasizes, "the abolition of slavery in Argentina" ended "almost two centuries ago." Implicit in the usage of the word "slavery" is the argument that the Koreans, with their atavistic feudal institutions and conservative mentality, are the ones reviving this anachronistic practice. They import this directly from Asia as one headline explicitly indicated: "La esclavitud que llegó desde el Oriente . . ." (Slavery coming from the Orient . . .).[12] I will analyze how this view of Korea as stuck in an "anachronistic space" is articulated with the contrary Argentine perspective that situates South Korea as a richer country than Argentina, as "almost the First World." In this schema "Koreanness" is oddly both inferior and superior to "Argentineness."

Race/Culture/Capital: The Economy of Power

While interviewing an Argentine female medical student who was the classmate of a Korean-Argentine woman in February of 2003, a middle-aged Argentine man overheard our conversation and intervened in our discussion.[13] He began a tirade that lasted well over half an hour that ended with this statement: "Nuestro país tiene muchos problemas. Pero tenemos una cultura superior a otros países latinoamericanos. Tenemos una cultura europea." (Our country has many problems. But we have a culture superior to other Latin American countries. We have European culture.) Later, during his heated monologue, he addressed me directly and said that the Japanese had a much more advanced culture than "you Koreans." These statements arose from an initial declaration that unlike some Argentines, he was not a racist. Indeed, for him these were matters of culture, not race.

How is a notion of culture deployed in this discursive structure? Isn't this merely another form of racism? Etienne Balibar's essay "Is There a Neo-racism?" participates precisely in this debate:

> Ideologically, current racism . . . fits into a framework of "racism without races." . . . It is a racism whose dominant theme is not biological heredity but the insurmountablility of cultural differences, a racism which, at first sight, does not postulate the superiority of certain groups or peoples in relation to others but "only" the harmfulness of abolishing frontiers, the incompatibility of life-styles and traditions.[14]

Although the man in question hierarchically stratified certain groups of people, he did so not by biological race, but by culture. That is to say, he did not simply state, "Argentines are superior to Bolivians" or "Koreans are inferior to the Japanese"; rather he said that the given nation's "culture" was superior to the other. Here I wish to examine the implications of this reconstruction of identity that is grounded on a notion of culture by analyzing the ways in which the categories of "nation" and "culture" replace that of "race" and continue to function like the prior notion of "race."

In the contemporary world, more often than not, the boundaries of a given culture are drawn along national borders so that in our quotidian conversations we uncritically refer to "Argentine culture," "Korean culture," and so on. By naturalizing the relation between nation and culture, we posit national identities as putatively holistic and homogenous: all Koreans have Korean culture. In this way, national identities act as an overdetermined bind that posits a priori one's cultural affiliation. It is in this sense that Balibar states, "culture can also function like a nature" to lock "individuals and groups a priori into a genealogy, into a determination that is immutable and intangible in origin."[15] Thus, by definition, national cultures are invested in the ideology of origins and in identities of a fixed and primordial nature. The culture of the nation-state, the established culture par excellence, legitimated by a network of institutions—the state, mass media, and other ideological apparatuses—demands that the "different" cultures within the nation, which are posited as a threat and an obstacle, must assimilate and be integrated into the dominant society. This is why in our present historical period immigration becomes articulated and narrated as a process of racialization that turns immigrants into racialized subjects. Bialogorski and Bargman suggest this when they claim "national categories become ethnic ones in the migratory process."[16]

In the contemporary context, the pretext is not the overt "whitening" of the nation, but the protecting of Argentine culture from the invasion of Oriental culture (in this case, Korean culture). Hence, mainstream Argentine society calls attention to the problematic "Koreanizing" of urban neighborhoods that have been "taken over" by signs in *hangul* (the Korean alphabet), the odor of Korean food, and the clamor of an unknown language. While concerns of nineteenth- and twentieth-century eugenics focused on eradicating degenerative Chinese and Indians, contemporary Argentine discourse expresses the dangers of cultural contagion.

Rita Segato, in her anthropological study on the re-ethnization of Afro-Brazilians in Argentina, maintains that "cualquier minoría que amenazase con mostrarse idiosincrática, sea esta indígena o europea, había sido presionada y llevada a diluirse en un concepto unitario de 'argentinidad,' bajo la acusación de constituirse, como mucho se habló, en 'una nación dentro de la nación.'" (Whatever minority group had seemingly been threatening by demonstrating itself to be idiosyncratic, whether it was indigenous or European, had been pressured and led to dilute itself into the unitary concept of "Argentineness," under the accusation that they were trying to constitute as they say "a nation within a nation.")[17] It is in this sense that Korean immigrants in Argentina are found guilty of preserving their culture with a Spartan-like fanaticism, of being unwilling to assimilate into their host society and thereby of attempting to create another nation in the country. They are repeatedly contrasted to the Japanese who are seen as "model minorities" who understand that their "community" can only operate as a subgroup that is framed by and circumscribed within the larger Argentine society. Marcelo G. Higa describes the Japanese-Argentine way of negotiating their dual identities in the following passage:

> The general agreement was that the interpersonal relationships of immigrants and their descendants inevitably had to incorporate the established demands of an Argentine national identity. These demands were privileged over claims either openly or weakly "ethnic." In consequence, even within the ambiguity of daily practices, the discourse of identification of those descended from Japanese immigrants did not admit doubts. That is why, in the Argentine context, there did not even exist a descriptive term such "Japanese-Argentine": one was "Argentine," a term that could be softened occasionally by adding the clarification "descended from Japanese."[18]

The Japanese are viewed as having a "superior" culture, as manifested by the view of Japan's First World economic status and by its widely advertised and popularized cultural practices and commodities embodied by items such as sushi, Zen meditation, or judo. In this perspective, the Japanese immigrants and their descendants' "willingness" to be incorporated into Argentine society only serve to prove Japanese superiority. For as Balibar states:

> No theoretical discourse on the dignity of all cultures will really compensate for the fact that, for a "Black" in Britain or a "*Beur*" in France, the assimilation demanded of them before they can become "integrated" into the society in which they already live (and which will always be suspected of being superficial, imperfect, or simulated) is presented as progress, as an emancipation, a conceding of rights. And behind this situation lie barely reworked variants of the idea that the historical cultures of humanity can be divided into two main groups, the one assumed to be universalistic and progressive, the other supposed irremediably particularistic and primitive . . . it immediately reintroduces the old distinction between "closed" and "open," "static" and "enterprising," "cold" and "hot," "gregarious" and "individualistic" societies.[19]

It is no surprise that the binarisms that Balibar highlights—"closed/open," "static/enterprising," "cold/hot," "gregarious/individualistic"—are deployed to differentiate the Koreans both from the Argentines as well as from the Japanese. One of the recurring comments on Korean immigrants in Argentina was the claim that "the Koreans are closed." When I asked the person in question what s/he meant by the term *cerrado* ("closed"), they could not quite explain themselves. After pushing the question, they would say: "Pues, viste, nosotros los argentinos somos bastante abiertos." (Well, you see, we Argentines are pretty open.) They could only define Koreans' "closedness" by opposing it to an Argentine "openness." Sometimes, s/he would try to describe the term by saying that "los coreanos son antipáticos, son fríos, sólo se juntan con otros coreanos" (the Koreans are unfriendly; they are cold; they only get together with other Koreans). When I asked if Argentines readily mixed with other groups of people, such as Koreans, Bolivians, Peruvians, etc., they seemed to think that I had missed their point.

The problem of language was often cited as an example of Korean "closedness" and as a manifestation of the "Korean problem" in Argentina. One Argentine man in his mid-thirties went so far as to suggest that the negative Argentine response toward Korean immigrants had nothing to do with race, but only with language. This linguistic turn in contemporary Argentine discourse is noteworthy for a number of reasons. First, it illustrates what George Yúdice has termed a transition from "bio-poder al poder cultural" (bio-power to cultural power).[20] Second, this emphasis on language further shows the racial hierarchical division that Balibar outlines between the universal (the hegemonic nation) and the particular (the nation of the immigrant).

The acquisition of proper Argentine Spanish, or what is called *castellano*, is posited as essential to the process of integration into the Argentine nation. In this respect, I wish to emphasize that in the context of Buenos Aires, speaking fluent Spanish is not enough; one must speak the proper *porteño* variant of the Spanish idiom. Immigrants from neighboring Latin American countries quickly realize the importance of this, such that after a short time in Buenos Aires, they learn to adopt the *vos* instead of the *tú* (for the word "you"), the *ché* (a colloquial slang used to mean "hey") emphatics, "*birome*" as opposed to *bolígrafo* (to refer to the word "pen"), and so on. Those who do not speak the Buenos Aires variant of Spanish risk being perceived (or "heard") by others and/or by themselves as subjects who dissociate themselves from Argentineness and assert their own particular identity. In this way, linguistic affiliation literally acts as an exercise of power that determines whether one does or does not belong to the imagined national community.

In the Latin American context, it is important to note that the Spanish language has been historically deployed to assimilate the native indigenous populations by subordinating the use of autochthonous languages. Indigenous languages did not become the linguistic tools with which to imagine and create a nation; rather they were relegated to the margins of the *criollo* nation or reified as a symbolic "ancestral" domain of the nation.[21] On the other hand, the language of the colonial and neocolonial elites was positioned as the foundation of Latin American national *bildung*.

In the Argentina of the late twentieth and twenty-first centuries, this cultural foundation serves as the basis for constructing an idea of Argentine racial and/or cultural superiority over Koreans that characterizes the discourses I analyze in this essay. The man who interrupted my interview with the female medical student clearly illustrated this view when he claimed that although Argentina suffers from economic and political problems characteristic of the Third World, it still retains a "superior" culture over other "non-European" countries, such as neighboring countries with larger indigenous populations (like Bolivia and Peru), and even over economically more stable non-Western nations such as South Korea. How does identification with the "civilizatory" myth of white European origin permit the hegemonic criollo imaginary of Argentina to construct a sentiment of superiority even in its peripheral condition?

In the case of Korean immigration to Argentina, which has been precipitated by the Argentine government's need for foreign investment and nationally generated capital, the logic of capital and race meet on an uneven national terrain. On the one hand, Korean immigrants are posited as producers of economic capital for the Argentine nation. This was the role that both the Argentine and South Korean governments assigned to the Korean immigrant. In 1985, the Argentine government signed an agreement with the Republic of Korea that established as a requisite for the securing of an immigrant visa a deposit of 30,000 US dollars per family (whose amount has increased to the point that in the present it exceeds 100,000 dollars). According to this agreement, the required sum would be refunded upon the completion of residence in the country (Acta de Procedimiento para el Ingreso de Inmigrantes Coreanos a la Argentina, [Certificate of Proceedings of the Entry of Korean Immigrants to Argentina], April of 1985). La Resolución de la Dirección Nacional de Migraciones (The Resolution of the National Management of Immigration) No 2.340 passed on June 26 of the same year declares that South Korean citizens are included as the exceptional cases that are listed by the said resolution: "migrantes con capital propio suficiente para desarrollar actividades productivas" (immigrants with proper sufficient capital for the development of productive activities).

On the other hand, Korean immigrants are viewed as "taking advantage of the nation" and "stealing its resources." Bialogorski and Bargman underline this contradiction by pointing out that "there is a discrepancy between the imagined Argentine idea of the rate of growth of the wealth of the Korean community, and the actual, slower rate of its social and symbolic integration."[22] That said, I think it is important to complicate this model and explore—by way of example—the complex connection between capital and race, not necessarily as an opposition, but as a conflictual relation.

When I lived in Buenos Aires, I was surprised to encounter numerous electronic, mechanical, and technological commodities produced by Korean multinational corporations: Samsung, Hyundai, Daewoo, LG, and so on. However, when I had previously asked "white" Argentines if Korean automobiles were sold in Argentina, they responded by asking, "Koreans make cars?" Ironically, one of the people who had voiced this question was an owner of a Samsung computer. When I asked her if she knew Samsung was a Korean company, she seemed shocked. I had further explored this phenomenon by asking Korean immigrants and Korean-Argentines who, of course, were all aware of the proliferation of Korean goods. Some had even worked in the Argentine corporate offices of these *chaebol* (South Korean conglomerates) companies before their evacuation during the Argentine financial crisis in 2001. When I notified them of the general "white" Argentine ignorance in respect to this, none of them seemed in the least surprised. "Of course, what do you expect," was the predominant way in which they would respond. Why is this link, no matter how imaginary or constructed, between Korean company branded commodities and "Korea" nonexistent in Argentina when, for instance, in the United States it has been one of the main ways South Korea has attempted to market itself as an "almost First World" nation? From the perspective of South Korea, is marketing to Argentina not worthy of investment? This was what the majority of Korean immigrants and Korean-Argentines seemed to think. If we take this opinion seriously, then we witness a paradoxical reciprocation of a blind spot, which is created by both the South Korean perception of Argentina as an "inferior Third World" nation and the Argentine construction of Korean cultural "inferiority." For the latter, Korean capital is welcomed as long as its "Koreanness" is obscured. If its connection to "Korea" were made visible, then the capital would be racialized, which has been the case for the Korean immigrant textile industry in Buenos Aires.

As for South Korea, the marketing of its national cultural identity only becomes necessary in its relation to economically "superior" nations. This case exemplifies the uneasy relation between the logic of capital domination and that of cultural superiority. The meeting of these two, which has been precipitated by globalization, causes conflicts and fissures that cannot be readily compared or opposed. What is the price for material and symbolic order that the Argentine nation pays for economic viability when those investing capital are not invisible account holders in Asia or racially unmarked corporate brands such as Samsung, but are rather visible inhabitants of the city—the Other in our midst? And on the other hand, can South Korea ignore the representation of its emigrants and of its national identity as a perception unworthy of response? Can it continue to limit its referent to the West, to the "First World"? These are the questions that arise from the critical interstices produced by a contradictory reality, in which national imaginaries, immigrant subjects, racial representations, and economic capital interconnect.

The liminal space between race and culture and between race/culture and economic capital in globalization is not an unsutured smooth surface. If the Korean immigrants in Argentina stumble between the fissures, "white"

Argentines also slip and slide between the crevices of this unpaved road. They must constantly negotiate between their "Third World" condition and their fictions of Europeanness, as well as between their privileged myths of "whiteness" and that disavowed "darkness" residing in the peripheries of the capital city and the provinces of Argentina.

Disrupting Identity: An Immigrant Response to the "White Myth"

The specter of capital does not completely disappear from the racial terrain. It reappears in the Korean immigrant discourse on Argentines and even in certain Argentine views on Koreans. As one Korean immigrant retail clothing store-owner in his twenties said to me: "You know Argentines aren't really white. Have you ever taken a close look at some of them? They definitely are mixed."[23] In another interview, a Korean business owner in his early sixties emphatically stated: "When Argentines are racist toward me, I just feel sorry for them. I make more money in a year than they will ever see in their lifetime." Both of these statements simultaneously question the myth of Argentine whiteness and its superiority vis-à-vis Koreans. For the former, Argentina as a white nation is a postulation that is not believable, while for the latter his economic capacity disproves Argentine racial and/or cultural superiority. However, neither of these views questions the position of the West nor do they critique the larger racial and ethnocultural framework which posits the West as superior; rather, what they refute is Argentina's autoperception of itself as Western. To these South Korean immigrants who immigrated in the 1980s and the 1990s, South Korea seems "more modern" than Argentina. In this sense, it is closer to the West than a peripheral Latin American nation. However, at the same time, they both agree that Argentine culture is more European. But this concurrence does not reiterate the same notion of "Europeanness" that has been articulated in the construction of the Argentine cultural dominant. For these Koreans, "Europeanness" becomes another characteristic like "Koreanness" or "Chineseness"; a descriptive statement that is not necessarily hierarchical.

By dissociating European culture from an idea of superiority, these Korean immigrants strip "whiteness" of its value, that is, of its potentiality. For as they emphasize, these nonwhite immigrants have secured a class status that many "white" Argentines will never acquire. Whiteness no longer can guarantee the capacity for economic mobility. It merely becomes another sign, a signifier among other signifiers. Korean immigrants will agree with "white" Argentines that the latter are more "white" and "European" than they are. If, in this process, these Korean immigrants disarticulate "whiteness" and "Europeanness" by delinking them from their significance—racial and cultural superiority—then we must examine how they enunciate their "Koreanness" or their "Argentineness."

For Korean immigrants in Buenos Aires, their very condition as immigrants necessitates an articulation of Korean and Argentine identities; it is this position that configures the locus of their auto-representation. Although the hegemonic Argentine discourse naturalizes an a priori "Koreanness," as well as a putative "Argentineness," in my interviews with Korean immigrants, I noticed that their construction of "Koreanness" was always in relation to both the host country and to their own position within Argentina. They were fully conscious that their "Koreanness" was only marginally connected to a South Korean national identity. As one young Korean-Argentine man told me on February 27, 2003:

> Irónicamente regresé a Argentina después de estudiar en Corea por un par de años porque extrañé a mis amigos de la colectividad coreana acá. Viste que los coreanos acá somos muy íntimos. Compartimos algo . . . ¿qué sé yo? Pero en Corea, a nadie le importa si sos coreano. Todo el mundo es coreano. Ser coreano no significa nada allá. Además ser coreano en Corea es distinto. Es difícil de explicar.
>
> [Ironically the main reason why I came back to Argentina after studying in Korea for a few years was because I missed my Korean friends here. I mean, here the Koreans are very close. We share something. But in Korea no one cares if you're Korean. Everyone is. Being Korean doesn't mean anything there. Besides Koreans in Korea are different. It's hard to explain.]

His testimony attests to the differential relation between Korean national identity in South Korea and that of its emigrants.[24] This yearning for the Korean immigrant culture and his Korean-Argentine friends caused him to return to Buenos Aires. In a sense, Argentina, for him, did not signify the dominant Argentine culture, but rather "being Korean" *in* Argentina. Rather than seeing this "Koreanness" as an importation from the country of origin, I wish to point out that it is precisely a product of the immigrants' relationality with the host country, in which s/he negotiates and reconstructs her position within it. By trying to make sense of their lives in Argentina, these Korean immigrants reinvent their understanding of Korean culture and creatively appropriate certain forms of Argentineness.

Moreover, it is through the economic sphere that they reformulate Korean and Argentine cultural/national identities and create a Korean-Argentine immigrant imaginary. I have purposely avoided the word "identity" since it implicitly implies a notion of distinct differences within fixed categories that suggest potential unchanging essences. In the case of the Korean immigrant population in Buenos Aires, there is no clear dividing line that can articulate their "difference" from Koreans elsewhere or from other Argentines. This complexity of "being Korean in Argentina" is revealed in the words expressed by the young Korean-Argentine businessman whom I interviewed on June 2, 2003:

> Nosotros [los coreanos-argentinos en los veintes] tuvimos una discusión bastante caliente con algunos coreanos [en Corea del Sur] en un *chat*. Decían que somos afortunados porque no tenemos que cumplir el servicio militar que es obligatorio en Corea. Y nosotros decimos que ellos no pueden entender ni siquiera las dificultades que nosotros tenemos que pasar acá. Viste, es recomplicado vivir afuera de su país. Pero claro, ellos no podían entender. Se calentaron re mal . . . los pibes en Corea viven con sus viejos hasta que se casan. No laburan como nosotros cuando son pibes, ¿viste? Tenemos que ayudar a los viejos. Y después laburar y ganar plata por nosotros mismos. Pero me parece que es imposible para ellos entendernos.
>
> [We (Korean-Argentine men in their twenties) had this heated debate with some Korean guys (in South Korea) in a chat-room. Well they were saying how we were lucky since we didn't have to serve the mandatory military service. And we were saying that they couldn't possibly understand the hardships we have to go through. You should understand how difficult and painful it is to live outside of the country. Of course they didn't. They got pissed off . . . I mean young people in Korea live with their parents until they get married. They don't have to work at a young age like we do. We have to help our parents. And then we have to make money ourselves. But I suppose it's impossible for them to understand.]

This chat-room discussion that turned into a cyber altercation between young men in Argentina and in South Korea centers on the determined incommensurable position between them and their localities. How can the other understand one's hardships? Who can say whose pain is necessarily greater? To the Korean-Argentine businessman, this dispute also re-evidenced the difficulty of representing the immigrant condition. Through South Korean media and stories of family members, Korean-Argentines have a certain mediated access to the young Korean man's experience of military service. To young Koreans living in South Korea, however, the experiences of Korean-Argentines are completely unknown and obscure. However, it is not merely the lack of visible representation of the Korean immigrant in Argentina that produces this incomprehensibility. Rather, underlying this Korean-Argentine's testimony is the suggestion that the immigrant experience intrinsically constitutes its own un-representability, or at least, presents a difficulty for representation.[25]

The language with which the interviewees narrate the typical immigrant's tribulations centers on the financial aspects of his life: "making money," "helping the family business." If we recall that Korean immigration to Argentina was officially construed as an entrepreneurial immigration, then we can see how the historical and legal basis of this immigratory process are mirrored and experienced in the immigrant's daily existence. In Argentina, the government actively produces the importance of the economic in their endorsement of Korean entrepreneurial immigration and yet public discourse condemns the Korean immigrant as capitalist exploiter. How do these immigrants, then, negotiate their economic role?

Contrary to the dominant discourse of the Argentine media in the beginning of the twenty-first century that racializes and culturalizes the economic by essentializing the Korean as a slave-driver, Korean immigrants present a complex articulation of the financial dimension of their lives: the economic is not overdetermined by essentialist notions of race and culture, instead it takes part in forming cultural and national affiliations. As the Korean-Argentine entrepreneur testified, it is through his/her occupation that the Korean immigrant articulates a notion of a "Koreanness" and an "Argentineness." The overwhelming majority of Korean immigrants work, in one form or another, in the textile industry. These small businesses are based on family units where each family member has an assigned role in the business. The Korean-Argentine interviewees directly comment on this when stating that although most young people in Korea do not "work," their counterparts in Argentina must help their parents in the family business. This inscribes the family unit—the apparatus through which notions of culture, history, and nationality are spread—within the economic sphere. Moreover, it is through these family-based businesses that relations with other Korean immigrant families are formed. The interconnection between social and economic encounters is not merely limited to relations within the Korean immigrant community, but also with other Argentines.

When I conducted interviews with Korean businessmen and women, I would ask the interviewee if they had relationships with "white" Argentines. Most of them said that their relations with "white" Argentines were limited to business encounters, but then would subsequently add that since the majority of their time was spent in maintaining the family business, most of their social ties were in one way or another connected to their work. The distinction that they construed between Korean immigrants and "white" Argentines was in regards to their work ethic; while they saw Koreans as being hard-working and industrious, they posited Argentines as "*tranquilos*" (laid-back), as lazy, and at times incompetent. However, when I followed the logic of these stereotypical representations by asking if that meant that they viewed Koreans as culturally and racially "superior," their response was ambivalent. As one middle-aged Korean immigrant woman said on August 31, 2003:

> You have to understand that they (white Argentines) have different values and different ways of working. It doesn't work well with our way of doing things. But then again Koreans can be "too much" sometimes. Also I think it's different since we are immigrants. We came here to make money. They like to have more leisure time . . . But then I think life here is better than in Korea since we do have more time. We're more "laid-back."

Although she at first delineates an opposition between us—the "hard-working" Koreans and them—the "laid-back" white Argentine, she, then, dissolves this distinction by saying that "we" too are "laid-back." This initial difference does not readily translate into a binary structure. This discursive framework is also reiterated in the way she relates "Koreanness" to the immigrant's supposed "industriousness." At first, she seems to suggest that Korean immigrants' work ethic arises from his/her "Koreanness." However she later reframes it as the product of the immigrant experience: "we came here to make money." Thus, the divergence in work ethic between the Korean-Argentine and the white Argentine is not linked to a cultural hierarchical difference, but rather to the different social position between the two. Here I want to suggest that the incongruous narrative of the Korean businesswoman arises from the conflictual and disjunctive position of the Korean immigrant, a position that is unable to translate into a holistic identity.

Furthermore, her statement—"we're more 'laid-back'"—implies that "Koreanness" itself is reinvented and moreover relocated in "another nation" during the process of immigration. This transformation does not imply an assimilation into the dominant Argentine culture nor a deculturation, but rather the contradictory articulation of the immigrant's "Koreanness," which cannot be readily identified with an official Korean cultural identity. How can we understand this Korean immigrant's testimony in light of our previous discussion on national cultural identity?

Luckily, through my contacts with the president of La Asociación Universitaria de los Coreanos en Argentina (AUCA), I was able to interview the writer of *Argentina: 25 Years of Korean Immigration*, Lee Kyo Bum. Unlike the majority of Korean immigrants, his reasons for emigration were not economic. His visit to Latin America twenty years ago had sparked a fervent desire in him to leave Korea for Argentina. When I asked him what aspect of Latin America had produced such an inspiration, he responded by saying: "I'm not sure if I can put it in words. A certain feeling, a certain beauty that this place has." He told me that in order to emigrate, he had to wait a few years for his children to become financially independent since they had refused to follow him and his wife to Argentina.

Out of all the Korean immigrants I had interviewed, Lee was the most overtly critical of the hegemonic idea that Argentine society was rooted in white European culture. His comments referred to the historical construction of the Argentine nation based on "the genocide of its indigenous population," and "the current racial backlash against Korean immigrants." At the same time, Lee contested the notion of a putative Korean national unity by locating it as the determining factor of the South Korean nation's hierarchical relation to the Korean diaspora and to its subsequent stratification of Korean immigrant communities:

> The South Korean nation-state in its aspiration to become a modern First World nation has turned its back on the Korean immigrants in places other than the United States. It considers them an embarrassment, a reminder of Korea's past when it used to be poor and subordinate to imperial powers. To leave this past behind, it has either expelled them from the national imaginary—by disavowing their existence—or relegated them to the margins. For instance, the way in which Korean-Chinese are seen as inferior to Koreans in South Korea.

Consequently, Lee underlines the South Korean government's uninterest in the Korean diaspora, as evidenced by the lack of studies and institutions of knowledge-production that examine Korean immigration in locations elsewhere than the United States. As he points out, this is a direct outcome of the South Korean auto-formulation of itself as a modern upcoming global power. South Korea seems to attempt, in this way, to substitute or "overcome" its own colonial history as a country that was colonized, dominated, poor, and "backward," in order to demarcate a rupture between its past and its present. However, the actual bodies of Korean immigrants appear as living proof of a Korean history with present fissures that remind us of the conflictual nature of its past. The displacement of these Korean immigrants caused by Korea's colonial and neocolonial historical situations serves to remind South Korea of the precariousness of the supposed discontinuity with this "past." Instead of examining and confronting this history as part of the present, South Korea merely circumvents this by either dissociating the South Korean national identity from Korean immigration or devalorizing it as an insignificant element.

Moreover, the circumscription of this "Korean national identity" within the boundaries of the nation-state facilitates a discourse that posits "Koreanness" as an unchanging essence that does not move. This discourse interpolates Korean immigrants and their subsequent children and their offspring as "second-class" Koreans. By right of "blood," they are *still* Koreans; however, in their adulteration by other cultures, they are not "full" equal Koreans. Instead of proposing a Korean cultural and racial identity that integrates these other types of "Koreannness," Lee asserts that we need to, in fact, rethink Korean identity. If we posit Korean immigrants and their descendants as equal to Koreans in South Korea, then this would resituate the problem of "Koreanness" itself. For as he eloquently expresses:

> It is no longer viable, if it ever was, to think that a Korean identity will continue and perpetuate itself with future generations. As the children, grandchildren, great-grandchildren, and their children proceed to live in places outside of the South Korean borders, they'll be influenced by their environment; they'll probably marry non-Koreans; and they most likely won't speak Korean or engage in "Korean" cultural practices. Of course, Korean identity is always in flux and in constant state of change. Even in South Korea. What I want to say is that the "Koreanness" we will subsequently witness will no longer be in a recognizable form. It'll have a different face, a different body and so on. We simply won't be able to identify it. But that's good. That's history.

When I consequently asked him how, then, can we call it a "Koreanness," his response was that it was Korean insofar that it was a manifestation of "our" history.

The understanding of "Koreanness" that he proposes is not an actual identity, an essence (racial or cultural), or even a difference that can be enunciated. Rather, it is a kind of communication with Korean history, that is, Korea as history. Lee's notion of history, though, is not equated with the notion of hegemonic History that postulates itself as a factual representation of a reified and fixed past, but rather is based on the understanding of history as the multiple articulations of the present's relations to the past. History's significance arises in the way we *know*, in the present moment, to negotiate and communicate with our past. However, this relation is neither transparent nor predetermined. Just as interruption and misunderstanding are part and parcel of communication, our relations with the past are partial, incomplete, conflictual, sutured, and, at times, obscure and illegible.

Lee's testimony suggests that a disruption and contestation of "the white myth"—that is, Argentine cultural/racial identity—cannot merely reconstitute an opposing Korean cultural and/or racial identity. The experience of the Korea immigrant in Argentina attests to the non-viability of formulating a counter-identity from which his/her position can be negotiated and articulated. At the same time, we cannot be certain what this communication with history will entail, in which form(s) it will take place, or what direct sociopolitical, economic, and cultural outcomes it will produce. As Lee suggests, it might not even be "recognizable," and that is why we have yet to wait to see what the present holds.

The experiences and discourses of the Korean immigrants in Argentina, thus, question hegemonic national narratives, reimagine nations and invite us to rethink its racial, ethnic, and cultural correlations. Which is the Argentina or the Argentinas that emerge in these conflicts that dispute belonging and non-belonging of immigrant subjects? How can we think of Korean immigrants in Buenos Aires not as an Other—"Oriental"—but as subjects who articulate new forms of citizenship and nationalities? Instead of positing "Korean," or "Asian," as always already in opposition to "Argentina," or "Latin America," the experiences of Korean-Argentines call attention to the porous and changing nature of cultural and national forms. As these immigrant stories suggest, Asian immigration to Latin America is not a curious anomaly, but a fundamental site where we can begin to redraw the map of a world construed not only of capital flows and governmental relations, but also of peoples, languages, and lives.

NOTES

An earlier version of this article was published in Spanish as "Desarticulando el 'mito blanco': la inmigración coreana en Buenos Aires e imaginarios nacionales," *Revista de Crítica Literaria Latinoamericana* 71 (September 2010): 169–193.

1. All translations are mine unless otherwise noted.
2. See Cristina Iglesia and Julio Schvartzman, *Cautivas y misioneros: mitos blancos de la Conquista* (Buenos Aires: Catálogos, 1987) and Susana Rotker, *Cautivas: olvidos y memoria en la Argentina* (Buenos Aires: Ariel, 1999).
3. In his book *The Afro-Argentines of Buenos Aires, 1800–1900* (Madison: University of Wisconsin Press, 1980), George Reid Andrews points out that the "disappearance" of Afro-Argentines in nineteenth-century Argentina was, in part, an outcome of the "whitening" of the middle class. Middle-class Afro-Argentines were seen as not-quite black unlike their poorer counterparts. In this historical process, class and race were constructed in conjunction with one another. See Viñas regarding Argentina and its indigenous peoples in the context of the end of the nineteenth century: David Viñas, *Indios, ejército y frontera* [1982] (Buenos Aires: Santiago Arcos, 2003).
4. See the respective studies of Sergio Caggiano, *Lo que no entra en el crisol: inmigración boliviana, comunicación intercultural y procesos identitarios* (Buenos Aires: Prometeo, 2005) and Alejandro Grimson, *Relatos de la diferencia y la igualdad* (Buenos Aires: Eudeba, 1999) on Bolivian immigrants in Buenos Aires. Also see Gerardo Halpern, *Etnicidad, inmigración y política: Representaciones y cultura política de exiliados paraguayos en Argentina* (Buenos Aires: Prometeo, 2009) on the Paraguayan community in Argentina.
5. Saskia Sassen, *Globalization and Its Discontents: Essays on the New Mobility of People and Money* (New York: The New Press, 1998), 56.
6. Kyeyoung Park, *The Korean American Dream: Immigrants and Small Business in New York City* (Ithaca, N.Y.: Cornell University Press, 1997), 41.

7. This percentage is not officially documented. However, according to the informal survey of the Korean Association in Argentina 70 percent is a relatively conservative figure. On the Korean immigrant community in Argentina, see Lee's pioneering study, originally published in Seoul, in the Korean language. Kyo Bum Lee, *Hanin imin 25 nyeonsa* [Argentina: 25 Years of Korean Immigration] (Seoul, South Korea: Sunyoungsa, 1992).
8. Explicit exploitation of garment industry workers is a major problem on a global scale that has been widely examined in works such as that of Ross. See Andrew Ross, *No Sweat: Fashion, Free Trade, and the Rights of Garment Workers* (New York: Verso, 1997).
9. Mirta Bialogorski and Daniel Bargman, "The Gaze of the Other: Koreans and Bolivians in Buenos Aires," *Patterns of Prejudice* 30, no. 4 (1996): 24.
10. Although I have searched for actual statistical data on tax investigation, it seems that the Argentine national tax bureau does not reveal its records to the public. Therefore, I will only submit this information in its capacity as ethnographic testimony.
11. Bialogorski and Bargman, "The Gaze of the Other," 22.
12. This vision recalls the discourse on the Chinese that was commonly held by Latin American criollo elites in the end of the nineteenth and the beginning of the twentieth centuries: the atavistic "yellow" race contaminates the Latin American nation by bringing with it Asia's backward premodern culture; a widespread discourse that can easily be found in the works of such dissimilar figures as Domingo Faustino Sarmiento, José Vasconcelos, or José Carlos Mariátegui. See Domingo Faustino Sarmiento, *Obras* XXIII (Buenos Aires: Luz del día, 1951), José Vasconcelos, *The Cosmic Race/La raza cósmica* [1925], trans. Didier T. Jaén (Baltimore: The Johns Hopkins University Press, 1979), and José Carlos Mariátegui, *Seven Interpretive Essays on Peruvian Reality* [1928], trans. Marjory Uriquidi (Austin: University of Texas Press, 1971).
13. Risking being labeled North American-centric, I use the term Korean-Argentine to refer to children of Korean immigrants who are born in Argentina. The other terminologies commonly used in Argentina, such as "the child of Korean immigrants" or "Argentines of Korean descent," seem to me to be lopsided where they either emphasize the individuals' Korean heritage or his/her country of citizenship.
14. Etienne Balibar, "Is There a Neo-Racism?" in *Race, Nation, Class: Ambiguous Identities*, ed. Etienne Balibar and Immanuel Wallerstein (London/New York: Verso, 1991), 21.
15. Ibid., 22.
16. Bialogorski and Bargman, "The Gaze of the Other," 23.
17. Rita Laura Segato, *La nación y sus otros: raza, etnicidad y diversidad religiosa en tiempos de políticas de la identidad* (Buenos Aires: Prometeo, 2007), 283.
18. Marcelo G. Higa, "The Emigration of Argentines of Japanese Descent to Japan," in *New Worlds, New Lives: Globalization and People of Japanese Descent in the Americas and from Latin America in Japan*, ed. Lane Ryo Hirabayashi, Akemi Kikumura-Yano, and James A. Hirabayashi (Stanford, Calif.: Stanford University Press, 2002), 262.
19. Balibar, "Is There a Neo-Racism?" 25.
20. George Yúdice, *El recurso de la cultura: usos de la cultura en la era global* (Barcelona: Gedisa, 2002), 8.
21. See Jorge Pavez Ojeda, *Cartas mapuche: siglo XIX*, vol. 2 (Santiago de Chile: CoLibris & Ocholibros & Fondo de Publicaciones Americanistas & Laboratorio de Desclasificación Comparada, Colección de Documentos para la Historia Mapuche, 2008) and Viñas, *Indios, ejército y frontera.*
22. Bialogorski and Bargman, "The Gaze of the Other," 24.

23. My interviews with Korean-Argentines were conducted in Korean, a mixture of Korean and Spanish, or Spanish; some words from both languages were used frequently. In order to facilitate comprehension, the interviews that were mostly conducted in Korean I present in their English translation, while the ones that were conducted mostly in Spanish I present both in Spanish and in English. However, I want to point out that even the Spanish "original" is also a translation of the hybrid *coreañol* that is used by Korean-Argentine immigrants.
24. Many Korean-Argentines, even those who are third-generation immigrants, go back and forth between South Korea and Argentina for reasons pertaining to family and work. The garment industry, along with all other industries, has been affected by globalization. Some Korean-Argentines have decided to utilize global chains by copying fashion designs in South Korea, Europe, and the United States, while outsourcing part of the production to China. There are also Korean-Argentines who have networks in other parts of Latin America such as Paraguay, Chile, Brazil, and Mexico. Given the context of globalization, national, ethnic, and linguistic identities have become more complex and porous.
25. The hybrid language used by the Korean immigrant community in Buenos Aires clearly exemplifies this problem of representation, or what I term "irrepresentability." The notion of homogeneous, uniform, and monolingual national languages governs the modes of representation that are readily available. For instance, we think of translation as going from one putative uniform language to another putative language: Spanish to Korean or Korean to Spanish depending on the audience. In this framework, however, the hybrid language used by the Korean immigrant community in Buenos Aires that fluidly moves between Korean and *porteño* Spanish, mixing one language with the other, inventing neologisms and creating different meanings to certain words, cannot be represented within the given established code.

3

Harnessing the Dragon

Overseas Chinese Entrepreneurs in Mexico and Cuba

ADRIAN H. HEARN

Three booking agents and two assistants were on duty at 4:30 P.M. when a brick shattered the window of the China Viaje travel agency in Tijuana's business district. At 6 P.M. they were sitting in a row before their manager and two representatives of the Chinese Association of Tijuana. Pedro, the owner of the business, spoke to me in a surprisingly calm voice: "Now do you see? This is what I was telling you about: it's been happening more and more to Chinese businesses. This has been a bad year. Is it because our employees are Chinese? When these things happen we try to hold our heads high and carry on without retaliating, and without drawing attention to ourselves. You're the anthropologist, so you tell me, what's going on? Have we done something wrong?"[1]

The incident at China Viaje was not isolated. In November, a month earlier, a Chinese supermarket just three blocks away had been vandalized and robbed, and the owners of a local department store specializing in imported Chinese home appliances discovered the words "Pinche Chinos" (Damn Chinese) spray-painted on its front window. When the mayor announced his support for the establishment of a Chinatown in downtown Tijuana, the opinion pages of local newspapers showed strong opposition: "How ridiculous, the damn Chinese have already inundated us with commercial piracy, and now they want to put a Chinatown in Tijuana."[2]

One thousand eight hundred miles away in the heart of Latin America's oldest Chinatown, a heavy-hearted group of Chinese descendants convened in Havana's Cuchillo Lane. Public hostility, inadequate legal protection, and official neglect were not among their concerns; on the contrary, they were worried about the growing attention and incessant commercial regulations they had attracted from the Cuban state. The goal of their meeting was to appraise, five years on, the 2006 dissolution of the district's coordinating body, the Grupo Promotor de Barrio Chino (Promotion Group of Chinatown) and the assumption of its administrative responsibilities by the Office of the Historian of the City. Everything from foreign donations to proposals for cultural festivals and tourism development had since been assessed and regulated by the office, signifying a total reorganization in the conduct of local business and politics.

Attending the meeting were Yrmina Eng Menéndez, Julio Hun Gerardo, and Carlos Alay Jo, three founding members of the Grupo Promotor. Each had been instrumental in Barrio Chino's "revival" in the 1990s and early 2000s, and each believed that the office's externally devised plan for growth and development had weakened the district's cultural and economic potentials. The irony of their predicament, they said, was plain to see: "The tourists come here to see the new gift shops, the restored restaurants, and streets with fashionable cafés. What they don't see is the human cost below the surface. Our social activities are not supported, our elderly residents are neglected, and our restaurants are paying higher taxes than ever. . . . The bureaucrats behind all this become suspicious whenever we try to do something really useful for our community."[3]

In both Cuba and Mexico, resident Chinese communities are confronted by the common perception that their commercial activities are strongly bound up in ethnic favoritism and therefore pose a threat to national interests. It is a recurring narrative that has resurfaced in both countries during times of economic hardship, most powerfully in the 1930s when the Great Depression provoked the forced closure of Chinese businesses in Cuba and the expulsion of some 10,000 Chinese people from Mexico. Today the narrative is fueled by China's growing global influence, and the role that overseas Chinese communities are thought to play in it.

It is striking that similar preoccupations should emerge in Cuba and Mexico, countries that occupy opposite ends of the spectrum in terms of economic openness and political ideology. A combination of downward coercion and upward nationalism continues to maintain the Cuban state's firm grip on civic administration; by contrast, three decades of contested privatizations in Mexico, driven since 1994 by the North American Free Trade Agreement (NAFTA), have eroded public confidence in the state's economic credentials. China's growing impact has reinforced existing tendencies. In Cuba it has revived historical anxieties about excessive foreign influence, evident in the state's recent attempt to assimilate Barrio Chino—and its emerging trans-Pacific ties—into a centralized scheme of governance and regulation. In Mexico it has undermined the government's already fragile credibility by provoking accusations from the private sector and the media that incompetent policymakers are to blame for China's negative economic impact. While China is now Cuba's second largest trading partner (with bilateral trade reaching $1.9 billion in 2013), it is Mexico's most obdurate competitor (with 2013 trade reaching $67.7 billion, but according to Mexican figures only $6.5 billion of this was in Mexico's favor).[4]

Diverging Cuban and Mexican reactions to China's rise have generated policy orientations whose implications are surprisingly similar for domestic Chinese communities. The Cuban tendency toward centralized management has produced top-down regulations unable to fully accommodate the priorities and productive capacities of Chinese ethnic associations and neighborhood leaders. Meanwhile, the hypersensitivity of Mexican politicians to public opinion has prevented them from openly collaborating with resident Chinese entrepreneurs to harness their unique business potentials. In both cases, national policy is out of step with local reality, impeding genuine engagement with Chinese communities and neglecting potentially useful sources of economic growth and political support.

The case studies presented below illustrate the political and cultural obstacles that have blocked productive outcomes, but they also suggest that these pressures are not insurmountable. The final case study from the Mexican state of Baja California demonstrates how overseas Chinese communities, when effectively integrated into local structures of governance, can provide important new opportunities for leveraging benefits from the world's fastest growing economy. The article concludes that overseas Chinese entrepreneurship can bring broad-based social and economic rewards, but also that this outcome requires approaches to regulation and rationalization that are sensitive to local concerns.

Engaging Overseas Chinese Networks

Chinese immigration to Cuba and Mexico can be traced to a shortage of labor in the late nineteenth and early twentieth centuries. Both communities shared the traumas of discrimination, but from the mid-twentieth century onwards they pursued different political, demographic, and economic paths. In Cuba, the revolution of 1959 led to the nationalization of Chinese businesses, the emigration of Chinese entrepreneurs to the United States, and mandatory recognition of the PRC among Chinese ethnic associations. Twelve associations and their coordinating body, the Casino Chung Wah, survived these pressures, and in the early 2000s were reinvigorated by the induction of over 2,500 enthusiastic second-, third-, and fourth-generation descendants.

Biologically and socially integrated with Cubans of European and African origin, the island's Chinese descendants have gradually climbed the ranks of the associations and initiated a range of dynamic initiatives. These include hosting international conferences on Chinese presence in Cuba, converting the associations' canteens into thriving restaurants with investment from the state and foreign sources, and increasingly, conducting commercial exchange with partners in mainland China. Deepening contact with mainland China has prompted many to study Mandarin Chinese, to set up language tuition programs in Chinatown, and in 2009, to oversee the establishment of a Confucius Institute with support from the PRC. Despite the Cantonese origins of the Chinese Cuban community, only the aging few born in China speak their native tongue.

In contrast to Cuba, the number of first-generation Chinese people resident in Mexico has grown rapidly since the mid-twentieth century, but owing to the undocumented status of many, Mexican scholars have little faith in official statistics. While the census of 2010 reports 6,655 Chinese-born residing in Mexico, the Chinese Embassy in Mexico counts 3,000, plus 20,000 Mexicans of Chinese origin, dedicated mainly to gastronomy, trade, and to a lesser extent, bureaucracy and professional services. The Overseas Chinese Affairs Office in Beijing calculates roughly half the number of naturalized Chinese, living primarily in the northern border cities of Tijuana and Mexicali, the urban metropolis of Mexico City, and the southern state of Chiapas. Unofficial accounts from Tijuana and Mexicali indicate that these two cities alone are respectively home to 25,000 and 35,000 Chinese immigrants and descendants, many of whom arrived since 2000 and are not legally registered. Whether in Mexico City or on the US border, Chinese people speak of a division between old and new arrivals, the former descending from the Cantonese-speaking immigrants of the nineteenth and twentieth centuries, with corresponding ties to the Kuomintang, KMT, and the latter hailing from the Mandarin-speaking urban centers of the eastern PRC.

China's growing influence in Mexico has subdued some of the differences between old and new arrivals, and aggravated others. Since 2000 the Chinese government has offered commercial partnerships and orchestrated prestigious visits from senior officials to persuade Mexico's Chinese associations to renounce recognition of the KMT and adopt Mandarin as their official operating language. However, the recent wave of Chinese immigrants, comprised largely of Mandarin-speaking young people with little interest in traditional ethnic associations, remains disengaged from older Cantonese-speaking communities, and from Mexican society in general. These individuals have generally focused on commercial activities, registered and otherwise, such as importing and retailing low-cost Chinese consumer goods, and have consequently drawn the scorn of their predecessors.

Despite their differences, Chinese communities in Cuba and Mexico endured similar historical pressures. Across Latin America Chinese immigrants endured and sometimes overcame repressive work regimes and discriminatory commercial regulations. But their hard-won progress, writes Evelyn Hu-Dehart, provoked harsh responses:

> The eventual success of Chinese in converting themselves into small urban business proprietors and the influx of free Asian immigrants to Latin America in ensuing decades were accompanied everywhere by anti-Asian agitation and mob action, as well as more organized state campaigns and persecution. In emulation of the U.S. Exclusion Act, Latin American governments in the early twentieth century enacted laws to severely limit further Asian, especially Chinese, immigration.[5]

Discriminatory laws influenced Chinese patterns of trans-Pacific immigration, settlement and commerce, but as Adam McKeown has argued, the impact of such laws was conditioned by specific contexts of place, time, and hierarchy.[6] Social forces were as important as legal codes, evident in the formation of solidarity networks to navigate and circumscribe official rules. Membership in mutual aid associations provided protection from discrimination, pathways to employment, and finance for small business development. But the same associations also deepened the segregation of their members from broader civic and social landscapes, perpetuating a vicious circle of external hostility and internal protection. Every rotation of this circle broadened the perception that resident Chinese groups were closed and self-serving.[7]

Repressive work regimes, discriminatory commercial regulations, and xenophobia in the late ninetieth and early twentieth centuries made membership in Chinese ethnic associations a matter of survival. Marginalization stimulated—as it has elsewhere—informal networks of protection, solidarity, and "bonding social capital."[8] Although conditions have since improved, twenty-first-century anxieties about China's growing global influence, compounded by competition between Chinese exporters and domestic manufacturers, have brought new pressures to bear on overseas Chinese communities. Ethnic associations therefore continue to fill important functions for their members, including economic advancement, protection against discrimination, and mechanisms for bypassing regulations that are perceived to be inappropriate or unfair.

Where external pressure has fomented in-group solidarities and loyalties over time, as is the case of Chinese communities worldwide, fairness is conceived not only in terms of individual advancement, but also as the protection of collective cultural and economic security.[9] Family ties and ethnic allegiances infused with *guanxi* (关系, relationship or connection) have furnished network members with benefits such as start-up capital, market access, a flexible labor force, a loyal customer base, and informal advice about opportunities. This has fostered the confidence necessary for foreign trade, informal loans, community mutual aid, and business partnerships.[10]

Chinese cooperative networks have sustained collective notions of exchange, loyalty, identity, and fairness, but their informality and ethnic partiality has sometimes led them into conflict with host country laws and public values. Internal affinities among ethnic Chinese people in Indonesia and Malaysia, for instance, provoked riots against them in the late 1960s, and continue to complicate the multicultural agenda in both.[11] Recent case studies presented in the *China Quarterly* show that perceptions of ethnic favoritism have also generated hostility toward Chinese immigrants across Africa.[12] The predicament of Chinese communities in Latin America is more subdued, but regional administrators have nevertheless struggled to incorporate them into domestic structures of governance and compliance.

From a policy perspective, tight-knit groups governed by internal regulations pose a challenge to civic administration and the rule of law.[13] As Alejandro Portes puts it, "the capacity of authorities to enforce rules (social control) can thus be jeopardized by the existence of tight networks whose function is precisely to facilitate violation of those rules for private benefit."[14] Informal networks impede the efforts of governments and markets to harness domestic talent and "scale up" local capacities for an ostensibly greater national good. This process is ideally characterized by the transformation of local norms and values into a wider system of procedural rules, and the "rationalization of social capital" through "the gradual replacement of informal associations and networks by formal administrative structures, and the impersonal market mechanism no longer tied to individual identities."[15] Emancipated from ethnic loyalties and bonding social capital, support networks and the trust they engender should—in the eyes of policymakers—become a public resource.

In the eyes of community actors, rationalization can bring opportunities for legal protection and commercial expansion, but these benefits must be weighed against the cost of subordinating immediate local needs to remote national priorities. The casualties of institutionalization, suffered by social movements and mutual aid networks across Latin America, include the erosion of internal commitments, the loss of cultural identity, and the cooption of interests by anonymous bureaucrats.[16] Cooperation across the "public–private divide" is not, however, a zero-sum game. Undocumented Mexican farm workers, Afro-Cuban religious congregations, Brazilian women's networks, and Chinese communities in northern Mexico (discussed below) have entered into formal synergies with states and markets when it has benefited them to do so.[17] As a series of policy papers from Harvard University's John F. Kennedy School of Government has argued, regulatory frameworks can earn public respect and become "embedded" within socioeconomic systems when they are sensitive to local interests. By contrast, "primitive metrics" of regulation that are not "tailored to take account of the culture, education, and priorities of intended audiences" afford little basis for state–society cooperation.[18]

Opportunities to build formal symbiotic partnerships with the Chinese diaspora in Latin America abound, but their potential is yet to be realized. Governments can endorse trade fairs organized by Chinese associations, facilitate work visas for potential Chinese investors, provide diplomatic support for resident Chinese entrepreneurs traveling "home" to seek out new markets and sources of investment, and promote public education about Chinese history, migration, and culture. When support has been forthcoming, Chinese communities have collaborated enthusiastically, but in its absence they have looked to alternative informal sources of affirmation, both within themselves and across the Pacific.

How should state and private actors harness the potential of their countries' emerging linkages to China? The political differences between Cuba and Mexico span the spectrum of state and market-oriented models, suggesting different responses to this question. However, regardless of their blend of public and private carrots and sticks, policymakers can harness a common resource: if handled appropriately and consensually, the ethnic solidarity of domestic Chinese networks can work for the broader national benefit. Case studies from Cuba and Mexico illustrate that governments and publics ignore the productive capacities of resident Chinese communities at their own peril; by contrast, they stand to reap substantial rewards if the activities of these communities are rationalized in more sophisticated ways—sovereign and intact—into broader strategies of economic development.

Formalizing the Informal in Havana's Barrio Chino

On January 2, 1847, 300 Chinese indentured workers, or "coolies" (kǔlì—苦力—literally "bitter use of strength") boarded the Spanish frigate *Oquendo* in the port of Amoy (present-day Xiamen), bound for Cuba. Contracted through the Manila and Tait Company in London, they were conscripted as laborers for eight years to the Spanish Real Junta de Fomento y Colonización. The 206 who survived the trans-Pacific voyage arrived in Havana's port of Regla on June 3 the same year, and were joined ten days later by 365 more aboard the British vessel *The Duke of Argyle*. By 1853 more than 5,000 Chinese had arrived in Cuba, and by 1873, an additional 132,453.[19] Chinese workers arrived in Cuba with the hope of fulfilling their contracts and returning home wealthy, but on four pesos per month, few returned home at all. Transcripts of an 1874 testimony recently analyzed by Lisa Yun demonstrate that whether or not the coolie trade constituted slavery, the social conditions in which Chinese workers and enslaved Africans lived were practically the same.[20]

When Chang Li and Laig Siu-Yi established a family restaurant and a fruit market in 1858, they set in motion a system of supply and demand that would underpin the development of Cuba's first and only Chinatown. By the early-to-mid-twentieth century, restaurants and convenience stores trading in fruits and vegetables, laundry services, and artisanry underpinned Barrio Chino's expansion to forty-four city blocks, making it the largest and most important Chinatown in Latin America, rivaling those of San Francisco and New York. Forbidden by law to live within the city center (today Old Havana), the Chinese community developed Barrio Chino as "an independent sector that sought to be the Cuban extension of the province of Canton."[21]

Despite their success in small agriculture and other niche sectors, wealth eluded most Chinese Cubans. Beyond the economically elite Chinese who arrived from post–gold rush California, it was only those involved in organized gaming and opium trafficking who prospered. Nevertheless, their perceived affluence provoked protests in the early 1930s, leading the government of Ramón Grau San Martín (1933–1934, 1944–1948) to implement laws (as Mexico had done in 1930 and as Panama would do in 1935) requiring them to diversify their workforces to include at least 50 percent (later 80 percent) non-Chinese Cubans. Jealousy and resentment toward the Chinese community is evident in the music of the time, featuring imitated accents and lyrics about Chinese immigrants and their descendants working multiple jobs, attracting Cuban women with their wealth, and buying up property both locally and in the United States.[22] Duvon C. Corbitt, who worked as a lecturer in Havana in the early 1940s, observed that behind the official image of harmonious ethnic integration, discrimination was widespread: "The good terms on which almost all Chinese live with their Cuban neighbors, and the relatively numerous marriages between the races, would seem to belie the fact that prejudice exists; nevertheless, close contact with the situation will reveal that the Cubans generally look on the Chinese as social, and even intellectual inferiors."[23]

Chinese business initiatives were protected and supported by ethnic associations organized according to members' family names, region of origin, and political affiliation. The associations' coordinating body, the Casino Chung Wah, was founded in 1883 and legally registered in 1893 under the honorary presidency of the Chinese consul general of Cuba, Tam Kin Cho. Together, the Casino and the associations linked local suppliers to consumers through networks of mutual aid and ethnic solidarity. They also fostered the development of Chinese restaurants as sources of employment and acculturation for new arrivals, and as social epicenters where community affairs were discussed and deals negotiated. The associations epitomized the development of the "social economy," relying on informal lines of trade with agricultural producers on the outskirts of Havana to supply their restaurants and canteens.

When Fidel Castro marched into Havana in 1959, Barrio Chino continued to function as a hub of unregistered commerce, economically and socially disarticulated from its surroundings. In an attempt to reign in the local informal economy, a special unit of the National Revolutionary Militia called the José Wong Brigade (named after the legendary young Chinese Cuban communist and founder of the illegal newsletter *Grito Obrero Campesino*, assassinated in 1930) entered the district on February 17, 1960. Comprised entirely of Chinese Cubans and operating in Cantonese, the brigade launched an outright campaign against gambling, prostitution, opium trafficking, and black market trading. The Sino-Soviet split of the 1960s strained diplomatic relations between Cuba and China, intensifying official scrutiny of Barrio Chino, particularly during the "great revolutionary offensive" of 1968. The district's businesses were nationalized, and only those properties linked to the Chinese associations remained in community hands, prompting the emigration of a significant (but unknown) proportion of Chinese Cubans. The associations continued to function quietly, relying on resilient informal networks to supply their canteens and social clubs.

By 1986 the rapidly declining number of first-generation Chinese immigrants prompted the Casino Chung Wah to advise its twelve remaining associations to open membership to second- and third-generation Chinese Cubans. In the early 1990s most did so, and by 2006 the associations together boasted a membership of 2,550 individuals (Montes de Oca Choy 2007). According to Jorge Chao Chiu, secretary general of the Casino Chung Wah, in early 2011 the Casino registered 171 surviving first-generation Chinese people in Cuba.[24] Unlike most of these individuals, second- and third-generation Chinese Cubans do not hold Chinese citizenship and are more biologically and culturally integrated into Cuban society. Despite this diversity, Chinese descendants have demonstrated a strong interest in the ethnic associations and now occupy senior (though not the highest) posts in the most important of these, including Min Chih Tang, Lung Kong Kun Sun, and the Casino Chung Wah.[25]

Governing or governed, native Chinese or not, all are aware that Barrio Chino harbors a legacy of informal support networks that are powerful even by Cuban standards. This legacy manifested itself in 1994 when a group of community activists marshaled support from the Casino Chung Wah and the ethnic associations to establish a grassroots organization called the Grupo Promotor (Promotion Group) of Barrio Chino. Using the Grupo as an administrative platform, they persuaded the municipal government of Central Havana to permit Chinese Cuban entrepreneurs to set up retail outlets for shoes, clothes, kitchen equipment, and other items imported directly from China. Led by Chinese descendant Yrmina Eng Menéndez, the Grupo was so successful that it attracted official pressure to register as a state institution, and in 1998 it conceded. Formalization brought executive power as the Grupo became officially responsible for Barrio Chino's economic development, but it also brought a raft of unforeseen regulatory provisos. For four years Eng and her team brokered deals between the Cuban state, the Chinese community, and business partners across the Pacific, but the complications of regulating expanding trade eventually saw the Grupo's founding members supplanted by external career administrators.

The transformation of any informal association into an official institution inevitably involves compromise. As grassroots loyalties and allegiances are rationalized, local autonomy should, in theory, be compensated by expanded economic and legal capacities for community protection and advocacy. In Barrio Chino this process was thrown off course by a convergence of structural and personal weaknesses. Official registration placed the Grupo under the jurisdiction of the Central Havana municipal government, an entity already overburdened with responsibility and lacking sufficient resources to develop regulations tailored to Barrio Chino's unique socioeconomic needs. Restaurants connected to the associations, for instance, were subjected to civil codes designed for Cuban nongovernmental organizations (NGOs), and as such were required to submit their profits (between $2,000 and $5,000 per day) to designated bank accounts accessible only with written permission from the Ministry of Justice. Monolithic acquittal procedures, combined with the Grupo's green light for commercial activity, generated easy opportunities for illicit personal gain. Irregularities became so pronounced that the Grupo, after eight years of official service, was disbanded and replaced by an entirely different system of economic and civic governance.

On January 1, 2006, administrative responsibility for Barrio Chino was transferred to the Office of the Historian of the City. As its name suggests, the office has distinguished itself by explicitly attempting to superimpose a temporal dimension onto its urban development projects in order to emphasize continuity with the cultural past. Since the early 1990s, the office has overseen the economic development of the adjacent municipality of Old Havana, whose historical charm it has leveraged as the centerpiece of tourism development.[26] The office's expansion into Barrio Chino represents a bold effort to grow its signature brand of historical tourism. Willing and able to finance the "revitalization of historical patrimony," it has set out to establish itself as the rightful steward of the district's economic affairs.

Directing its efforts at the associations and restaurants, the office attempted to do what one Cuban urban development agency believes is the most pressing task facing the island: "formalize the informal" in order to "bridge the widening gap between state structures and community life."[27] Employing a proven formula, it set about converting Barrio Chino into a mainstream tourist destination by providing opportunities for residents to participate actively in their neighborhood's "revival."[28] These opportunities were initially embraced, but local entrepreneurs soon became frustrated with the office's prefabricated bookkeeping requirements. Commerce with Chinese exporters quickly diminished as a generalized system of trade credits replaced cash payments. The associations' restaurants were required to continue submitting profits to designated bank accounts, and subjected to centralized sourcing restrictions that sought to formalize their supply chains through officially nominated providers.[29] The office's attempt to rationalize local activities also involved a new tax: in addition to an existing levy charged by the Organización Nacional de Asuntos Tributarios (National Organization of Tributary Affairs, ONAT), private (*cuenta propia*) restaurants like those in Cuchillo Lane would now have to pay a "donation" to fund neighborhood development projects.

Association elders believed that the new environment would force them to curtail or abandon their 150-year-old tradition of charitable service, including complimentary meals for the most needy local residents. Stricter regulations were also introduced to community organizations that openly maintain foreign linkages, such as the Residencia China, which provides housing, medical attention, and other services to many of Barrio Chino's remaining 159 first-generation Chinese residents. According to the Residencia's director: "We've always received donations from foreigners. Usually these have been private individuals, and many of them have been from China. There has always been a high level of understanding and trust. But now, if I need to get a new sofa for the Residencia I have to first go through a long approval process, and every penny needs to be accounted for."[30]

The office's attempt to incorporate collaborative ties and social capital—what the Residencia's director called "understanding and trust"—into a general scheme of rationalized governance was criticized openly by the Casino Chung Wah. Two days before the office's takeover, and shortly before his death, its president, Li San, commenced a public speech in Cuchillo Lane by invoking a sense of imperiled local authority: "Our unity is under threat, and we must be stronger now more than ever before."[31] Whether or not this comment was intended to incite noncompliance, deepening informality over the following five years turned the office's objectives on their head. A community leader described the situation in early 2011:

> We are governed by a series of bureaucrats whose eyes have become rounder over the years. Most of them live in El Vedado [a comparatively whiter and wealthier district of Havana], and they know little about our culture. From 5:01 P.M. until 8:59 A.M. they are not concerned with Barrio Chino. . . . The new system has problems, for example, the leaders of the

associations take a cut of about 25 percent before submitting their profits to the Ministry of Justice bank account. That way they can live more comfortably and invest more freely in their restaurants.[32]

Taking personal charge of profits was not the only strategy employed by restaurant administrators, who also privately flouted the office's requirement that they purchase supplies from state-designated stores. The informal sector, as it had for decades, continued to play a key role in local supply and demand. Furthermore, family connections compensated for the collapse of formal commercial ties between Barrio Chino entrepreneurs and Chinese suppliers. A district administrator estimated that between 2006 and 2011 approximately twenty Chinese investors financed the conversion of relatives' homes into restaurants and small businesses. Not only do such operations skirt the office's foreign investment laws and property rental fees, but they also enable a 96 percent saving on electricity, water, and gas, since utilities are charged to citizens in *Moneda Nacional* (Cuban pesos) rather than *Convertibles* (convertible pesos).

The attempt of the Office of the Historian to rationalize norms and practices in Barrio Chino indicates its awareness of the need to engage informal networks, but as yet it has been unable to harness their potential. The approach developed in Old Havana by the office's director, Dr. Eusebio Leal Spengler, is commendable: "We're trying to preserve schools and houses, create jobs, and encourage true participation, for which we've created dynamic fiscal structures that allow reinvestment of profits in the historic center."[33] Not so commendable, and less effective, is the attempt to transfer commercial regulations across distinct contexts with little adjustment for local conditions, cultures, and priorities. As a senior office administrator put it: "Chinese immigrants and their descendants have always been integrated into Cuba. Remember, one of our most famous national icons is the *mulata cubana* [the racially mixed Cuban woman]. Because of Cuba's long history of racial integration we have been able to work in Barrio Chino with no problems. It's just like working here in Old Havana."[34] In Barrio Chino this optimism is counterproductive, as it underestimates the efficacy of bonding social capital and *guanxi* accrued over generations and perpetuated by ongoing perceptions of external interference. Scholars have argued that social capital is generally not fungible across distinct contexts; it stands to reason that the same holds true for attempts to rationalize it.[35]

Although community leaders complained about the office's accountability requirements, some nevertheless perceived benefits in the formalization of local governance. Former director of the House of Chinese Arts and Traditions, Carmen Eng noted that: "with a solid organizational structure, getting things done will be easier. No more doing deals by word of mouth. Instead we'll do things in a more disciplined manner."[36] Despite reservations about the bureaucracy of handling foreign donations and acquiring furniture, the Residencia's director also expressed confidence in the new executive framework: "An advantage is that the Office of the Historian has contacts with foreign NGOs and sources of funds, including in China. Now there's an official mechanism for linking up with donors."[37]

The above comments support the finding that public, private, and civil sectors can accrue mutual benefits from the rationalization of grassroots values, affinities, and social capital.[38] Despite Max Weber's anxieties about the bureaucratic "iron cage" inherent in this process, and arguably its manifestation in Cuba, since 1959 state command of economic and human resources has produced impressive outcomes in life expectancy (79 years), infant mortality (5/1,000), expected years of schooling (17.7), environmental performance (9th out of 163 countries), and other development measures.[39] Cuban citizens, official and otherwise, are proud of these achievements and are concerned about their sustainability as the market assumes a more prominent place in their lives. As urban development specialist Mario Coyula put it, "There is a fear that we could lose the results of 50 years of experiments, failures, lessons, and achievements in a day."[40] Their concern is reflected in the Central Report of Cuba's April 2011 Communist Party Congress, which attempts to balance economic liberalization with restrictions on the accumulation of private property.[41]

Commercial regulations that accommodate the entrepreneurial initiative of local networks do not imply a wholesale adoption of a free-market policies and renunciation of state stewardship over national development goals. On the contrary, the evidence from Barrio Chino suggests that a balanced combination of state and market forces would produce an optimal platform for rationalizing the district's capacities. The president of the Casino Chung Wah, Juan Eng, notes that his associates in China are eager for opportunities to invest in Cuba, and that they are comfortable operating in a state-oriented environment.[42] Nevertheless, as a member of Hu Jintao's 2008 delegation to Cuba revealed, they are also concerned that unsophisticated and outdated commercial codes will impede their ability to conduct profitable business.[43] Greater administrative space for the conduct of business would alleviate these concerns and improve local conditions. This outcome, writes Cuban economist Ricardo Torres Pérez, is a key objective Cuba's recent reforms: "If greater capacities for local management are achieved, this will enable economic synergies . . . that today are overshadowed by the weight of national priorities. This will produce development alternatives that account for regional conditions, improving the microeconomic use of resources and the wellbeing of residents."[44]

Barrio Chino's community leaders command knowledge, connections, and *guanxi* that could enable them to attract investment and capital goods from China, and potentially open new channels for exports to China. To do so they will require state support in the form of diplomatic engagement, trade intelligence, and regulatory oversight that permits private business networks to function under legal sanction. Locally tailored strategies are prerequisite if Chinese communities are to willingly permit their entrepreneurial capacities to be rationalized into official codes of governance. This is the case not only for state-led societies such as Cuba, but also for market-oriented economies such as Mexico. There is a need in both countries to recognize the historical and contemporary pressures driving the formation of bonding social capital in Chinese networks, and to transform this potential threat into a competitive advantage. This process is yet to run its course in Havana and Mexico City, but there are signs of progress in the northern Mexican cities of Mexicali and Tijuana.

From Threat to Opportunity in Mexico

China's unparalleled economic growth, on the order of 10 percent per year since 1970, is sustained by a massive flow of worldwide exports, and overseas Chinese communities have played an important role in familiarizing mainland suppliers with domestic markets. In 1978 the State Council of China created the Overseas Chinese Affairs Office (OCAO) to consolidate a sense of belonging, loyalty, and Chinese cultural identity among emigrants. OCAO assists overseas Chinese communities to create opportunities for trade with China, overcome linguistic and cultural misunderstandings, and build "harmony with the governments and communities that host them."[45] In the case of Mexico, bilateral trade has accelerated rapidly, but the prospect of bilateral harmony is remote. As China's consul general in Tijuana, Gao Shoujian, points out, the convergence of economic competition with persisting diplomatic and social tensions constitutes a formidable challenge to any efforts to build cooperation and understanding.[46]

As in Cuba, Chinese communities in Mexico have faced pressure to integrate into their surrounding economic and legal environments. Accusations in the national media of obscure and unregulated business practices among Chinese importers have emanated mainly from small and medium-sized Mexican enterprises unable to compete with the flood of inexpensive Chinese consumer goods. These sectors perceive a chronic lack of fairness and transparency in the ethnic exclusivity of Chinese trade fairs, the labor conditions and low wages in Chinese factories, the piracy of traditional Mexican handicrafts, and the seemingly ungovernable expansion of illegally imported Chinese textiles, shoes, toys, office equipment, and steel products.

According to Mexico's most recent (2010) census, the country is home to 6,655 Chinese-born individuals (the twelfth largest foreign group), a small populace compared to the 738,103 expatriates from the United States (the largest group).[47] Unofficial reports estimate the number of US citizens residing in

Mexico to exceed 1 million, many of them unregistered. These figures are not surprising considering that in 2013 US–Mexico trade amounted to $487.7 billion (more than seven times that of China's).[48] Commercial ties, though, are only part of the explanation; the other part concerns the aging US population: in 2005 some 250,000 US senior citizens were living in gated villages on Mexico's Pacific coast, where Spanish is barely spoken and "you can't really tell you're in Mexico."[49] Such communities are growing, and the Mexican government reportedly hopes to attract some 5 million US retirees by 2025.[50] This objective reveals a sharp divergence of public attitudes toward US and Chinese migrants, though the reasons for this probably extend beyond historical familiarity, trade integration, and other economic considerations. As a student under the author's supervision at the Autonomous University of Baja California explained, "Even though we hate the *gringos* [North Americans], we wish we could be like them. It bothers us that they look down on us, so we pass this feeling on, especially to Chinese people."[51]

The uncomfortable predicament of Chinese communities in Mexico owes much to national economic insecurities generated by thirty years of ineffective industrial policy, the debilitating socioeconomic impact of the war on drugs, and the global financial crisis. This politically charged backdrop has intensified the bitterness of the nation's unsuccessful economic competition with China, which one trade unionist described as "the global force that is taking away what little we have left."[52] Unlike the Chinese government, President Felipe Calderón's conservative PAN party has followed the tendency of its predecessors since Miguel de la Madrid (1982–1988) to shy away from proactive industrial policy as a legitimate solution to macro-economic problems. The much-touted Sino-Mexican "strategic partnership" has consequently played out on uneven economic terrain, generating correspondingly slanted perceptions of China and its people.

A pervasive social symptom of the economic imbalance, writes Francisco Haro Navejas, is a homogenizing tendency in the Mexican public sphere to equate Chinese businesses, products, and people with the global ambitions of the Chinese state.[53] This tendency is strengthened by the mass media's frequent publication of domestic and foreign articles critical of human rights abuses in Chinese state-operated factories, the substandard quality of the products they manufacture, and the unfair competition they represent for Mexican businesses.[54] As illustrated at the beginning of this chapter, suspicions extend to Chinese communities resident in Mexico, which are viewed by many as the foot soldiers of China's commercial "invasion."

It does not require detailed investigation to reveal that multiple ethnic origins, historical backgrounds, political affiliations, and economic aspirations have produced considerable diversity in Mexico's Chinese diaspora. Communities descended from nineteenth- and twentieth-century Chinese migrant laborers, for instance, did not automatically embrace the 1949 triumph of New China, and have generally maintained only thin relations with its diplomatic missions. For thousands of Chinese Mexican entrepreneurs, diplomatic indifference has stemmed less from political considerations than a reluctance to expose their blend of local, trans-Pacific, formal, and informal business activities to the scrutiny and regulatory designs of Chinese and Mexican authorities. For their part, the governments of both countries have shown little interest in Mexico's Chinese community, or even in each other, instead focusing what little cooperation they maintain on the upper echelons of transnational business. Their failure to find bilateral solutions to Mexico's chronic trade deficit with China has not as yet provoked serious efforts from the Mexican government (with the exception of Baja California) to harness the entrepreneurial capacities of resident Chinese communities.

Identifying missed opportunities for engagement, ethnic Chinese entrepreneurs in Mexico City have—like those in Havana—attempted to develop commercial initiatives with partners in China. Conscious of these thickening trans-Pacific ties, the Chinese embassy has pressured resident Chinese communities to officially register their activities, advance opportunities for Chinese firms through local political and business connections, and explicitly articulate support for the PRC's "One China" policy. In response, the Confederation of Chinese Associations of Mexico (CACHIMEX) has sought public support from the Mexican and Chinese governments for its commercial expos and trade fairs. However, official endorsement from either government is unlikely considering the political sensitivity of Mexico's trade deficit with China, and popular perceptions that such activities are dedicated to importing Chinese products—legally and otherwise—into Mexico.

Despite the lack of official support, in 2009 CACHIMEX coordinated the first "Expo China-Mexico," which brought together some 250 companies, half of which were from Mexico and the other half from China, Vietnam, and other Asian countries. The second Expo, held in November 2010, made headway in facilitating fruit, vegetable, and scrap metal exports to China. According to CACHIMEX Secretary General Jimmy Li, "we hope this will reduce the perception that these fairs are all about bringing 'made in China' products into Mexico."[55] Li adopts an "integral" approach to Sino-Mexican commerce by complementing these trade fairs with educational seminars delivered by local scholars, such as the director of UNAM's Centre for China-Mexico Research (CECHIMEX), Enrique Dussel Peters. According to Dussel Peters: "CACHIMEX brought in 15,000 people to its last Expo, but this could, and should, be 50,000. Since the Chinese and Mexican governments won't get involved, the Expo is run 100 percent by the business community. This won't work because it results in a focus on importing over exporting, and leaves no space for policy strategies that could turn this around."[56] The lack of policy engagement with resident Chinese entrepreneurs, paired with substantial trade tariffs on imports from China, has created an environment conducive to unofficial alternatives. A Chinese student at UNAM spoke of his family business:

> My sister has lived here in Mexico City for seven years, and I have come to help her. We import watches, clothes, and shoes from our contacts in China, and we can order any brand you want. I get the watches via UPS, and my sister handles the clothes and shoes. She sends a van to Guatemala to pick them up because tariffs there are lower, and it's easier to bribe customs officials. The tariff is low on watches because Mexico doesn't produce them, but clothes and shoes are between 50 percent and 200 percent. When the clothes come straight to Mexico we ask the suppliers to write a lower price on the papers to reduce the tax.[57]

Destined for urban marketplaces and street kiosks, imported Chinese consumer goods have become a major source of dispute. The country's most notorious outlet for unregistered merchandise is Tepito, on the eastern perimeter of Mexico City's Historic Center. Customers are drawn to the district by its commercial catchphrase: "dress yourself with 100 pesos [US $8]." Unable to compete with low-priced contraband, owners of the Historic Center's 17,670 registered enterprises are increasingly converting their shopfronts into warehouses to service the 40,000 unregistered merchants who have now spilled over from Tepito.[58] In Tepito alone it is thought that some 150,000 people are dedicated to street vending, and according to one local representative of 500 vendors, "Our basic needs are more important than official legal regulations; street vending is a safety valve."[59] Former Economic Counsel to the Mexican Government in China Juan José Ling agrees:

> Mexicans should realize that their informal sector, which constitutes something like 40 percent of business in the country, is something they need. The official figure of 5 percent unemployment is a blatant lie. There is an abundance of people we call "*nini*": *ni trabajan ni estudian* [neither work nor study]. They need informality to survive. The real problem is the lack of government support for education and training, and for Mexican companies, which should be actively finding new markets—including in China—and creating jobs.[60]

The absence of a coherent strategy for dealing with China and a reliance on trade tariffs to quell domestic political fallout have restricted formal economic opportunities for Chinese entrepreneurs in Mexico City. Family connections, *guanxi*, and the informal sector have logically filled the void, though in ways that generate business only within relatively small circles of ethnic entrepreneurship. Resulting perceptions of disproportionate advantages enjoyed by Chinese communities and their networks further impede formal strategies of engagement. The problem is circular: public hostility toward Chinese communities obstructs state support of their commercial initiatives, provoking informal alternatives confined to tight-knit ethnic networks, in turn generating further suspicion and hostility. In this environment, the prospect of rationalizing Chinese initiatives into formal structures of governance is remote.

The same circle that revolves in Mexico City extends to the northern cities of Mexicali and Tijuana, but geographic and legislative distance from the metropolis has enabled regional policymakers to more effectively reach out to resident Chinese communities. Despite the public pressure these communities have faced, official partnerships have enabled their leaders to explore tentative solutions. Recent steps taken by the state of Baja California government and Chinese business networks to cooperate with each other demonstrate that rationalization, when premised on the fulfillment of local aspirations, can produce both local and national benefits.

From 1990 until 2006 Eduardo Auyón Gerardo served as president of the Chinese Association of Mexicali, a position he used to build ties with the growing number of outward-looking commercial exporters in China. In 2001 his efforts to connect Chinese exporters with Mexican retail networks were recognized by OCAO, which appointed him as one of thirty-two worldwide "assessors." Providing a stable nexus for bilateral trade, together with the related advertising, matchmaking, and visas have made Auyón a key node of contact for entrepreneurs from both sides. Building commercial networks under the auspices of OCAO, he says, has provided a robust and enduring framework for business development:

> The important thing is security. Some Chinese businesses have shipped their products over only to find that the market has turned against them because of exaggerated media reports about product safety and competition with Mexican producers. As an assessor for the Overseas Chinese Affairs Office I am responsible for selecting trustworthy clients who will follow through with their commitments. This has worked very well for us with electronic products and home appliances. Mexicali is on the same latitude as the Sahara Desert, so we are sourcing a new line of powerful air conditioners under our "Kooling Air" and "Dragón Refrigeraciones" brands, and selling these through the network.[61]

Throughout his career, Auyón has cultivated a series of official and unofficial relationships to facilitate cultural and commercial initiatives between Mexico and China. In 2004 he began arranging meetings for the governor of

Baja California, Eugenio Elorduy Walther, with Chinese counterparts such as the governor of Jiangsu Province, Liang Baohua. When President Hu Jintao visited Mexico in 2005 to discuss strategies for diminishing the trade imbalance, he personally recognized Auyón's protagonism in facilitating new business linkages. The government of Baja California praised the potential benefits of these connections during National Immigration Week in October 2008. While seven Mexican states participated in the festivities, the Baja California branch of the National Institute of Migration (INAMI) dedicated the week specifically to Chinese immigration, holding all related events and ceremonies in the Chinese Association of Mexicali. The city's mayor, Rodolfo Valdéz Gutiérrez, described the Chinese community as "a motor of the local economy," while Baja California's INAMI delegate, Javier Reynoso Nuño, promised to simplify the process of visa acquisition for relatives of the local Chinese community.[62]

In partnership with the Chinese Association of Mexicali, in June 2010 Auyón oversaw the establishment of the Chamber of Chinese Enterprises of the Northeast, a coordinating body for some four thousand Chinese businesspeople resident in the states of Baja California, Sonora, Coahuila, and Chihuahua. The chamber benefits from the logistical support of OCAO's Guangdong office, illustrating the Chinese government's interest in building ties with overseas Chinese associations and in "becom[ing] the central force of the Chinese community."[63] Through the chamber, Auyón aims to "generate a bridge to support commerce between Chinese entrepreneurs and producers in Asia and those in this region of Mexico," particularly in the *maquiladora* [manufacturing/assembly] and auto sectors.[64]

Auyón's talent for matchmaking has established mutually beneficial linkages between Mexico and China. The chamber has begun to research the placement of Mexican products in the Chinese market and work with Chinese investors seeking opportunities in Mexican copper mining and the development of renewable energy technologies in Mexicali's Silicon Border initiative. Such activities are sorely needed both for Mexico and its Chinese communities, which have faced hostility precisely because of public perceptions that they have monopolized economic opportunities rather than extend them beyond their tight-knit business networks. Support from the Baja California state government, its Chinese counterparts, and OCAO may prove decisive in this regard, as institutionalized cooperation will enable the diversification and formalization of previously narrow trade ties, thereby reducing external perceptions of unfairness and illegality.

One hundred thirty-five miles west of Mexicali, the Chinese Association of Tijuana has also positioned itself as an intermediary of bilateral trade. Its secretary general, Willy Liu Ke Wei, was recently involved in lobbying the Mexican airline Aeroméxico to open a direct flight between Shanghai and Tijuana. His efforts paid off, and in May 2008 the new route was launched with the ambition of attracting 30,000 Chinese tourists per year, inspiring Liu to set up a travel agency catering to Chinese entrepreneurs exploring opportunities in Mexico. While Chinese businesses in Baja California are reported to have seen a 30 percent decline in earnings due to the global financial crisis, the agency aims to generate new trade and investment directly from China.[65]

For Liu, a critical first step is to build Mexican appreciation for Chinese traditions; in his words, "Commerce and culture are like sisters, and if you go down the path of culture, you arrive at the path of business."[66] The path forged by Liu's agency is paved with both, bringing Chinese entrepreneurs to Tijuana three times a year to meet Mexican business partners in conventions and banquets that coincide with the Chinese New Year, New China Independence Day, and the Chinese Day of Light. Since 2005 these events have been accompanied by public parades and Chinese-themed street markets in the downtown area, coordinated by his association at the invitation of the Tijuana city government. The Chinese Consulate has contributed resources to these events, for as Liu says, "the PRC needs our help in creating a good public image."[67]

As well as seeking to build a more positive image, the Chinese government has also requested that Mexico's Chinese associations break off linkages with Taiwan. To this end, in 2001 OCAO established the "Chinese Peaceful Pro-unification Alliance of Baja California," which the state's three Chinese associations (Tijuana, Mexicali, and Ensenada) immediately joined, adopting Mandarin Chinese as their operating language as a condition of entry. For the Association of Tijuana, 2001 marked the first time since its 1918 establishment that it did not conduct its annual meeting in Cantonese, the first language of 98 percent of its members. This adjustment, along with vigilance against anti-PRC and pro-Taiwan activities, appears to be the price of institutional recognition. Indeed, without the backing of the Chinese government it is unlikely that the Chinese Association of Tijuana will attract sufficient support from regional authorities to achieve officially endorsed business outcomes like its counterpart in Mexicali. Conscious of this, Liu has prioritized engagement with Chinese and Mexican authorities in order to set the Association of Tijuana on a virtuous circle of diversified partnerships, more open disclosure of business activities, and improved public relations.

A combination of administrative distance from Mexico City and creative policymaking has enabled officials in Mexicali and Tijuana to reach out to resident Chinese communities in an attempt to harness their strengths. By supporting commercial partnerships with China, facilitating trade fairs, and inviting Chinese associations to conduct public festivals, administrators are discovering that their territories stand to gain when local social capital, *guanxi*, and business networks are rationalized—sovereign and intact—into broader strategies of economic development.

Conclusion

Overseas Chinese communities in Latin America are uniquely positioned to broker trans-Pacific cooperation, and have begun to do so in Cuba and Mexico. The manner in which they engage with Mainland partners depends on the extent to which their activities are formally institutionalized. If policymakers are out of touch with local dynamics, or lacking political will, then they will fail to elicit compliance and generate formal agreements. If, on the other hand, overseas Chinese communities are approached with regard for their historical development, priorities, and ways of doing business, then the rationalization of their networks into official regulatory frameworks can bring local and national economic benefits. In the prior scenario, the ties binding domestic Chinese communities to business partners in China are likely to remain unregistered, limited in scope, and only beneficial for small circles of ethnic entrepreneurs. In the latter, trans-Pacific ties are likely to be legally endorsed, publicly disclosed, and broadly beneficial.

In Cuba, Barrio Chino's assimilation into a twenty-first century system of civic governance is complicated by previous top-down regulatory designs. The commercial injunctions of the anti-Chinese movement, the nationalization campaign of the early Revolution, the monolithic acquittal procedures of the Central Havana municipal government, and the rigid accountability codes of the Office of the Historian each reinforced the informal practices they set out to eradicate. While Barrio Chino harbors strong entrepreneurial capacities, local perceptions that commercial codes are too rigid and out of step with community priorities have discouraged compliance. The consequent profusion of undisclosed business ties and family connections within Barrio Chino and across the Pacific constitutes a significant challenge for policymakers. There are signs that more sophisticated approaches are now being formulated: the April 2011 Communist Party Congress recognized that locally sensitive regulations are a prerequisite if private enterprise is to alleviate pressure on the overburdened public sector and diminish the appeal of the black market. This recognition may herald new approaches to governance that permit Barrio Chino's informal business networks to function under legal sanction, in the process enticing them into formal registration and tax compliance.

In Mexico, media reports of substandard labor conditions in Chinese factories, coupled with public perceptions of domestic Chinese networks dedicated to importing and smuggling underpriced consumer goods, have fueled fears of a Chinese "invasion." This volatile environment has inhibited policymakers from openly engaging with resident Chinese communities to harness their local and global linkages for broader national benefit. The economic rewards of trade fairs and commercial networks operated by Chinese nationals and naturalized Chinese Mexican impresarios consequently remain restricted to group members, perpetuating a vicious circle of external hostility and internal solidarity. While creative strategies for breaking this circle are yet to emerge in Mexico City, several branches of the Baja California state government have openly engaged with the Chinese Associations of Mexicali and Tijuana. Rationalization in northern Mexico has therefore begun to generate a virtuous circle of institutionalized cooperation with Chinese investors and opportunities for the placement of Mexican products in the Chinese market.

For a century and a half Chinese communities in Cuba, Mexico, and elsewhere in Latin America have drawn on informal connections, personal determination, and trust to sustain connections with their motherland. Premised on shared ethnicity, these relationships have deepened in the twenty-first century, joining together people on opposite sides of the Pacific. An important task facing Latin American societies is to recognize the historical pressures and injustices that shaped early Chinese experiences of the region. This history illuminates the central role of trust in the initial formation and later dynamics of diaspora communities. Taking account of these past and present developments is the surest way for Latin America to harness the trust and potential of Chinese communities for a more inclusive and mutually beneficial future.

China's thickening ties with Latin America have brought new opportunities for overseas Chinese communities to enter into global business partnerships. Their pursuit of these opportunities, whether driven by internal interests or what Benedict Anderson has called "long-distance nationalism," are recognized and praised in China.[68] China and Latin America stand to benefit if resulting connections develop in an open and legal manner. In the absence of locally sensitive policies and regulations, ethnic cleavages will widen; by contrast, open engagement with Chinese communities premised on respect for cultural history and business customs will produce mutually beneficial outcomes on both sides of the Pacific. The prospects for harmonious global integration with China may, in sum, depend on how effectively Latin American governments harness local ambitions.

NOTES

This chapter originally appeared as "Harnessing the Dragon: Overseas Chinese Entrepreneurs in Mexico and Cuba," *China Quarterly* 209 (March 2012): 111–133. Reprinted with the permission of Cambridge University Press.

1. Interview with author, October 16, 2008.
2. Comments in response to Daniel Salinas, "Buscan crear barrio chino en la 'Revu,'" *Frontera*, March 1, 2008, 1.
3. Interview with author, February 22, 2011.
4. Figures are from the United Nations Commodity Trade Statistics Database (Comtrade), accessed September 8, 2014, http://comtrade.un.org/db/default.aspx.
5. Evelyn Hu-Dehart, "Latin America in Asia-Pacific Perspective," in *Asian Diasporas: New Formations, New Conceptions*, edited by Rhacel S. Parreñas and Lok C. D. Siu (Stanford, Calif.: Stanford University Press, 2007), 51.
6. Adam M. McKeown, *Chinese Migrant Networks and Cultural Change: Peru, Chicago, and Hawaii, 1900–1938* (Chicago: University of Chicago Press, 2001), 26–27.
7. David W. Chang, "Current Status of Chinese Minorities in Southeast Asia," *Asian Survey* 13, no. 6 (1973); Anil Hira, *An East Asian Model for Latin American Success* (London: Ashgate, 2007).
8. Stephen Castles and Alastair Davidson, *Citizenship and Migration: Globalisation and the Politics of Belonging* (London: Macmillan, 2000); Alejandro Portes and Julia Sensenbrenner, "Embeddedness and Immigration: Notes on the Social Determinants of Economic Action," *American Journal of Sociology* 98, no. 6 (1993): 1320–1350; Robert D. Putnam, *Bowling Alone: The Collapse and Revival of American Community* (New York: Simon and Schuster, 2000), 22–23.
9. St. John Robinson, "The Chinese of Central America: Diverse Beginnings, Common Achievements," in *The Chinese in Latin America and the Caribbean*, edited by Walton Look Lai and Tan Chee-Beng (Leiden: Brill, 2010); Catalina Velázquez Morales, *Los inmigrantes chinos en Baja California 1920–1937* (Mexicali: Universidad Autónoma de Baja Californa, 2001).
10. Alan Smart and Jinn Yuh Hsu, "The Chinese Diaspora, Foreign Investment, and Economic Development in China," *Review of International Affairs* 3, no. 4 (2004): 544–566; Yunxiang Yan, *The Individualization of Chinese Society* (New York: Berg, 2009).
11. Michael Yahuda, *Towards the End of Isolationism: China's Foreign Policy after Mao* (New York: Palgrave Macmillan, 1985), 222–223.
12. Julia C. Strauss and Martha Saavedra, eds., "China and Africa: Emerging Patterns in Globalization and Development," Special issue, *China Quarterly* 199 (2009).
13. Tina Hilgers, "Recentering Informality on the Research Agenda: Grassroots Action, Political Parties, and Democratic Governance," *Latin American Research Review* 43, no. 2 (2008): 272–281; Guillermo O'Donnell, "Informal Institutions, Once Again," in *Informal Institutions and Democracy: Lessons from Latin America*, edited by Gretchen Helmke and Steven Levitsky (Baltimore: Johns Hopkins University Press, 2006).
14. Alejandro Portes, "Social Capital: Its Origins and Applications in Modern Sociology," *Annual Review of Sociology* 24 (1998): 15.
15. Johannes Fedderke, Raphael de Kadt, and John Luiz, "Economic Growth and Social Capital: A Critical Reflection," *Theory and Society* 28, no. 5 (1999): 719.
16. Sonia E. Alvarez, Evelina Dagnino, and Arturo Escobar, eds., *Cultures of Politics, Politics of Cultures: Re-envisioning Latin American Social Movements* (Boulder, Colo.: Westview Press, 1998); Ariel C. Armony, *The Dubious Link: Civic Engagement and Democratization* (Stanford, Calif.: Stanford University Press, 2004).
17. Sonia E. Alvarez, *Engendering Democracy in Brazil: Women's Movements in Transition Politics* (Princeton: Princeton University Press, 1990); Jonathan Fox, "How Does Civil Society Thicken? The Political Construction of Social Capital in Rural Mexico," *World*

Development 24 (1996): 1089–1103; Adrian H. Hearn, *Cuba: Religion, Social Capital, and Development* (Durham, N.C.: Duke University Press, 2008).

18. Archon Fung, David Weil, Mary Graham, and Elena Fagotto, *The Political Economy of Transparency: What Makes Disclosure Policies Effective?* (Harvard University, John F. Kennedy School of Government, 2004); Mary Graham, *Information as Risk Regulation: Lessons from Experience* (Harvard University, John F. Kennedy School of Government, 2001); David Weil, *The Benefits and Costs of Transparency: A Model of Disclosure-Based Regulation* (Harvard University, John F. Kennedy School of Government, 2002).
19. Leonardo Padura Fuentes, *El Viaje más Largo* (Havana: Ediciones Unión, 1994).
20. Lisa Yun, *The Coolie Speaks: Chinese Indentured Laborers and African Slaves in Cuba* (Philadelphia: Temple University Press, 2008).
21. Luz María Fornieles Sánchez, "El Barrio Chino," *Contrapunto* 3, no. 27 (1993): 25–26.
22. Johnny López, "El Chinito Pichilón," New York: Decca [format: 78–10, publish # 21266–1], 1942; Armando Oréfiche, "Chino Li-Wong," recorded with Billo's Caracas Boys, Venezuela: Billo's [format: 78–10, publish # 4056–1], 1953.
23. Duvon C. Corbitt, "Chinese Immigrants in Cuba," *Far Eastern Survey* 13, no. 14 (1944): 131.
24. Interview with author, February 23, 2011.
25. Gregor Benton, ed., *The Chinese in Cuba: 1847–Now* (Lanham, Md.: Lexington Books, 2009), xxii–xxv.
26. Ethnographic case studies of the Office of the Historian's activities in Old Havana are presented in Hearn, *Cuba: Religion, Social Capital, and Development.*
27. Mario Coyula, Miguel Coyula, and Rosa Oliveras, *Towards a New Kind of Community in Havana: The Workshops for Integrated Neighborhood Transformation* (Havana: GDIC, 2001), 12; Grupo para el Desarrollo Integral de la Capital, *La Maqueta de La Habana* (Havana: GDIC, 2001), 1.
28. Kathleen López, "The Revitalization of Havana's Chinatown: Invoking Chinese Cuban History," *Journal of Chinese Overseas* 5, no. 1 (2009): 197.
29. Cheng Yinghong, "Fidel Castro and 'China's Lessons for Cuba': A Chinese Perspective," *China Quarterly* 189 (2007): 40.
30. Interview with author, January 16, 2006.
31. Li San, public speech, December 30, 2005.
32. Interview with author, February 27, 2011.
33. Interview with author, April 29, 2002.
34. Interview with author, February 28, 2011.
35. Armony, *The Dubious Link*, 26; Elisabeth S. Clemens, "Securing Political Returns to Social Capital: Women's Associations in the United States, 1880s–1920s," in *Patterns of Social Capital: Stability and Change in Historical Perspective,* edited by Robert I. Rotberg (Cambridge: Cambridge University Press, 2001), 247; Umut Erel, "Migrating Cultural Capital: Bourdieu in Migration Studies," *Sociology* 44, no. 4 (2010): 646; Robert D. Putnam, "E Pluribus Unum: Diversity and Community in the Twenty-first Century," *Scandinavian Political Studies* 30, no. 2 (2007): 138.
36. Interview with author, March 12, 2006.
37. Interview with author, January 16, 2006.
38. Fedderke, de Kadt, and Luiz, "Economic Growth and Social Capital," 719–720; Nan Lin, *Social Capital: A Theory of Social Structure and Action* (Cambridge: Cambridge University Press, 2001), 39–40.

39. United Nations Development Programme, *Human Development Index 2010* (New York: Palgrave Macmillan, 2010), 146, 2000; "Environmental Performance Index 2010," accessed June 16, 2011, http://epi.yale.edu.
40. Interview with author, April 2, 2002.
41. Arturo Lopez-Levy, *Change in Post-Fidel Cuba: Political Liberalization, Economic Reform, and Lessons for U.S. Policy* (Washington, D.C.: New America Foundation, 2011), 6.
42. Interview with author, February 23, 2011.
43. Interview with author, November 21, 2008. Chinese officials have been urging their Cuban counterparts to adjust their blend of state and market strategies in favor of the latter ever since Fidel Castro's meeting with Chinese premier Li Peng in 1995. See Yinghong, "Fidel Castro and 'China's Lessons for Cuba'"; Jiang Shixue, *Cuba's Economic Reforms in Chinese Perspective* (Beijing: Chinese Academy of Social Sciences, 2009).
44. Ricardo Torres Pérez, "La actualización del modelo económico cubano: continuidad y rupture," *Temas*, accessed June 17, 2011, www.temas.cult.cu.
45. Milthon Minor, "Abren en Mexicali Cámara de Empresarios Chinos del Noroeste," *Frontera*, March 6, 2010.
46. Interview with author, November 5, 2008.
47. Instituto Nacional de Estadísticas y Geografía (INEGI), *Censo de Población y Vivienda 2010*, accessed October 11, 2011, www.inegi.org.mx.
48. Figures are from the United Nations Commodity Trade Statistics Database (Comtrade), accessed September 8, 2014, http://comtrade.un.org/db/default.aspx.
49. "Retiring Americans: Go South, Old Man," *The Economist*, November 24, 2005, accessed October 10, 2011, www.economist.com/node/5214922.
50. Andrés Oppenheimer, "La gran esperanza de México: Lograr tener 5 millones de norteamericanos retirados," *Excelsior*, April 30, 2010.
51. Interview with author, October 31, 2008.
52. Interview with author, September 3, 2008.
53. Francisco Haro Navejas, "El dominio de las emociones: percepciones mexicanas sobre China," in *China y México: Implicaciones de una Nueva Relación*, edited by Enrique Dussel Peters and Yolanda Trápaga Delfín (Mexico City: La Jornada Publishers, 2007), 457.
54. Rocio González Alvarado, "Piratería china de artesanías amenaza subsistencia del mercado de la Ciudadela," *La Jornada*, July 14, 2008; "Acusan a China de competencia desleal," *La Prensa*, January 30, 2005.
55. Interview with author, June 11, 2010.
56. Interview with author, June 16, 2010.
57. Interview with author, June 17, 2010.
58. Mario López, "Cambian giros de comercios a bodegas," *Reforma*, June 5, 2006, 6.
59. Santos Mondragón, "Ambulantes invaden el Centro Histórico," *Noticieros Televisa*, December 25, 2006, 1.
60. Interview with author, June 8, 2010.
61. Interview with author, October 7, 2008.
62. Javier Mejía, "Festejó Asociación China la 'Semana de Migración,'" *La Voz de la Frontera*, October 24, 2008, 1; "Prometen a chinos traer a sus familias," *La Crónica*, October 24, 2008, 5.
63. Elena Barabantseva, "Trans-nationalising Chineseness: Overseas Chinese Policies of the PRC's Central Government," *ASIEN* 96 (2005): 17.
64. Minor, "Abren en Mexicali Cámara de Empresarios Chinos del Noroeste."
65. Guadalupe López, "Expanden cultura china," *Frontera*, February 12, 2009.
66. Interview with author, October 21, 2008.

67. Ibid.
68. Benedict Anderson, "The New World Disorder," *New Left Review* 193 (1992): 13; Francisco Haro Navejas, "China's Relations with Central America and the Caribbean States: Reshaping the Region," in *China Engages Latin America: Tracing the Trajectory*, edited by Adrian H. Hearn and José Luis León Manríquez (Boulder, Colo.: Lynne Rienner Publishers, 2011), 209–210; "Jia Qinglin Voices Five-Point Hope for Overseas Chinese," *Xinhua*, September 15, 2007, accessed June 19, 2011, http://news.xinhuanet.com/english/2007-09/15/content_6729877.htm; Lisheng Zhan, "Event Lauds Role of Overseas Chinese," *China Daily*, December 4, 2002, accessed June 19, 2011, www.highbeam.com/doc/1P2-8797193.html.

PART II

Historicities

Interlude

KATHLEEN LÓPEZ

As Asians moved throughout the Americas and the US sphere of influence in the late nineteenth and early twentieth centuries, they experienced another kind of encounter—one with the state and its gatekeeping policies. Governments linked Asian immigrants with concerns about domestic public health and crime and enacted policies to regulate their movements and interactions with locals or to exclude them altogether. At the heart of official gatekeeping policies lay the relationship between race and national identity. Traveling discourses of Asians as yellow peril circulated not only throughout the hemisphere but also to US-occupied spaces in the Pacific and white settler nations around the globe.

The two historical essays in this section examine the centrality of Chinese immigrants to debates on the construction of a cohesive political entity enclosing an obedient, productive population, whether the new Cuban republic or "protocolonial" Kingdom of Hawai'i. They also highlight the role of the United States in promoting and extending exclusionary immigration laws. The regulation of Chinese bodies became a central prong of a strategy used by the United States to manage and control its burgeoning empire in the Caribbean and the Pacific.

Politicians and elites sought political stability, economic prosperity, and international legitimacy in the recently formed Latin American republics. Public debates arose on how to integrate the nonwhite populations of former colonial societies and on the preferred racial composition of the new nations. Cuba's independence from Spain came much later than the other colonies, after thirty years of military struggles, yet its sovereignty was midwifed by a formal US occupation in 1899. As US military forces prepared to withdraw from Cuba in

1902, the US government insisted that the new nation adopt a Chinese exclusion law. Other countries in the Americas followed with their own bans on the entry of Chinese laborers. On the path toward modernization and progress, an anti-Chinese immigration law became a marker of status (ironically, even for nations with few Chinese). José Amador demonstrates how, at the moment of the birth of the Cuban republic, Chinese and black immigrants became linked in the Cuban racial imaginary as threats to public safety and health. Elite reformers based their agenda of political sovereignty and social whitening on published scientific studies about different racial groups' propensity for crime and disease. According to some commentators, the offspring of Chinese and blacks who intermixed were the most degenerate among society.

Around the same time, the United States extended its imperial reach across the Pacific to Hawai'i and the Philippines, where its actions disrupt the hemispheric category "Asians in the Americas." The 1882 exclusion of Chinese laborers from the United States reverberated throughout the Americas and to US overseas possessions. However, as Julia Katz reveals in her essay on opium regulation toward the end of the Hawaiian kingdom, sustained attempts to control Chinese mobility actually reveal the extent of daily intimacies with the native population. She demonstrates how opium regulation intersected with mechanisms of immigrant exclusion similar to those practiced in the early Cuban republic, such as surveillance, quarantine, incarceration, and deportation. Opium licensing laws were intended to protect native Hawaiians from Chinese, considered morally depraved. Similarly, promoters of racial gatekeeping laws in Cuba claimed they were protecting the native Cuban worker from unnatural competition from Chinese workers, who supposedly could survive on nothing in their crowded and unsanitary residences.

Like all of the authors in this volume, the two historians here read against the grain of the archival record to generate new insights about Asian encounters with the state and with other communities. The voluminous documentation on the regulation of opium, crime, and public health tells us much about who the authorities perceived to be dangerous to national and imperial projects and therefore in need of policing. Government officials attempted to extend their reach into the private, localized spaces of homes, shops, and neighborhoods, where everyday interactions and intimacies among Asians with locals defied elite conceptions of proper decorum and progress.

4

Caught between Crime and Disease

Chinese Exclusion and Immigration Restrictions in Early Twentieth-Century Cuba

JOSÉ AMADOR

In 1906, criminologist Fernando Ortiz stood before government officials and public health specialists gathered at the Fifth National Conference of Charities and Correction held in Santiago to assess the so-called "immigration problem" in Cuba. With a mixture of modesty and self-assurance, the lawyer told the crowd that the problem required "specialists from multiple fields of human knowledge," but that he would only approach it from the "criminological point of view." While immigration was a matter of border control and international relations, only modern science could provide a clear view of the problem. For Ortiz crime was not only a "juridical entity," but also a manifestation of an "anomaly in the social coexistence" of delinquents that criminology could identify and gage. To assess the value or danger of potential migrants and to safeguard the future of Cuba, it was necessary to consider race as the "most important factor" in the proper "selection of immigrants."[1]

Because theories about racial predisposition predicted criminal behavior, not all immigrants were regarded equally. Early in his presentation, Ortiz noted that the psyche of blacks and Chinese was inherently more "primitive and barbarous" than that of whites and thus more prone to delinquency. Using statistical data from the 1866 census, he claimed that Chinese were not only more delinquent than any other race in Cuba, but that they committed "six times" more violent and nonviolent crimes than whites. By eliciting different racial fears, he urged delegates to restrict the entry of "immigrants from the black and the yellow race" and to pass policies that ensure white immigration.[2] Ortiz's racial comparisons served to legitimate the logic of restrictive immigration.

Ortiz was not alone in his policy recommendations. Physicians attending the conference also sounded the alarm against Chinese and black immigration and encouraged white immigration. Doctor Federico Córdova y Quesada, for example, made a case for selective immigration based on medical and cultural grounds. Although agricultural lands in Cuba were vastly unpopulated, he opposed bringing Chinese and black immigrants into Cuba because of their allegedly unhealthy "habits" and "vices." As natural bearers of disease and immorality, Chinese and black laborers would make the new republic prone to disease outbreaks and social instability. Fearing waves of nonwhite transient laborers arriving to Cuba, Córdova y Quesada promoted instead the colonization of Canary Islanders because they spoke Spanish and were already adapted to tropical island living. He concluded by proposing a white-only rule as the single "advantageous immigration policy."[3]

For white professionals like Ortiz and Córdova y Quesada the truth-claims of science offered a way to both define bodies in transit and manage national borders. Objectivity, they maintained, superseded politics. Four years after the Cuban republic was inaugurated, criminologists and public health officials attempted to remake Cuba into a nation free of degeneration and disease by endorsing selective immigration policies. Ortiz and Córdova y Quesada, like most of the participants gathered at the Santiago conference, were part of a new class of urban reformers that sought to use their scientific authority to propel the young nation onto a path of social stability, economic development, and political sovereignty. This chapter reassesses political tensions between the demand for transient labor and the aspirations for a white settled society by examining how Chinese exclusion became an important factor in casting all nonwhite immigrants as disruptive to the social order and the health of the nation.[4] In Cuba, the political yearning for a white sovereign republic went against the race-transcendent nationalism forged during the wars of independence and the expansion of the US-dominated sugar industry. With tools to scrutinize the bodies of immigrants, criminologists and public health officials were decisive in consolidating an ideology that disqualified nonwhite transient laborers from the promise of democracy and equality.

Within this context, it is worth noting that historians of Cuba have mostly analyzed the fields of public health and criminology separately to explore the relationship between racialization and state formation and its impact on Cubans of African descent. However, they have rarely highlighted how these two fields worked in tandem to exacerbate the vulnerability of nonwhite transient laborers and how Chinese exclusion powerfully shaped the politics of immigration in Cuba.[5] If in the early years of the republic criminologists and public health officials were emboldened by the possibility of shaping immigration policy, they were also inspired by a military order established under the US military occupation (1898–1902) that restricted Chinese immigration into Cuba.[6] Working in the shadow of US empire, reformers like Ortiz and Córdova y Quesada fashioned an ideal of nationality that enhanced the promises of settlement for white Europeans and excluded nonwhite immigrants from full participation. What is striking about the Cuban case is that the target of immigration policy varied in light of changing relations between Cuba and the United States.

By exploring the assumptions, accomplishments, and failures of criminologists and public health officials, this chapter traces the continuities and cleavages in the gatekeeping ideology during the first decades of the twentieth century. It will demonstrate how the legal construction of Chinese as excludable aliens under the US occupation influenced the racialization of Jamaican, Haitian, and Spanish immigrants. For these professionals, the scientific rationale underpinning Chinese exclusion justified building a new bureaucratic infrastructure to regulate the movement of low-wage, short-term labor promoted by US sugar capitalists in Cuba. Over time the economic reliance on this foreign labor fueled the growth and diffusion of anti-imperial sentiment in the island. Criminologists and physicians responded to these pressures with coordinated calls to control national borders as an assertion of national sovereignty. As members of state bureaucracies and civic organizations, as well as in the pages of scientific and popular media, they articulated a vision of Cuba that later became a formidable force in narrowing definitions of national belonging.

Imperial Precedent and Immigration Restrictions

The consolidation of the ideology of racial gatekeeping in the early years of the republic was less an expression of scientific confidence than a recognition of the precariousness of national sovereignty. After three decades of independence struggles against Spain, the end of the war in 1898 did not guarantee political sovereignty. Instead it brought a four-year US military occupation that severely curtailed the possibility of a truly independent Cuba. To worsen matters, the imposition of the Platt Amendment to the 1901 Cuban Constitution as a condition for ending US military rule underscored the uncertainty of sovereignty since the amendment guaranteed the right of the United States to intervene in the domestic affairs of Cuba. For example, political turmoil could lead to new military intervention, but so too a disease outbreak.[7] Gatekeeping thus evolved in concert with changing spheres of US involvement in Cuba.

The last time the United States exerted direct influence over Cuba's immigration policy was five days before the end of the occupation. On May 15, 1902, Governor Leonard Wood, a physician serving in the US Army, locked the idea of gatekeeping into the legal framework of the new republic by issuing Military Order No. 155. Modeled after the 1882 Chinese Exclusion Act of the United States, the military order was the first immigration law following Cuba's independence that restricted an immigrant group based on their nationality, race, and class. While the law banned the entry of contract labor from any nation, it explicitly prohibited the immigration of Chinese, with the exception of merchants, diplomats, students, and tourists.[8] This national-origin exclusionary language made Chinese immigrants the model to assess the desirability of other immigrant groups. Moreover, it made the military order a referent point for discussing immigration policy. As Kathleen López has shown, "although the origins of anti-Chinese restriction in Cuba can be found partly in US-imposed legislation, equally if not more important was a deeply engrained ideology among white political intellectuals and elites concerning the ideal composition of a progressive and prosperous nation."[9] Indeed, after the occupation ended, many of these intellectuals and elites invoked the military order imposed by the United States to promote immigration restrictions.

Besides establishing a precedent for restrictionist legislation, an important but understudied article of Military Order No. 155 resonated with those who sought to allay fears that crime and disease traveled with nonwhite immigration. The law also mandated the exclusion of "all idiots, lunatics, or homeless people that could become a public charge; those afflicted by a repugnant, grave or contagious disease; and those convicted of grave or depraved crimes."[10] That is, any immigrant who upon inspection was deemed disabled, diseased, or criminal could not enter Cuban soil. The order thus set malleable grounds for exclusion based on the prediction of who was liable to become destitute or dangerous in the future. The criminological and public health reasoning of this restrictive legislation facilitated the ways opponents of nonwhite immigration would respond to pressures of foreign interests to bring transient labor to sugar plantations.

Envisioning a White Nation: Criminology and Public Health Converge

After the US military withdrawal, debates about state-favored immigration intensified until it became official state policy. During the administration of President Tomás Estrada Palma (1902–1906), criminologists and public health officials found a welcoming platform to promote European immigration and colonization. These immigrants, they argued, would replace the population lost during the wars of independence and help develop agricultural enterprises in sparsely populated areas. Amid concerns about their settlement and assimilation, criminologists and public health officials stressed the white racial identity of Spanish immigrants as a sign of desirability. Conversely, they stressed the inferiority of nonwhite immigrants to justify a selective immigration law. Criminologists, for instance, cobbled together insights from hereditary theories, psychology, and physiognomy to explain criminality based on race and national origin. Similarly, public health officials sought to prevent the importation of epidemic diseases through the targeted screenings of immigrants. Despite their difference in perspectives, both were able to conjure up dramatic images of foreign dangers to present immigration as a national security problem. What was at stake, they believed, was the very survival of Cubans as a people.

Taking their cue from President Estrada Palma, who in 1904 rejected demands of sugar companies to flood the labor market with black Caribbean laborers, lawyers and physicians lobbied to pass legislation that would favor white immigration. When in 1906 Fernando Ortiz and Federico Córdova y Quesada spoke at the Santiago conference, they were responding to the selective immigration bill debated in Congress. Despite their distinct approaches, both used the Chinese to develop a scale of desirability according to which Spanish immigrants occupied the highest position and blacks occupied the lowest. The relational construction of blacks and Chinese as a menace meant that the solution to the immigration "problem" was to sponsor the immigration of white laborers that allegedly had a greater capacity for assimilation. Criminological and medical discourses about the moral and physical failings of nonwhite immigrants provided a scientific foil that either undermined the official race-transcendent ideology or reproduced the muted racist assumptions inscribed in it.

Even though criminologists and physicians claimed the right to speak for the rest of the country, they still had to grapple with creating a policy that would boost European immigration. Criminological and public health appeals to whiten Cuba were often followed by linguistic and cultural justifications. Ortiz, for instance, proposed to follow the model of Australia and New Zealand, which banned the entry of any immigrant that did "not speak a European language," a measure that would assure that no immigrant from Africa or China would enter the country.[11] Since even Europeans could pose a threat if their immigration was not regulated by solid scientific principle, he recommended standardized procedures to document their upbringing, marital status, educational level, professional training, and criminal record.[12] To avoid the formation of ethnic enclaves that bred criminality, Ortiz suggested dispersing immigrants among different towns throughout the countryside. Fearing that European immigrants exposed to socialist ideals would promote "revolutionary upheaval," he advised legislators to pass labor measures that guaranteed proper working conditions, accident insurance, pension plans, and the protection of women and children from exploitation.[13] Because nonwhite exclusion was taken as a given, the underlying logic of Ortiz's proposal was to foster the full integration of European immigrants and their dependents.

Ortiz's recommendations were premised on the truism that immigrants committed a "greater number of crimes than the natives born in the country."[14]

He therefore framed the right of deportation as a legitimate expression of sovereignty. "Any recurring foreign criminal," he stated, "should be expelled from the national territory." Deportation was not contrary to international law, but rather a "faculty that, just as all states have, the Cuban state has."[15] To properly exercise this right, Ortiz continued, the government needed to build a permanent border control facility. He modeled his General Registry of Immigrants after the General Registry of Prisoners established in 1901 by US military officials. In this immigration facility, officers would keep personal records of all new arrivals and issue identification cards. Ortiz borrowed from penal bureaucratic procedures so the state could track and scrutinize arriving immigrants, applying imported technologies of surveillance to Cuban border control.[16]

The assimilation of European immigrants also occupied a prominent place in the presentations of physicians. Diego Tamayo, a doctor who served as secretary of state during the occupation and the Estrada Palma administration, encouraged the formation of benevolent associations to assist incoming European families with housing, work, and health care. By defending white immigrants "against the threat of speculation, vice, and disease," Cubans would fulfill their patriotic duty to guarantee Cuba's "future prosperity."[17] On top of assimilation concerns, physicians had to debunk allegations that tropical degeneration threatened the survival of European immigrants. To appease these fears, Juan Santos Fernández, the president of the Academy of Medical, Natural, and Physical Sciences of Havana, argued that "diseases that frightened the white man" had been effectively eradicated. He rejected the claim of an American physician who suggested that white soldiers in the Philippines had become unnerved by the tropical environment. American soldiers, Santos Fernández noted, traveled to the war-torn Philippines without their families, and these strenuous conditions caused their neurasthenia. In contrast, a policy that promoted the settlement of white families, including spouses, children, and siblings, facilitated the adoption of the "new country as their own." In addition, a reliable public health system based on "sound scientific principles" would ensure success in the tropics. Santos Fernández reminded the audience that they should focus on proven public health efforts like the campaign that eradicated yellow fever, rather than on worrying about antiquated miasmatic theories that had been proven wrong.[18]

One month later, in a ceremony that included as audience members President Estrada Palma, the president of the University of Havana, and the secretaries of state, agriculture, and education, Santos Fernández expanded his assurances about white viability in the tropics.[19] He acknowledged that Cuba's sugar industry was underdeveloped, but he opposed importing laborers from Africa, Yucatán, and Asia to expand the economy. Instead, he championed policies that favored selective immigration restrictions like the ones in place in Germany and the United States.[20] He drew on the work of French anthropologists

Jean Louis Armand de Quatrefages and Paul Topinard about European races to counter the widely held belief that racial mixture has led to the "political crime of rebellion" and climate has contributed to the "depressed character" Of tropical people. Cubans, like their European counterparts, were not a pure race but the stabilized outcome of racial mixture.[21] With the progressive loss of African presence due to Spanish immigration and racial mixture, Cuba could develop just as Europe had. As for the environment, Cubans had already transformed the island into a salubrious utopia by waging war against filth and disease. "We will not be the ones to negate Spanish immigrants the best conditions to colonize the tropics," Santos Fernández concluded.[22] The dangers about the effects of the tropics on whites had changed, but racial gatekeeping did not. Spanish settlers were reassured and enthusiastically welcomed. Nonwhite immigrants were not.

In the early twentieth century, criminologists and public health officials influenced legislative debates about the desirability of different immigrant groups by bolstering assumptions about the compatibility of Spanish settlers and the incompatibility of nonwhite labor. Their boundary work ultimately undermined the race-transcended conception of Cubanness expounded only decades earlier. Three months after the Santiago conference took place, a selective immigration bill was signed into law, when the Estrada Palma administration set aside $1 million for subsidizing the passage of European immigrants to Cuba: $800,000 of this money was earmarked to pay for bringing immigrants from Spain and the Canary Islands, and the remaining $200,000 was for bringing immigrants from Sweden, Norway, Denmark, and northern Italy.[23] With a whitening policy firmly in place, immigration debates became increasingly defined by the scrutiny of the conduct and health of racially suspect migrants.

Political Mobilization and Surveillance Technologies

Over the next decade, tens of thousands of Spanish immigrants entered Cuba soil, increasing their percentage of the Cuban population from 11.1 in 1909 to 13.9 in 1919.[24] This demographic shift coincided with mounted pressures exerted by US-owned sugar companies to chip away provisions prohibiting the entrance of nonwhite laborers. Throughout the 1910s, the boom in the island's agro-export economy, driven by increased US investments and rising sugar prices during World War I, led to an increased demand for immigrants from Jamaica, Haiti, and China. Seeking to take advantage of rising profit margins, sugar producers successfully lobbied the Cuban government to shift its immigration policy. In 1911 the ban against black Caribbean laborers (*braceros*) was relaxed, and in 1917 a law lifting the ban against contract labor, including Chinese labor, was passed. The pressures of US companies to lift immigration bans deepened the growing resentment toward low-wage, nonwhite transient labor.

Political mobilization within Cuba also heightened anxieties about non-white immigration. In 1908, a group of veterans of color founded the Partido Independiente de Color (PIC) to fight government discrimination. President José Miguel Gomez responded by outlawing the party, which led to an uprising in 1912 and its violent repression by the government. The 1912 revolt was often portrayed as the result of outside influence and not of entrenched racial prejudice. Widespread anxieties about foreign African influence were largely based on Fernando Ortiz's pioneering study *Los negros brujos* (The Black Wizards). Published in 1906, the book made the brujo the epitome of Cuban criminality by linking African-derived religious practices to the murders of white children.[25] Before and after the 1912 revolt, criminologists and physicians often projected these fears onto Haitian and Jamaican laborers and pointed to their foreignness and blackness as the source of irreconcilable social and political conflict.

In 1909, the Cuban government responded to political unrest with the creation of the National Bureau of Identification. To predict criminal behavior and develop new technologies of surveillance, the new institution applied criminal anthropology by taking anthropometric measurements and documenting the physical marks of criminality of all convicted criminals.[26] To keep track of recidivism, the National Bureau also implemented the "Dactilophotographic" system of registration in which fingerprints and mug shots were kept for identification purposes. Following this model, immigration authorities implemented similar technologies to register migrants at points of entry. In 1914, the Department of Immigration, under the supervision of the director of public health, began to take fingerprints and photographs of all arriving immigrants. The racial scrutiny at immigration checkpoints converted newcomers, particularly black and Chinese immigrants, into potential criminals or disease carriers that needed to be catalogued and tracked.[27]

Nowhere were shifts in the target of gatekeeping more evident than in the works of criminologist Israel Castellanos and physician Juan Guiteras. The lives of these two professionals often overlapped through personal relations, civic organizations, and state institutions. Israel Castellanos, a criminologist following in the footsteps of Fernando Ortiz, was able to pursue his career under the mentorship of the powerful physician Diego Tamayo. Under his guidance, Castellanos gained access to insane asylums and prisons to measure, photograph, and record confined bodies. Moreover, Tamayo published Castellanos's criminological findings in the pages of his journal *Vida Nueva*. Castellanos became the director of National Bureau of Identification in 1921.[28] Following the theories of Italian criminologist Cesare Lombroso, he linked suspect signs such as body size, facial angles, cranial circumference, and physiognomic crevices, hair texture, and tattoos to criminal tendencies.[29] In 1916, Castellanos's book on black brujos and black secret organizations received the best book award by the Academy of Sciences and consolidated his reputation as one of the leading criminologists in Cuba.[30]

Whereas Castellanos based his system of information collection on registering hereditary stigmas of criminality, Guiteras screened immigrants to prevent epidemic outbreaks. A close friend of Tamayo, he was appointed director of public health in 1902 and remained in that post for nearly two decades. In that role, Guiteras oversaw the Quarantine and Immigration Departments, the institutions in charge of issuing quarantines and scrutinizing immigrants.[31] An advocate of whitening since the Spanish–American War, Guiteras pursued selective quarantine measures to protect Cuba from real and imaginary public health threats.[32] In 1916, for example, he recommended a mandatory quarantine against Jamaican immigrants based on unsupported, but widespread, fears that they were the source of a recent malaria outbreak. Spanish immigrants, however, were not subjected to the same treatment. Speaking about the malaria outbreak a year later, Guiteras maintained that the "free introduction of braceros" had gravely threatened "the public health of Cuba."[33] While this selective measure did not stop the flood of braceros from arriving at Cuban shores, the targeted quarantine portrayed them as agents of disease transmission.

The Panama Canal and the Scrutiny of Chinese Bodies

Just as the flood of black Caribbean laborers (*braceros*) increased the nativist rhetoric of criminologists and public health officials, so too did speculations about the introduction of cheap Chinese laborers crossing the Panama Canal. Even though Cubans took pride that the eradication of yellow fever in the island paved the way for the public health efforts that made possible the construction of the canal, they feared that its opening in 1914 would have increased Chinese immigration. In 1908, Fernando Ortiz represented Chinese immigration as a "yellow peril" that would only increase "after the inauguration of the interoceanic isthmus."[34] Five years later, another commentator lamented that the canal not only would expand Chinese immigration, but also expand the immigration of braceros because they could afford to pay the 30 pesos required by the Cuban government after work on the construction of the canal ended.[35]

Rumors about the dangers of an increasingly interconnected world fueled new anxieties about Chinese immigration among public health officials and criminologists. In fact, in the previous decade these experts had only mentioned the alleged dangers of the Chinese in passing, without devoting full-length articles to their study. Instead, their writings used the "vices" of the Chinese as a proxy to exalt the virtues of European immigration. This lack of intense scrutiny derived from the perception that the 1902 military order had erected an ironclad gate to forestall Chinese immigration. It thus seemed unnecessary to classify their bodies in ways that led to their exclusion. The opening of the Panama Canal, coupled with the rapid expansion of the Cuban sugar industry, undermined the idea of a "closed gate" in Cuba. These anxieties created a window of opportunity for the arbitrary assessment of Chinese bodies. Despite these fears, until 1917 the Chinese population in Cuba remained about 17,000, nearly equal to that of the closing days of Spanish rule.[36]

Juan Guiteras was among the first to portray the "pending opening of the Panama Canal" as a source of public health concern. In 1913, he warned members of the Academy of Sciences that "direct contact with China" would expose Cuba to a deluge of diseases. Chinese immigrants, he maintained, would bring "to our territory" either "utterly exotic diseases" or "those that are showing a tendency to vanish."[37] Guiteras claimed that exotic diseases such as the plague, cholera, and malaria that were rare in Cuba but widespread in the southern provinces of China would spread once Chinese immigrants reached the island. At the same time, other diseases such as dysentery, hookworm, and tuberculosis that were currently under control in Cuba could easily return. In an historical revision that obscured the reliance on Chinese labor as an alternative to African slave labor, he blamed the coolie trade of the mid-nineteenth century for introducing hookworm and beri-beri to Cuba.[38] Guiteras, who had been a professor of tropical medicine at University of Pennsylvania and the University of Havana, lumped these diseases together even though he knew that each of them had a different etiology, regional intensity, and mode of transmission. In associating these diseases with Chinese labor, he reintroduced obsolete conceptions of geographic and racial determinism.

Guiteras's defense of a closed door policy against Chinese contract laborers also relied on elite and popular imaginings of Cuban nationality. As exiled independence leader in the late 1890s, he had embraced Jose Martí's claim that the alliances forged by white and black soldiers during the wars of independence transcended racial divisions.[39] On the eve of the opening of the Panama Canal, Guiteras reinterpreted this nationalist saga to justify a deeply racist immigration policy. "Together our two races, the white and the black," he warned, "constituted the Cuban nation whose interests we need to guard. And surely we do not defend those interests by introducing a race that does not amalgamate in the country."[40] To wall off Cuba from Chinese immigrants, Guiteras denied Chinese their rightful place in the nationalist narrative by casting them as culturally inassimilable. His narrative omitted the significant participation of *chinos mambises* (Chinese freedom fighters) in the independence movement.[41] In addition, Guiteras fueled anxieties about Chinese immigration by warning about labor competition and depressed wages. He maintained that single, cheap Chinese laborers had an advantage over black and white Cubans, competing for jobs in "small business, small industries, and certain classes of labor."[42]

Israel Castellanos followed the lead of both Ortiz and Guiteras in his study of the effect of race on Chinese criminality. However, he questioned the alleged "supremacy of the Chinese in Cuban delinquency," an assertion proposed by Ortiz in 1906 at the Santiago conference and repeated by Guiteras in 1913. While Castellanos conceded he could not obtain the crime statistics cited by Ortiz, he used data from the National Bureau to answer one central question: "Are Chinese in Cuba a cursed race, a criminal and malevolent people?"[43] Drawing on penitentiary records, anthropometric data, frontal and profile facial photographs, and the 1907 census, Castellanos arrived at an entirely different conclusion than Ortiz. He found that of the 3,898 prisoners recorded in 1907, only twenty-seven were "yellow," and of that number only twenty-one were Chinese. In other words, less than 1 percent of the prison population was either "yellow" or Chinese. In contrast, of the total prisoners, 1,156 were blacks, or almost 30 percent. "It is evident," Castellanos wrote, "that those [blacks] who introduced brujería and ñañiguismo are the true representatives of Cuban criminality; and their descendants, the mestizos, feel the barbaric impulsivity of their parents vibrate in their veins." Not surprisingly, despite the fact that of the total prisoners 562 were Spanish, or almost 15 percent, Castellanos did not feel compelled to highlight the criminality of Spanish immigrants.[44] On the contrary, he spoke of the ethnographic improvements that would result from Spanish immigration.

According to Castellanos, Chinese criminality was relatively benign. He emphasized their inherent affinity for minor crimes such as gambling and loitering. Like blacks, Chinese have a "specific delinquency," nonetheless their criminal tendencies differ not because of the environment but rather because of the "temperament of their race." Both were inferior races, but whereas blacks were "impulsive" and "arrogant," Chinese were "tranquil" and "vulnerable." This difference may be interpreted in relation to the growing political mobilization of black Cubans. Still haunted by the 1912 revolt, Castellanos asserted that Chinese, in contrast to blacks, had neither participated in "bloody rebellions nor in barbaric explosions."[45] Moreover, they did not organize to commit crimes or established illegal associations. In connecting blackness with political instability and organized crime, Castellanos underlined the utility in criminology for policing black activists and political opponents.

Castellanos's confidence on new technologies to register on the marks of criminality broke down in his examination of Chinese physiognomy. Because he was convinced that the normal features of Chinese bodies were considered abnormal in white ones, analyzing Chinese criminality required additional expertise. According to Castellanos, Chinese lunatics, thieves, and murderers lacked the "physiognomic repugnancies" specific to their crimes. In contrast, "black Cubans, as well as white, stamp in the face the barbarity of their crime."[46]

For this reason, upholding clear racial distinctions proved particularly difficult. This was especially challenging when attempting to maintain a coherent argument about the criminality of *mestizos achinados*, the offspring of Chinese and blacks. Castellanos claimed that mestizos achinados were "more violent, than . . . pure blacks."[47] Yet earlier in the article—as well as in other books and articles—he had stated that blacks had the highest and most violent rates of criminality. The fissures of his argument are apparent in his attempt to apply theories that rely on distinct racial categories in people of mixed African and Chinese descent.

Although Castellanos failed to assemble incontrovertible evidence about the impure process of racial mixture, or *mestizaje*, he ended the article showcasing how cultural whitening would both "lessen" and "harmonize" the traits of the races composing the "complex mosaic of Cuban nationality." While his contradictory data could not provide certainty for the present, he found relief on the progressive loss of African and Chinese influences through whitening. Cuba's future progress, he concluded, would be assured since the vestiges of black "fetishism" and Chinese "deviations" would be offset by the "powerful gust of Hispanic American culture."[48] At stake was an attempt to consolidate the power of whiteness at a time when black political mobilization and the opening of the Panama Canal threatened its stability.

The disparate conclusions of Guiteras and Castellanos not only reveal the important role of public health and criminology in the racialization of immigration, but also how these disciplinary knowledges derived their power from the institutional context in which individuals interpreted them. As director of public health, Guiteras portrayed Chinese immigrants as more menacing than blacks because they allegedly brought exotic diseases. At the same time, when he depicted Chinese as unassimilable based on the discourse of race-transcendent nationality, the contraction between celebrating racial tolerance and promoting racially exclusive immigration policies became evident. In contrast, Castellanos portrayed blacks as more menacing than Chinese because the recent revolt of the Partido Independiente de Color had challenged racial hierarchies and political stability in an unprecedented manner. As a criminologist, the real fear of a black uprising endangering the political order of the state outweighed any alleged threat posed by the Chinese. In a world of heightened nonwhite migration and political mobilization, Guiteras's and Castellanos's intense scrutiny of nonwhite bodies illustrates the arbitrary ways racial anxieties were mobilized by specific institutional concerns.

The Rise of Anti-Imperialist Nativism

Supporters of immigration restrictions frequently invoked the writings of public health and criminological experts. For example, when *La Reforma Social*, a journal of domestic politics and international affairs, reprinted Guiteras's piece on Chinese immigration, the editors included an excerpt of Ortiz's 1906 article in a footnote. This footnote, the editors claimed, further proved Guiteras's assertion that Chinese immigration was "deeply menacing and pernicious to our country's interest."[49] This trend took a more populist, anti-imperial turn after World War I, when organized labor began to demand more social guarantees from the state. Elites took advantage of this change in orientation by using the 1902 military order to recast their restrictionist fantasies as a desire to protect Cuban workers and sovereignty.

As early as 1915, journalist Pelayo Perez used the Guiteras piece to invoke images of Chinese, Jamaican, and Haitian immigrants as disease carriers and argue that the cost in public health expenditures far outweighed the savings in the cost of labor. Alluding to US sugar interests, Pérez complained that the "same representatives of our agricultural wealth" who are now advocating for Chinese immigration had previously introduced dangerous waves of Haitian and Jamaican contract laborers.[50] Ultimately deep-seated resentments against the economic influence of the United States linked nonwhite immigration to the greed of foreign agricultural interests. Pérez expressed outrage at the hypocrisy of US lobbies that promoted an "open door" immigration policy in Cuba while the United States kept a "closed door" policy at home. He accused companies that argued for the importation of transient labor to boost the economy as misleading since developed countries like the United States, Canada, Australia, and New Zealand kept restrictions against "undesirable immigrants" in place. "In Cuba," he lamented, "the first North American intervention passed an Immigration Law inspired in this healthy principle, [but] the lust for profit and the incessant clamor of property owners asked for cheap labor." Pérez then compared sugar interests to opponents of the abolition of slavery who had delayed the advancement of Cuba by repeatedly asking for "one more harvest." Today, he complained, foreign companies used their outweighed "influence to loosen the mesh of the law."[51]

The rise of sugar prices during World War I increased pressures to lift immigration restrictions. During the hearings of a 1917 bill to increase contract workers, Senator Cosme de la Torriente, one of the founders of the Conservative Party, attacked the notion that the importation of cheap immigrant labor was part of the war effort. He expressed dismay over the "suspension" of Military Order No. 155 and noted that the US government had tightened its immigration restrictions, even as it sent "ten million vigorous men" to war.[52] Aggravating his indignation was the fact that the United States had kept these restrictions in place in Hawai'i, Puerto Rico, and the Philippines.[53]

De la Torriente turned again to racial fears to propose the activation of a deportation mechanism once the war ended. Cheap Chinese laborers, he claimed, would arrive to Cuba by the tens of thousands, lured by higher wages. If the economy took a downturn in the future, they would remain on the island because the prospects in their country would surely be worse than in Cuba. "There is no doubt," he told fellow congressmen, "that the Chinese, whose wages in their homeland are insignificant, will prefer to stay here, earning forty, fifty, or sixty cents, rather than to return to their country." Unwilling to work for such low wages, Cuban laborers would become "public charges in their own homeland." Passing a bill lifting immigration restrictions, he warned, would assure the future "unhappiness of the Cuban and his family."[54] De la Torriente's proposal was underwritten by an immigrant group's proximity to whiteness, not their foreignness. He argued, for example, that Spanish immigrants were needed for "developing the land" and "strengthening the white race" in the tropics. Rather than denying Spanish laborers entry because of their foreign status, "they should be defended and protected against other immigrants as if they were Cuban laborers, whites or blacks."[55] Both the affirmation of the "white" racial identity of Spanish immigrants and their protection "as if" they were Cuban workers reinforced the acute vulnerability of nonwhite transient labor.

Despite de la Torriente's passionate pleas, the rising demand for labor—and the growing political clout—of the agro-business pressed the government to open the gates of Cuba to new waves of immigration. Only one other Cuban senator opposed lifting the immigration ban. President Mario G. Menocal signed the bill into law in August 1917. De la Torriente and his predecessors, however, succeeded in laying the foundation for making the gatekeeping ideology central to the nationalist, anti-imperialist rhetoric that eventually gave way to broader, more insidious policies. After the sugar industry peaked in 1920, the steady decline of the Cuban economy renewed calls for mass deportations and citizenship requirements. This position gained traction strengthening the nativists' calls that ushered the repatriation of tens of thousands of Haitian and Jamaican workers in the late 1920s. When the provisional government of Rámon Grau San Martín took power in 1933, workers and politicians drew on gatekeeping to demand for legislation that required that 50 percent of the agricultural, industrial, and commercial workforce were Cuban born. The following year this workforce legislation was promulgated.

Conclusion

An analysis of the 1902 military order and Chinese exclusion forces us to rethink the role of gatekeeping in the construction of the Cuban Republic. In the early twentieth century, US legislation to restrict immigration in Cuba brought increasing numbers of individuals under the scrutiny of criminologists and public health officials. For the most part, US authorities and white Cuban elites agreed that a race-based system for regulating transient labor would secure a healthy society free of social conflict. Yet shifting debates about immigration following the end of the occupation illustrate the important precedent set by Military Order No. 155. Proposals for selective immigration gained even more legitimacy as criminologists and public health officials used the putative "objectivity" of science to introduce new technologies of surveillance and screening. As members of the professional elite, these racial gatekeepers saw themselves as the true standard bearers of Cuban democracy—an educated, intelligent vanguard of committed citizens loyal not to markets or politics but to scientific progress and national sovereignty.

Although the whitening logic of gatekeeping did not change significantly in the first decades of the twentieth century, the context in which it was interpreted dramatically changed. In the first years of the republic, prominent criminologists and public health officials championed state-sponsored European immigration. While criminological and public health arguments underscored the need to exclude black and Chinese immigrants, they focused primarily on ways to better integrate white immigrants—whether by avoiding the formation of ethnic enclaves, reforming labor laws, eradicating diseases or debunking myths about tropical demise. It was only when the guarantees of Military Order No. 155 began to erode in the 1910s that gatekeeping efforts shifted away from concerns about assimilating white immigrants toward preventing the entrance of nonwhite transient labor. Criminological and public health discourses that compared immigrant groups were forcefully seized upon by Cuban professionals, as evidenced by the frequent scrutiny of Chinese bodies during the construction of the Panama Canal. Calls for immigration restrictions, however, took a clear anti-imperialist, nationalist tone only after US sugar capitalists successfully lobbied for loosening immigration restrictions to satisfy labor demands. At a moment when Cuban control over their borders was severely undermined, dramatic scenarios of criminal and public health dangers—disseminated and consumed by various publics—were crucial to the rise of virulent anti-imperial nationalism.

The story of gatekeeping, thus, complements existing scholarship on race and science in that it underscores the role of racialization in shaping immigration policy. Gatekeeping efforts were not solely determined by black and white binaries, but by relational, and often contradictory, hierarchies of difference. Criminologists and public health officials, for example, distinguished among Chinese, Jamaican, Haitian, and Spanish immigrants. Paying close attention to the formation of these racial boundaries allows scholars to reevaluate the emergence and the workings of the gatekeeping ideology by bringing into relief the contingent relation among race, labor, nation, and empire. Modern gatekeeping in Cuba not only drew on the Chinese exclusion codified in the 1902 military order, it was fundamentally transformed by the plurality of immigrant laborers that agricultural capitalism demanded and by the scientific technologies developed to scrutinize them.

NOTES

1. Fernando Ortiz, "Consideraciones criminológicas positivistas acerca de la inmigración en Cuba," in *Memoria oficial: Quinta conferencia de beneficencia y corrección de la isla de Cuba*, edited by Jorge Dehogues (Havana: La Moderna Poesía, 1906), 343–344. The article was reprinted as "La inmigración desde el punto de vista criminológico," in *Derecho y sociología* 1, no. 5 (1906): 54–64.
2. Ortiz, "Consideraciones criminológicas," 345.
3. Federico Córdova y Quesada, "Clase y procedencia de la inmigración que debe proteger el estado," in Dehogues, *Memoria oficial*, 389–390.
4. On the history of Chinese influence in early twentieth-century Cuba, see Kathleen López, *Chinese Cubans: A Transnational History* (Chapel Hill: University of North Carolina Press, 2013) and "'One Brings Another': The Formation of Early-Twentieth-Century Chinese Migrant Communities in Cuba," in *The Chinese in the Caribbean*, edited by Andrew R. Wilson (Princeton, N.J.: Markus Wiener, 2004), 93–127. See also Miriam Herrera Jerez and Mario Castillo Santana, *De la memoria a la vida pública: identidades, espacios, y jerarquía de los chinos en la Habana republicana, 1902–1968* (Havana: Centro de Investigación y Desarrollo de la Cultura Cubana Juan Marinello, 2003); Duvon C. Corbitt, "Chinese Immigrants in Cuba," *Far Eastern Survey* 13, no. 14 (1944): 130–132. For valuable testimonies on the experience of immigration, see Mitzi Espinosa Luis, "Si tú pleguntá, a mi me gusta hacer cuento: Felipe Luis narrates his story," in *The Chinese in the Caribbean*, edited by Andrew R. Wilson (Princeton, N.J.: Markus Wiener, 2004), 129–142. For representation of Chinese in the literature of this period, see Ignacio López-Calvo, *Imagining the Chinese in Cuban Literature and Culture* (Gainesville: University Press of Florida, 2008), chapters 4 and 5. On the coolie narrative in the transition from slavery to freedom, see Lisa Yun, *The Coolie Speaks: Chinese Indentured Laborers and African Slaves in Cuba* (Philadelphia: Temple University Press, 2008).
5. On criminology and race in Cuba, see Stephan Palmié, *Wizards and Scientists: Explorations in Afro-Cuban Modernity and Tradition* (Durham, N.C.: Duke University Press, 2002), 201–259; Alejandra Bronfman, *Measures of Equality: Social Science, Citizenship, and Race in Cuba, 1902–1940* (Chapel Hill: University of North Carolina Press, 2004), 67–86. On public health, see Consuelo Naranjo Osorio and Armando García Martínez, eds., *Medicina y racismo en Cuba: la ciencia ante la inmigración canaria en el siglo XX* (La Laguna: Taller de Historia, 1996); Mariola Espinosa, *Epidemic Invasions: Yellow Fever and the Limits of Cuban Independence, 1878–1930* (Chicago: University of Chicago Press, 2009); Marc McLeod, "'We Cubans are Obligated Like Cats to Have a Straight Face':

Malaria, Quarantine, and Race in Neocolonial Cuba, 1898–1940," *The Americas* 67, no. 1 (2010): 57–81; José Amador, *Medicine and Nation Building in the Americas* (Nashville: Vanderbilt University Press, 2014), 39–67.

6. Recent work on immigration focuses mostly on black contract workers from the Caribbean. See Marc McLeod, "Undesirable Aliens: Race, Ethnicity, and Nationalism in the Comparison of Haitian and British West Indian Immigrant Workers in Cuba, 1912–1939," *Journal of Social History* 31 (1998): 599–623; Aviva Chomsky, "'Barbados or Canada?': Race, Immigration, and Nation in Early-Twentieth Century Cuba," *Hispanic American Historical Review* 80 (2000): 415–462; Barry Carr, "'Omnipontent and Omnipresent'? Labor Shortages, Worker Mobility, and Employer Control in the Cuban Sugar Industry," in *Identity and Struggle at the Margins of the Nation-State: The Laboring People of the Central America and the Hispanic Caribbean*, edited by Aviva Chomsky and Aldo Lauria Santiago (Durham, N.C.: Duke University Press, 1998), 260–291.
7. On the impact of the Platt Amendment, see Louis A. Pérez, *Cuba under the Platt Amendment, 1902–1934* (Pittsburgh: University of Pittsburgh Press, 1986); Juan Pérez de la Riva et al., eds., *La républica neocolonial: Anuario de estudios cubanos* (Havana: Editorial de Ciencias Sociales, 1975).
8. On the history of Chinese exclusion in the United States, see Erika Lee, "The Chinese Exclusion Example: Race, Immigration, and American Gatekeeping, 1882–1924," *Journal of American Ethnic History* 21, no. 2 (2002): 36–62; Lucy Salyer, *Laws Harsh as Tigers: Chinese Immigrants and the Shaping of Modern Immigration Law* (Chapel Hill: University of North Carolina Press, 1995); Mae Ngai, "Legacies of Exclusion: Illegal Chinese Immigration during the Cold War Years," *Journal of American Ethnic History*, 18, no. 1 (1998): 3–35; Lisa Lowe, *Immigrant Acts: On Asian American Cultural Politics* (Durham, N.C.: Duke University Press, 1996).
9. López, *Chinese Cubans*, 145.
10. Military order 155, May 15, 1902; reproduced in *Documentos para la historia de Cuba*, edited by Hortencia Pichardo (Havana: Editorial de Ciencias Sociales, 1969), 2:199–201.
11. Ortiz, "Consideraciones criminológicas," 345.
12. Ibid., 353–355.
13. Ibid., 349.
14. Ibid., 350.
15. Ibid., 352.
16. See, for example, Ricardo Salvatore and Carlos Aguirre, eds., *The Birth of the Penitentiary in Latin America: Essays on Criminology, Prison Reform, and Social Control, 1830–1940* (Austin: University of Texas Press, 1996); Ricardo Salvatore, Carlos Aguirre and Gilbert Joseph, eds., *Crime and Punishment in Latin America: Law and Society since Late Colonial Times* (Durham, N.C.: Duke University Press, 2001).
17. Diego Tamayo, "Necesidad de asociaciones particulares de carácter filantrópico que protejan a determinados inmigrantes," in *Memoria oficial: Quinta conferencia de beneficencia y corrección de la isla de Cuba*, edited by Jorge Dehogues (Havana: La Moderna Poesía, 1906), 337–338.
18. Juan Santos Fernández, "Clase y procedencia del inmigrante que debe proteger el estado," in Dehogues, *Memoria oficial*, 379, 380.
19. Juan Santos Fernández, "La inmigración," *Anales de la Academia de las Ciencias de la Habana* 43 (1906): 4–25.
20. Ibid., 4.
21. Ibid., 7.
22. Ibid., 19.

23. On debates that led to the passage of this law, see Lillian Guerra, *The Myth of José Martí: Conflicting Nationalisms in Early Twentieth-Century Cuba* (Chapel Hill: University of North Carolina Press, 2005), 146–150.
24. María del Carmen Barcia, "Un modelo de inmigración 'favorecida': el traslado masivo de españoles a Cuba, 1880–1930," *Catauro* 2, no. 4 (2001): 41.
25. Fernando Ortiz, *Hampa afro-cubana: Los negros brujos (apuntes para un estudio de etnología criminal)* (Miami: Ediciones Universal, 1973 [1906]). For the reception of *Los negros brujos*, see Reinaldo Román, *Governing Spirits: Religion, Miracles, and Spectacles in Cuba and Puerto Rico, 1898–1956* (Chapel Hill: University of North Carolina Press, 2007), 82–105; Bronfman, *Measures of Equality*, 37–52.
26. See Fernando Ortiz, *La identificación dactiloscópica. Informe de policiologia y de derecho publico* (Havana: Imprenta la Universal, 1913).
27. Manuel F. Alonso and T. Valero Martínez, eds., *Cuba before the World at the Panama-Pacific Exposition* (New York: Souvenir Guide of Cuba Co., 1915), 74–76.
28. For autobiographical information, see Israel Castellanos, "Confidencias de Israel Castellanos, de la Habana," *Higia* 2 (1917). For biographical information, see Andrés Galera Gómez, "El resurgir de una nueva escuela: Israel Castellanos y el atavismo del delito," *Asclepio* 15, no. 2 (1988): 81–97. For an analysis of his work, see Bronfman, *Measures of Equality*, 124–134, and "The Allure of Technology: Photographs, Statistics and the Elusive Female Criminal in 1930s Cuba," *Gender and History* 15, no. 2 (2007): 60–67.
29. Articles published by Castellanos include "Anomalía atávica en el occipital de un criminal," *Vida Nueva* 6 (1914): 222–225; "La forma geométrica de la cara en los delincuentes cubanos," *Gaceta Médica del Sur* 22 (1915): 217–219; "Los músculos faciales y la fisonomía de un delincuente," *Vida Nueva* 34 (1916): 30–33.
30. In 1916, Castellanos received a prize from the Academy of Sciences for *La brujería y el ñañiguismo bajo el punto de vista medico-legal* (Havana: Imp. Del Lloredo, 1916).
31. For biographical information on Guiteras, see José López del Valle, "Biografía del Dr. Juan Guiteras Gener," in *Papeles del Dr. Juan Guiteras* (Havana: Consejo Científico, Ministerio de Salud Pública, 1962), 7–26.
32. For Guiteras's role in promoting whitening ideology in the 1890s and the 1910s, see Amador, *Medicine and Nation Building*, 45–46, 59–60.
33. McLeod, "'We Cubans," 62.
34. Ortiz, "El Peligro Amarillo," *Cuba y América* 25, no. 15 (January 22, 1908): 3.
35. Pelayo Pérez, "El peligro amarillo y el peligro negro," *Cuba contemporánea* 9, no. 3 (1915): 257.
36. See Corbitt, "Chinese Immigrants in Cuba," 131; López, "One Brings Another," 95. Although the 1902 military order was still in place throughout much of the 1910s, Chinese laborers entered Cuba with falsified documents.
37. Juan Guiteras, "La inmigración china," *Anales de la Academia de Ciencias Médicas, Físicas, y Naturales de la Habana* 50 (1913): 558. Reprinted as "La imigración china y el Canal de Panama," *Reforma social: revista mensual de cuestiones sociliales, económicas, políticas, parlamentarias, estadísticas y de higiene pública* 1, no. 1 (1914): 1–6.
38. Ibid., 565.
39. Guiteras had embraced a similar argument in 1899, when he promoted a campaign against yellow fever in order to encourage white immigration. See Amador, *Medicine and Nation Building*, 45.
40. Guiteras, "La inmigración china," 560.

41. On Chinese participation in the wars of independence, see López, *Chinese Cubans*, 117–143. See also Pedro Eng Herrera and Mauro G. García, *Martí en los chinos, los chinos en Martí* (Havana: Grupo Promotor del Barrio Chino de la Habana, 2003).
42. Guiteras, "La imigración china," 560.
43. Israel Castellanos, "Los chinos en Cuba: Su criminalidad," *Gaceta Médica del Sur* 33 no. 4 (1915): 74. This is the first article of a two-part series.
44. Ibid., 75, 76.
45. Ibid., 76–77.
46. Ibid., 102.
47. Ibid., 105.
48. Ibid., 105.
49. Guiteras, "La inmigración China y el Canal de Panamá," 1.
50. Pérez, "El peligro amarillo y el peligro negro," 257.
51. Ibid., 255.
52. Cosme de la Torriente, "Inmigraciones peligrosas," in *Cuarenta años de mi vida, 1898–1938* (Havana: Imprenta El Siglo, 1939): 101–102.
53. Ibid.
54. Ibid., 102.
55. Ibid., 103.

5

The Politics of the Pipe

Opium Regulation and Protocolonial Governance in Nineteenth-Century Hawaiʻi

JULIA KATZ

During the last two decades of the Hawaiian monarchy, cultural, political, and economic struggles converged in the regulation of opium, and nearly every faction of Hawaiian society had a stake in the debate. What made opium regulation such a salient site of struggle? How did the debate come to consume the attention and resources of the nation, and what does this captivation tell us about the sociological imagination of the late nineteenth-century Hawaiian body politic? As with our contemporary War on Drugs, the discursive and empirical record of the regulation of opium tells us less about who was actually using and selling the drug than it does about who was already perceived to be criminal, which improper and abject subjects needed to be policed and purged.

The discourse around opium reveals a lurid public imaginary, one preoccupied with the precarious fate of an island kingdom always on the precipice—whether of demographic failure, financial ruin, or annexation. Opium, whose sensational tragedies and alleged abuses circulated through rumor and published accounts across the imperial world, lent these fears a sordid urgency. It became, in the eyes of the state and respectable society, a crisis of criminality in the case of the Chinese, a crisis of public health for the Native Hawaiians, and a crisis of governance for a protocolonial state unable to extend its reach into those corners of society deemed most threatening—the interiors of Chinese and Hawaiian life.[1] I argue that opium, when taken as an optic, reveals both the vexing blind spots of protocolonial governance, as well as its strategies of sovereignty, including sinophobia, paternalism, and exclusion. Each tactic was crucial to the maintenance and extension of American hegemony in the islands.

While the traffic in opium generated fortunes for some, squandered the meager holdings of many, filled jails and government coffers, and scandalized the native monarchy, it has been largely ignored by contemporary historians of Hawai'i. However, its strength as an optic for viewing Hawaiian history is evident in its wide scope. The discourse around opium regulation deserves critical analysis because of its high-stakes terms, the urgency and anxiety generated by the perceived drug crisis, and the material impact it had on Hawaiian politics, economy, and society. Furthermore, historicizing opium as a site of struggle reveals the stumbling, frustrated, contingent, and improvised nature of American imperialism in the islands. It is precisely in these vexations, in the rehashing and testing and failure of schemes of colonial governance, that an alternative history of colonialism lies—one that reveals its insidious processes to be both endless and incomplete.

Reciprocity and American Hegemony

Inter-imperial rivalry overshadowed the political history of the nineteenth-century Pacific Islands. American involvement in Hawai'i was plagued by perpetual fears that the islands were being pulled away from the North American mainland—specifically, toward Britain and China. It was against the former pull that the Reciprocity Treaty of 1875, the inaugural triumph of King Kalākaua's reign, was passed. The culmination of years of previous efforts to negotiate, draft, and ratify an agreement facilitating trade between the United States and Hawai'i, the treaty fastened the fate of the Hawaiian economy, particularly the sugar industry, to the US market. Stipulating that the Hawaiian government recognize the United States as its favored trading partner, the treaty excited popular suspicions of American annexation. Amid these fears, American ministers in the Hawaiian government had a tricky path to negotiate. While lobbying for the extension of American power into the archipelago, they dissembled their imperial intentions through assurances that a closer alliance with the United States would secure Hawaiian independence.[2]

A loud champion of the Reciprocity Treaty and American supremacy in the islands, Walter Murray Gibson delivered his "Address to the Hawaiian People" in 1876 with two purposes: to assuage their fears that the treaty was effectively a blueprint for colonization, and to convince them to expend their civic energies elsewhere—namely, in reproduction. For the minister, reproduction had more than a biological connotation. Reproduction meant assimilating to the modes of capitalist labor and behavior by which American economic activity in the islands was structured. By measuring population increase against assimilation, Gibson displaced blame for the decimation of the Hawaiian people from *haole* (white, foreign) colonists to the Hawaiians themselves. He contrasted the islands to the "many countries where . . . the red skins have increased from one million to many millions since the whites went to live among them, because the native people have become as orderly and industrious as the white foreigners."[3] It was the Hawaiians' own failure to civilize and adapt, and not their exposure to promiscuous propagators of disease and extractive policies, that had caused their great loss of life. Their cooperation with the aims of the Reciprocity Treaty would be a new test of their fitness as a race, and as individual members of the global capitalist market.

Gibson argued that only the proper adoption of Anglo-American culture and habits could redeem the Native Hawaiians, warning, "If you do not prosper there must be some cause of decay in your blood or in your situation."[4] In a cunning metaphor that couched the imperatives of the global market in contemporary theories of morbidity and epidemiology, Gibson claimed Hawai'i's supposed isolation was the cause of her people's demographic distress: "You have been so long, so many ages isolated in the great ocean, and have so long interbred and associated in your narrow isles under the destructive influences of a polluting heathenism, that your blood has become corrupt and weakened, and predisposed to receive and succumb to every new disease that comes to desolate your beautiful islands."[5] In Gibson's epidemiological imaginary, Polynesian cultural, racial, and economic pathologies—represented as heathenism and isolation—had been absorbed into the blood as pathogens.

His address recorded the condescension that saturated haole propaganda, and demonstrated an important dimension of political discourse: namely, that few political claims were made in late nineteenth-century Hawai'i that did not attach themselves to the demographic crisis. For the state and haole officials, this crisis was an embarrassing indictment of colonial mismanagement. For the indigenous people, it was a devastating reality of loss and vulnerability ranging from the economic to the epidemiological. Throughout the archive of political rhetoric are promises that successive programs and policies would stem the decline of the native population and reinvigorate the islands. As in Gibson's case, these promises masked the more urgent goal of profiting from the land, its inhabitants, and its proximity to the United States.

It is no small irony, then, that the Reciprocity Treaty did not resolve Hawai'i's demographic crisis, but in fact created new ones. The treaty's bolstering of Hawai'i as a sugaring island produced an immediate and rapacious need for labor that could be easily assimilated to the demands of cane cultivation. Evidence from across the sugaring world pointed to China as the source of cheap, tractable, exploitable labor. Imperial accounts spoke of China as a land of starving masses—the first place one would look for workers who could be underpaid and heavily disciplined. Furthermore, China had, arguably, the most available pool of labor in the world. While the coolie trade from South

Asia had come under serious regulation by the British colonial government, the weak and quasi-colonized Chinese state could barely enforce its own restrictions on emigration, much less oversee the trajectories and treatment of its nationals abroad. After much lobbying, the organized sugar interests succeeded in persuading the government to sponsor Chinese contract migration and to facilitate a private trade in Chinese coolie labor. This traffic would radically transform the demographic composition of the islands, setting off social panics that would influence Hawaiian politics for decades to come. Chief among these was opium, which shifted from a problem to a crisis after the Reciprocity Treaty was enacted.[6]

Opium Regulation in Hawai'i: Sovereignty, Paternalism, Sinophobia

Opium regulation has been studied extensively within colonial historiography, most notably in Dutch, French, British, and to a lesser extent, American Southeast Asia. Scholars have also looked to opium to narrate nationalist historiographies, particularly in the Pacific frontier of the American West.[7] Each of these contexts served as cases of comparison and precedent to Hawaiian policymakers, who frequently cited colonial practices in Java, and always kept an eye on the policies of the United States in relation to its Chinese subjects. But compared to Asian and North American contexts, opium regulation in Hawai'i was unique for three major reasons. The first is that the kingdom did not fit neatly into either category of nation or colony. While it was, in fact, a sovereign nation, its sovereignty was considered—with both anxiety and hope—to be precarious and negotiable. Though Hawaiian diplomats had labored to secure international recognition of the kingdom's independence, foreign agents and imperial powers continued to intervene in the political affairs of nearly all Oceanic polities, whether by claims to economic supremacy or campaigns of outright conquest. Indigenous statesmen deftly played these forces off against each other, but each alliance with a foreign power legitimized imperial hopes of eventual accession.[8]

To many influential haole politicians in Hawai'i, colony was the future tense of a nation unlikely to stave off imperialist advances. Furthermore, in their arrogant ideologies of race and rule, they deemed Hawaiians fundamentally unfit for self-governance, their very independence a tenuous bargain with generous imperial powers, delivered by the genius of haole political advisers. Despite international recognition of their independence, the internal logic of protocolonial governance cast Hawaiians as semi-civilized subjects in desperate need of Anglo-American tutelage, even as they bucked it off. Indeed, their recalcitrance was taken by white ideologues as further proof of indigenous people's ineligibility for autonomy.[9]

Hawaiian patriots were not easily deceived by the treacherous motives of haole leaders, and experienced nationhood in crisis. In their exercise of power they remained acutely aware of the threat of foreign conquest. Hawaiian leaders understood that their recognition as a sovereign people had been conditioned upon their ostensible submission to the codes of Euro-American governance and morality. Their political autonomy was at least partially premised on their strategic reproduction of idealized social conduct and cultural norms. Thus, even in matters of social reform, sovereignty was always explicitly at stake. If civilizing missions within official colonies fetishized indigenous sovereignty as something to be (eventually) gained, within Hawai'i it was under the perpetual threat of being lost. This sense of managing a state and society under the implicit threat of colonization marks nineteenth-century Hawaiian national politics as particularly fraught.[10]

The second unique quality of opium regulation in Hawai'i was the belief that the drug had to be kept away from an indigenous population that was already dying. While colonial policies throughout Southeast Asia contained what we will call the "Chinese exception," which legalized the distribution and consumption of opium for Chinese subjects alone, it was seen as a preventative measure to ensure the health of their native population. In Hawai'i, the express prohibition of opium for natives was more urgent than a matter of prevention—public officials and policymakers were already struggling to prevent the immense and ongoing loss of native life. While haole ministers justified their authority through claims that they could rescue a degenerating race, death and depopulation haunted Hawaiian political discourse. By the time opium use gained salience as a source of public concern in the kingdom, it appeared as a kind of opportunistic infection, a scourge on an already imperiled population that government officials had been failing to protect.

The third and final reason regulation efforts in Hawai'i were unique had to do with the sheer volume of Chinese migrants present in the islands. Hawaiian ministers were not struggling to govern cohesive and coherent communities located in hypervisible urban pockets, as authorities in cities like London and San Francisco were. Certainly, the Hawaiian government and haole reformers fretted and fixated over Honolulu's Chinatown but by the 1870s Chinese migrants were everywhere, dispersed across the archipelago from bustling port cities to remote rural towns, with countless numbers roaming in between as peddlers and runaways. Their apparent ubiquity was confirmed when the census of 1872 recorded more Chinese men than haole, and again in 1884 when it was revealed that Chinese men composed half of the adult male population of the islands.[11] While numbers alone do not suffice to account for the vitriolic rhetoric and social panic that arose in response to the growing Chinese population, these statistical realities anguished policymakers and reformers.

Uncontained Chinese migrants in Hawai'i were more than an inconvenience for Hawaiian ministers. They constituted a crisis of governance.

Regulating Opium, Regulating Migrants

This crisis was reiterated throughout the course of Hawaiian politics and across the spectrum of daily life. It spoke through the figures of Chinese incarcerated in prisons and insane asylums, where typically their numerical dominance was second only to Native Hawaiians. It manifested itself in the regulations imposed on virtually all forms of Chinese economic activity, from laundries to poi factories to the roving carts of fishmongers. It was articulated in the restrictions devised to control and curb further Chinese migration to the kingdom. Beginning in 1882, these efforts ensured that Chinese arrivals to the islands did not exceed departures, resulting in the gradual decrease of the Chinese population between 1884 and 1890. But the crisis of governance was given its most consistent and profound expression in the political status of the Chinese themselves, subjects with near-impossible access to formal political representation whose slim chances of enfranchisement through naturalization were altogether rescinded by the Bayonet Constitution of 1887. While scholars have shown that the regulation and exclusion of Chinese bodies was a central project of statecraft in white settler nations, in Hawai'i it provided the material and discursive pretext for the establishment of a colonial state.[12] Though some partisans feared that the influx of Chinese migrants would render the islands racially undesirable to the United States, haole politicians invoked the perpetual crisis of Chinese regulation as an invitation for American intervention.[13]

Opium regulation became one mechanism in a regime of exclusion gradually developed by the protocolonial state. It engaged modern techniques of governance including surveillance, quarantine, incarceration, segregation, and deportation. The supposed transits of opium mapped the problems posed by the Chinese population, and the strategies and institutions devised for its regulation doubled as the architecture of exclusion of the Chinese themselves. In the name of drug regulation, white citizens demanded intensified policing of Chinatown and Chinese social space. "It is high time that the Chinese Theatre were either shut up by the authorities or placed under vigilant police surveillance," demanded one author in the *Daily Bulletin*. "The Chinese Theatre is said to be the common resort of gamblers and opium-smokers, where they commit their illegal practices with a feeling of comparative security from detection."[14] The increased scrutiny and hypervisibility of Chinese in the eyes of law enforcement agents resulted in the criminalization of entire communities, which were categorically suspected of using and dealing opium.

Opium regulation was even written into immigration laws to mark certain bodies as unfit for entry. The Act to Regulate Chinese Immigration of 1887 disqualified any resident Chinese from reentering the Hawaiian kingdom unless he could "make it appear to the satisfaction of the Minister of Foreign Affairs that he has resided within the Kingdom for two years, and that he is not a vagrant, criminal, professional beggar, user of opium, or one likely to become a charge upon the country."[15] It is difficult to imagine what constituted sufficient proof that one was not an opium user considering the widespread suspicion that virtually all Chinese consumed the drug. In response to the intense disciplinary focus of the Hawaiian state and haole society, the Chinese innovated strategies to circumvent their laws and undermine their order. They mobilized community networks adept at operating below state radar. They smuggled opium into and across the islands, escaped from carceral institutions like jails and sanatoriums, and, it was suspected, illegally shared reentry permits in order to sustain lifeways and livelihoods organized around mobility and circulation.[16]

Opium Law and the Chinese Exception

Legislative efforts to regulate opium trafficking and consumption can be categorized into four phases. The first regulations, enacted between 1856 and 1860, authorized licensed physicians and surgeons to sell opium for medicinal use only. When authorities realized that Chinese migrants were taking opium "recreationally," a law was passed specifying that doctors could not sell to Chinese customers without prescriptions.[17] The perceived misuse of opium by Chinese consumers resulted in the second phase of regulation, the Chinese licensing laws. From 1860 to 1874 the importation, sale, possession, and consumption of opium was authorized for Chinese subjects only. This in turn reproduced popular understandings of opium as a Chinese drug.

The routine subversion of these regulations by smugglers, merchants, and indigenous consumers caused some in government to become disillusioned with the practical reality of the opium license and Chinese exception. "It is estimated that when the prohibitory act went into effect, not less than 500 to 1000 natives had acquired the opium habit," wrote prominent attorney and prohibitionist William R. Castle in 1884.[18] From 1874 to 1876 opium was outlawed in the kingdom, marking the third phase of regulation: prohibition. But beginning in 1876, the great influx of migrant smokers revived the opium question, leading to the fourth phase of regulation, characterized by perpetual debate. On one side were those who called for a return to the licensing laws; on the other, those determined to extend prohibition. The legislative struggle was ultimately silenced in 1893 when the provisional government established after the overthrow of the monarchy ruled to prohibit opium once and for all, a decision upheld under annexation.

The most intense period of contestation, between 1876 and 1892, was marked by growing sinophobia and shifting interest groups made up of missionaries, planters, merchants, and reformers—each with a high stake in the future of opium in Hawai'i. Haunting these struggles was the continued failure of the protocolonial government to improve the health and life chances of the Native Hawaiian population, many of whom had come to appreciate the allure of opium. Although virtually excluded from the halls of government, Chinese and Hawaiian dealers and smokers contested all attempts at regulation through elaborate networks of underground consumption and trafficking. Given the volume of the opium trade, the state itself had a major vested interest in licensing its sale. So lucrative was opium to the elite Chinese merchants who oversaw its distribution and to the cash-poor kingdom that collected its fees that in 1874, on the eve of prohibition, the license to sell opium in the kingdom sold for $19,266—purchased on the *chance* that it might be validated.[19]

The factions and allegiances that formed through these debates were porous and changing. Missionaries generally favored prohibition, viewing opium as a vice incompatible with proper Protestant morality. Planters were split on the issue, with some convinced that opium hindered the productivity of their plantation workers, while others—perhaps more informed—were willing to tolerate its consumption as a concession toward their foreign laborers. Undoubtedly, some planters even benefited from the use of opium by addicts, as cases of dependent coolies locked into labor contracts by mounting debts attest. There was no consensus to be found among Native Hawaiian or Chinese communities, either. Bourgeois elites in both groups tended to echo missionary views of opium use as a transgression against morality, decency, and racial uplift as their humbler members actively partook of the drug. In all camps hypocrisy, venality, and ulterior motives complicated the official positions and narratives of opium's supporters and detractors. It was frequently alleged in legislative debates that those ministers supportive of prohibition were themselves engaged in the illegal trafficking of opium, and Castle alleged that certain Chinese were "offering large amounts to procure the passage of license laws."[20]

The first Chinese license law was passed in 1860 and set practical precedents that were rearticulated by all subsequent versions. While opium remained a licit medicinal substance to be dispensed by doctors, the act allowed for its importation and distribution by licensed Chinese entrepreneurs, to be sold to Chinese consumers only. The license to sell opium in a particular district was sold at auction, the government hoping to generate as much of a profit as possible from wealthy merchants eager to monopolize the trade of a precious commodity. These hopes were thwarted, however, by the cooperative spirit of the merchants themselves, who refused to bid against each other for the profit of the state, and instead agreed to rotate ownership of the license by year. These agreements were not always successful, interrupted periodically by interethnic antipathies and personal economic competition. In 1874 the moral panic around opium culminated in the passage of the Prohibitory Act, the first regulation ever to criminalize the possession of opium.

Bills were proposed in 1878, 1880, and 1884 to reinstate the Chinese opium license. Each passed the assembly, only to be vetoed by King Kalākaua. Finally in 1886 a new licensing law was passed, providing for a single four-year license to be sold without auction. The ensuing scramble among Chinese entrepreneurs to secure the license resulted in a major bribery scandal, at the center of which was King Kalākaua himself. The embarrassing incident became potent ammunition for haole propagandists, and ultimately served as one pretext for the Bayonet Constitution of 1887, which stripped the native monarch, as well as his nonwhite subjects, of meaningful political power. The mostly white vigilantes who forced Kalākaua to ratify the document under threat of violence moved to prohibit opium in the kingdom, but honored the Chinese license of 1886.

Throughout this period Chinese merchants negotiated regulations and penalties in the courts, which, along with bribes, served as surrogate institutions through which they participated in the political life of the kingdom. Concurrently, the penalties for violating the Prohibitory Act were lessened. Then in 1892, in the midst of an economic depression, a final licensing law was proposed with strict and specific provisions to restrict the sale, location, clientele, and consumption of opium to authorized sellers in opium dens with Chinese male clients over the age of twenty. Almost immediately after the "Opium Den" Act was passed, a new vanguard of vigilantes staged a coup with the backing of American marines that brought an end to the Hawaiian monarchy.

The cultural significance of the licensing laws, which operated on the principle of Chinese exception, has been oversimplified by scholars of opium and empire. Some attribute the solution, implemented across colonial Southeast Asia, to sinophobia, cultural relativism, and paternalism in relation to indigenous populations, whether Malay or Polynesian. To a certain extent, each of these ideologies and techniques of governance animated the laws and lent them their traction. But if we consider some insights offered by scholars of colonial law, and particularly those focused on the British Empire, we must recognize that law was more than a tool of legislative governance. It was an instrument of social and cultural engineering. Laws like those pertaining to the Chinese opium license relied on racial taxonomies that evaluated persons differently based on their perceived membership in specific groups. These categorizations, it has been argued, did not passively reflect social realities—which became ever complicated by the intractable intimacies engendered by colonialism itself—but actively produced them. Colonial, and by extension, protocolonial governments, did not rule stable and transparent racial groups, but governed through the production and distinction of specific groups whose perceived differences were classified as racial in the eyes of the law.[21]

Castle alluded to the difficulties of separating Hawaiian from Chinese in the years before mass migration, noting that in the census of 1860, the year the first Chinese license law was passed, Chinese "were counted with Hawaiians at some places."[22] At a crucial moment of demographic transformation, Chinese licensing laws performed more than the legal operation of determining who could and could not partake of opium based on race. They performed the social and cultural labor of producing racial groups—a codified Chinese community distinct from both Native Hawaiians and the mixed progeny that descended from both. These groups, the laws themselves betrayed, could not be kept apart, and it was their quotidian interactions, which occurred most disturbingly in the lowest registers of society, that created a panic of protocolonial governance beyond the actual traffic of opium.

Chinese Mobility: Unsettling the White Pacific

But what was at stake in regulating Chinese–Hawaiian intimacy? In the Malthusian terms of the late nineteenth century, which reframed life as a racialized bid for survival, Chinese were described as a uniquely competitive race, not because they had evolved through virtue and civilization into a higher form of life, but because they had adapted to suffering. They survived by virtue of their lower life form, their willingness to feed from the bottom, their ability to cheat and skimp. Where the European went with his torch of enlightenment, to bestow the gifts of knowledge and progress upon lesser creatures, the Chinese lurked in the shadows, eager to siphon even the humblest dregs of wealth back into his celestial kingdom. The licensing laws, then, were meant to protect the Native Hawaiians from the Chinese as much as from opium. Their forced separation, some hoped, would protect the former from the supposedly predatory machinations of the latter. Further, it would prevent the Hawaiians from adapting the soiled habitus of the heathen Chinese, whose gritty cosmopolitanism threatened to spoil the natives.

"The Hawaiian has not the cunning and secretive qualities of the Chinese," Castle stated, giving voice to the common racial–moral taxonomies embraced by haole reformers and activists. Their social geography of the islands was landscaped by sinophobia and hypocrisy. In white minds, the Chinese were an invasive species who overwhelmed the native race and derailed the Anglo-American Protestant civilizing mission. Their putative power and criminality eclipsed the exploits of white adventurers often engaged in the same activities of smuggling and dealing. Hawai'i was, after all, a small nation in the vast expanse of a maritime frontier. It was no great surprise to anyone that enterprising rogues and pioneers converged on the islands from three continents to gamble on a future in the young kingdom.

But to the haole establishment, the missionaries, businessmen, and planters whose fathers and grandfathers had come to the islands to evangelize and trade, not all migrants deserved equal opportunities to stake claims to the islands. For this faction that had risen to political and economic power, the struggle for dominance in Hawai‘i was as much against the Chinese as it was against the Native Hawaiians. This struggle was betrayed by the fixation on opium, which came to stand in white protocolonial discourse as the ultimate sign of Chinese influence and intractability. Opium did not create new hatreds; rather, it illuminated the antipathies that structured the social, cultural, and political life of the islands by revealing which subjects were deemed abject by the Hawaiian state and dominant society.

Chinese migrants occupied a troublesome place within the haole power structure of Hawai‘i. To this seasoned diasporic people, who knew the islands as the Sandalwood Mountains, Hawai‘i was one mooring spot in a churning Pacific that had beckoned young men for centuries. There, they established what would become the two most lucrative industries of the kingdom, sugar and rice cultivation, and facilitated a trade in people that recruited tens of thousands of Chinese migrant workers during the four decades preceding formal exclusion.[23] While their labor recruitment efforts aided and abetted Euro-American imperialism across the Pacific, they also frustrated white settler colonial projects in Hawai‘i.

Chinese entrepreneurs facilitated a contract labor system that landscaped two hemispheres under the terms of imperial capital. It was the super-exploitation of Chinese (and South Asian) labor that built railroads, powered ships, and cultivated cash-crops in the age of capital. These systems of labor exploitation were underwritten by the contract, a collaboration between capital and the governments of the territories the migrants entered, devised to discipline and immobilize racialized labor after liberalism and humanism declared slavery too crude a mechanism for the modern market.[24] Contract migrants across the globe were predominantly male, and this was especially true of Chinese emigrants. Overwhelmingly, women stayed in southern China to maintain domestic lives ruptured by the demands of imperial capital. Virtually all of the Chinese migrants to the Kingdom of Hawai‘i were men, whose arrival exacerbated the skewed gender dynamics of the islands and gave rise to sexualized anxieties and moral panic. Nevertheless, supposing that they could be confined to the status of coolies and kept within the boundaries of plantations, the Chinese were essential to the economic future of Hawai‘i envisioned by haole capitalists.

There was a small but vocal faction of white workingmen who had come to the islands without the pretension and power of the missionary-planter elite, and they objected to Chinese labor—contracted and free—from the start. The laboring vanguard of the white settler Pacific, these men resented coolies as the units of human capital that enriched greedy planters, and despised Chinese merchants, mechanics, and craftsmen as competition in territories that they believed should be the exclusive domain of white colonial prerogative.[25] To them, the Sandalwood Mountains were "*Pake* [Chinese] Paradise," a nightmare of white settlement where "John Chinaman" lived easy and reigned supreme.[26]

In a pamphlet provocatively entitled "The Planters' Mongolian Pets," the polemicist Z. Y. Squires aimed his racist invective at all levels of Chinese society, rehearsing common arguments against Chinese migration. He decried the innate criminality of the Chinese, who were "trained . . . from infancy in all the arts of vice and villainy and deception"; proclaimed their unfitness for democratic citizenship, claiming "no other race or tribe of people would submit tamely to tyrannical laws and rules put in force by most of our plantation managers"; and highlighted their corrupting influence on Hawaiians, warning that the Chinese were "demoralizing our once respectable Hawaiian citizen and inhabitant."[27] The author's most urgent critique was of the unbridled economic power embodied by Chinese migrants, who were fit to "cause the disappearance of the white laborer . . . from our shores."[28] It was the perceived financial savvy and economic mobility of the Chinese that most threatened white settler colonials and protocolonial sovereignty in the kingdom. Hawai'i was on track to become a racially amalgamated plantation colony, and this was a matter of despair for the white laboring classes.[29] But for the planter elite, it was a lucrative concession.

Unfortunately for haole planters and workingmen alike, the Chinese had designs of their own. The post-Reciprocity migrants who came as fieldhands had been recruited by various combinations of kin, Chinese firms, haole planters, and the Hawaiian government to work in sugar and rice plantations. But the planters who imported them could neither predict nor prevent the trajectories they pursued once in the islands. The historian Clarence Glick has argued that "occupational mobility among the migrants in Hawai'i was far greater than among the Chinese in the continental United States or in many overseas Chinese colonies."[30] This was due partly to the vacancies left by Hawaiians across the economic landscape, and largely to the maneuverings of the Chinese themselves.

Despite serial ordinances passed by the state that increasingly linked Chinese belonging with plantation labor, migrants' persistent resistance, mobility, and cooperation destabilized the very category of "coolie" in Hawai'i.[31] Migrants whose journeys had been sponsored by sugar planters evaded their contracts upon arrival and went to work in rice, where cooperation and collective ownership created the discipline so desired by contract. Others ran away before their contracts expired. The majority, however, served their terms, and upon their release assumed or innovated jobs that were at once marginal and central, disruptive and supplemental, to the bustling plantation and port economies of Hawai'i. They engaged in a kind of colonialism of the pocket, staking claims to the small change of Native Hawaiians, haoles, and fellow Chinese alike. As peddlers and hawkers they traveled between urban centers and rural interiors, stocking up on goods from Chinese merchants and selling them for cash—or barter, with the stubborn Native Hawaiians who refused to be proletarianized. They set up shop in plantation towns and expanded into trading houses in the ports of Hawai'i. They worked in agriculture, from petty market gardening to enormous rice plantations that shipped their harvests to the growing Asian populations on the West Coast of North America.[32] Opium was just one of many commodities imported and smuggled, peddled and pushed, across sprawling networks of mobile Chinese.

The menace of opium merely highlighted networks and circuits of Chinese economic life that had long been construed as a danger to the islands. In truth, the scourge of opium and Chinese activity were mutually constitutive. It was the rumor of opium that made Chinese trade suspect, and Chinese capital and combination that made opium toxic. Chinese economic activity beyond the sugar plantation caused enough concern to the Hawaiian government that in 1890, for the first time, the census tabulated occupation by "nationality."[33]

William Castle's pamphlet on opium prohibition can be read as a map of Chinese economic activity, highlighting its marginality, subversion, insidiousness, and criminality. Landmarks included the porous borders of the islands, the paths of peddlers running from ports to interiors, urban opium dens, and plantation barracks. The extent of smuggling activities—in which haoles and Native Hawaiians were also engaged—registered in the figure of 3,632 pounds of opium reportedly seized by the Custom House between 1875 and 1884.[34] Bribery and artifice allowed these smugglers to subvert the sovereign technology of customs and border control. Within the islands themselves, peddlers and hawkers were pervasive, extending the ring of distribution as far as even the most remote plantation.

"Large quantities of opium were sold by the licensee to people who went all over the country, from Hawaii to Kauai, peddling it, and it was sold and furnished to natives—and it will be again,"[35] Castle warned, pointing out the fact that even licensed distribution did not conform to legal mandates. These illicit interracial transactions occurred across the vast network of opium distribution. "The native in the country can procure opium as easily as in Honolulu; perhaps he is not as likely to become addicted to its use as in town."[36] This speculation betrayed anxieties beyond the sinophobic conceptualization of Chinese urban space, hinting at fears of indigenous urbanization, especially if Chinese from "the opium using class" were serving as tutors.[37] While "the old [licensing] law prohibited the sale [of opium] to natives . . . it did not prevent them from visiting the frequent opium dens and partaking with the Chinese, of the drug, for which they paid, not the holder of the license, but the proprietor of the den."[38] Indeed, the great danger of Chinese mobility and space lay not only in the sprawling, roving networks that organized economic activity but also in the fixed enclaves that harbored and hid Chinese-Hawaiian social life.

Racing Bodies: Public Health and Haole Paternalism

Before we can discuss the cultural and political implications of haole anxiety around opium's interiors, and the interracial intercourse that occurred within them, we must further clarify the racialist thinking about Chinese and Hawaiians that cast the former as villains and the latter as victims. As mentioned before, opium regulation was crucial to constructing regimes of racial knowledge and institutions of separation and segregation meant to extricate the two groups. The extent of their entanglement was broad and profound, occurring in all registers of life, from economic ventures to conjugal homes. In 1935, the sociologist Romanzo Adams estimated that before 1900, between 1,200 and 1,500 Chinese men had established families with Native Hawaiian women.[39] These figures say nothing of the fleeting, casual, and platonic interactions that served as sinews connecting Chinese and Hawaiians in a shared social world.

While some welcomed Chinese men who adequately performed Protestant patriarchal roles, stabilizing "half-caste" families and linking them to the modern market, most observed interracial interaction with growing unease.[40] After all, Chinese and Hawaiians composed two populations in desperate need of rationalization through civilization, evangelization, and integration into the global capitalist market. That these two irrational—and often illegible—groups appeared to collaborate so fluently posed its own problem for protocolonial governance and the imagined destiny of Hawai'i. Each group would have to be rationalized and assimilated to the haole colonial vision of Hawai'i separately: while Hawaiians were to be proselytized, tutored, and groomed for positions within the nation according to the dictates of paternalism and white settler colonialism, Chinese were to be immobilized, criminalized, and segregated as guest-workers and outsiders within a growing regime of exclusion.

These dual programs of paternalism toward Hawaiians and exclusion of Chinese manifested themselves in the discourse around care, health, and opium use. Castle described opium, perhaps sardonically, as "a drug so poisonous and deadly that on no account could it be sold or furnished *to any but Chinese*."[41] His own concern for the drug's effect on their health was confined to the productive bodies of plantation workers. "If the Government wishes to have regard for the physical condition of the laborers in the country," he argued, "it will not license opium."[42] Speaking in 1852 to the Royal Hawaiian Agricultural Society, the planter E. H. Allen prefigured the protocolonial economy of care and affect in which the Chinese were to become impoverished. "You must have sympathy with honest labor," he advised his cohort.[43] Decades into the Chinese experiment, haole planters, workingmen, missionaries, ministers, and reformers had little sympathy left. They were not alone, as licensing laws across the imperial world revealed the pervasiveness of this lack of concern for the welfare of migrant Chinese. From French Indochina to the Dutch East Indies, colonial governments profited from the gradual deterioration of Chinese bodies. And indeed, these systems operated by the identical logic that promoted the global exploitation of coolies as a universal good.

For Hawaiians, the paternalistic care of the state and haole establishment was no simple gift. The historian Warwick Anderson describes hygienic reform as among the most invasive and insidious tools of colonial intervention. The "goal of hygiene," he explains, "is to reform the individual body." It is a "disciplinary" technology, operating at the level of the body and the home to restructure the interior and domestic cavities of indigenous life.[44] From missionary days, Native Hawaiians were the targets of near-obsessive campaigns to rationalize their modes of dress, movement, consumption, and sexual and family relations. This ethos of reform persisted even as missionary influence waned, with government officials taking up the mantle of civilizing mission. Their concern, yet another pretext for increased state oversight and management of marginalized life, was in accord with the principles of late imperialism: namely, that colonial governments had to demonstrate that they were doing some good for the native population.

Care, then, was a highly problematic and complicated category in the context of colonial governance. One might ask, for example, why so many programs of hygienic intervention focused on maternal and infant health while so few concerned themselves with the suffering of the elderly. The answer is that care was never synonymous with altruism. The Hawaiian protocolonial state recognized the discourses of colonial violence in which it was embedded—they circulated across the entire white settler Pacific, from North America to Australia. And it was this discourse—which highlighted the ironies and hypocrisies of so-called "enlightened" rule by pointing to the decimation of native populations wherever these rulers seemed to go—that forced the Hawaiian state to reckon with the demographic crisis it had created and continued to exacerbate. What happened to coolies, kept discursively and materially outside of the nation, only came into the biopolitical purview of the protocolonial state when native bodies were implicated.

Few documents outline more clearly and completely the assumptions and imperatives of the protocolonial state in relation to indigenous health and hygienic intervention than Walter Gibson's "Sanitary Instructions for Hawaiians." The product of a special committee (including Castle) convened by the legislature in 1878, "Sanitary Instructions" remains remarkable for its lofty goals and meticulous practicalities. Over the course of some two hundred pages, Gibson concerned himself with the salvation of a precarious people, endangered by their exposure to Western civilization and simultaneous alienation from traditional ways of living. For Gibson, Hawaiians occupied a liminal place between tradition and modernity, nature and culture. They could neither return to their idyllic past, nor navigate the modern world without falling victim to its excesses. They needed to be protected and prepared, informed of their constitutional vulnerabilities and taught the proper defenses against pollution and disease, and thus shepherded into modernity. Hawaiian bodies, homes, and communities had to be re-formed. In this project of reconstituting a declining population into hygienically well-behaved units, no detail of biological and material life was too small, from the picking of teeth to the wearing of undergarments.

Alongside these minute prescriptions were expansive meditations on the very nature of decay. Gibson's treatise was deeply concerned with the presumed medical–moral nexus of health, sexuality, and productivity that informed much of the social scientific and evangelical discourse that circulated among public officials and reformers in late nineteenth-century Hawai'i. According to this moral and epidemiological conception of the body, disease was not simply the outcome of contact with biological contagions, but the result of misappropriated energies, particularly sloth and licentiousness. Warned Gibson: "A woman who lies on a mat all day, soon wastes her strength in lasciviousness at night," and these twinned indulgences produced an internal filth that sedimented itself in the body, eventually manifesting itself as disease.[45]

Gibson's lens was especially trained on reproductive women, in whose bodies he located the suffering of the race. "The hope of her country is in her womb," he wrote with strained ambivalence of Hawaiian women.[46] Throughout his instructions he fretted over the young indigenous female body, specifically its protection and exposure. Girls should sleep in nightgowns in private and secluded quarters. They must take care to wash and cover their private parts. These precautions were almost obsessively reiterated throughout the text, intended to protect young women from the sexual pathologies harbored by native families and the very souls of Hawaiian girls themselves. Still, the greatest threat from which young women required protection, a threat positioned at the center of a treatise on feminine, reproductive, and national hygiene, was the threat of interracial intimacy with Chinese men.[47]

At the very beginning of the text, while brooding on the origins of indigenous depopulation, Gibson blamed interracial intimacy as the chief cause.[48] He argued against the claim that Native Hawaiians were inherently doomed, pointing instead to the disturbing social realities of sugar culture, which in 1879 had become dominated by Chinese labor. According to Gibson, the source of Hawaiian decline could be located in the besieged wombs of Hawaiian women, whose reproductive energies were being usurped and sapped by the hypersexualized demands of "large numbers of men without women," an obvious allusion to the Chinese.[49] It was by these men, entangled in their own web of sexual pathologies, that "*the wombs of [Hawaiian] women [were] made sterile*."[50]

Several points are important to note here. First, that Gibson, despite his own condescending attitudes toward Native Hawaiians, denied the inevitability of their extinction. There was hope, and that hope lay in the intervention of the protocolonial state and the missionary-planter establishment, in the salve of Christian morality and the stimulant of capitalist agriculture. To deny this would be to deny the central rationale for the persistence of haole authority despite its devastating outcomes. Second, the blame for indigenous decline did not fall solely on Hawaiian women. Rather, their—and by extension their race's—deterioration was the result of intimate contact with a demographic believed to be more sexually pathological than the natives themselves. Within the text and the popular discourses of public health in which it circulated, we can see Hawaiian girls and Chinese men paired as dangerous subjects of perversity and decay.

Contagion and Collaboration: Opiated Intimacy and Interracial Exchange

This menacing pairing haunted the discourse on opium regulation. While opium appeared only once in the text of "Sanitary Instructions," under the heading of "Vegetable Poisons," the fears around its quotidian exchange between Chinese and Hawaiians, especially Hawaiian women, were illuminated throughout Gibson's writings. As a commodity it facilitated the social interpenetration of both groups; as a substance it supposedly lubricated their destructive passions. The threat of opium, and of Chinese migration more broadly, was a profoundly sexualized threat, and racial reproductive anxieties were embedded and sublimated within the discourse around its containment.

No case better illustrated the sexualized threat of opium and Chinese men than the murder of a Chinese shopkeeper by a young Hawaiian woman in Wailuku, Maui, on March 1, 1879.[51] The facts of the case were summarized by Chief Justice Harris at the woman's sentencing, and published in the *Hawaiian Gazette* as follows: "By your confession it appears that for the smallest temptation, you undertook to assist in the murder of a man who had been your paramour for many years, with whom, it does not appear, you had any cause of quarrel, from whom you had separated yourself at your own will, and with whom you still continued intimate and friendly enough to pass the night previous to his death, in company with your husband, under his roof."[52] The "smallest temptation" amounted to ten dollars. Although she acted with two accomplices, her husband, Alonzo Davis, and their Chinese friend, Asham, Keliihanaiwi Davis was the only one sentenced to death. Following the outcry of elites against the decision of a native jury, King Kalākaua commuted her sentence to life imprisonment.

Seven years later, during the legislative debates on licensing of 1886, prohibitionist Lorrin A. Thurston retold her story to illustrate the dangers of opium to Hawaiian reproductive life:

> A young man on the island of Maui who was a very clever, able and good looking man had married as nice a native girl as ever he (the speaker) had seen. He and his wife contracted the opium habit. He became a miserable, degraded worthless fellow. His wife murdered a Chinaman to get out of his store a few tins of opium which she had not the means to buy. She was sentenced to be hanged, but the sentence was commuted by His Majesty, and now she is serving out her life sentence over the reef [on Maui].[53]

Whether his inclusion of opium was a modification or elaboration of the actual case, the narrative was given coherence by the discourse around the drug, Chinese dealers, and the destabilization of native reproductive life. His emphasis on the seemingly viable couple, who might have had a chance of establishing a proper domestic life, narrated opium as a disruptive Chinese agent that penetrated intimate spheres of Hawaiian conjugality. This point was strongly articulated in the "Report of the Special Committee on Opium" of 1892, which argued in favor of prohibition, citing "the decrease of reproduction and unhealthy progeny of all opium-smokers." The authors summarized the natalist, paternalist, and prohibitionist mandate of the protocolonial state thus: "In this country where the reproduction of the natives is already so naturally deficient, we cannot allow any extraneous causes to increase the evil and accelerate the extinction of the Hawaiians."[54]

Despite the tireless efforts of the haole establishment to reform indigenous life, evidence points to popular insistence on the self-management of bodily intimacies through native systems of care and pleasure. Though skewed by the perspectives of their editors, newspapers offered a rough map of the social landscape of Hawai'i, and registered in their crime and arrests section the daily rebellions of unreformed natives against the dictates of public health and social order. Among the most common crimes listed were those that pertained to practicing medicine without a license and selling *'awa*, an indigenous spirit distilled from kava root, to Native Hawaiians. The first was likely a reference to *kahuna*, indigenous healers and intermediaries of the divine, whose expertise Hawaiians commonly sought in matters medical and spiritual. Much like the irresponsible young Hawaiian woman and the lecherous Chinese man, the superstitious and tricky kahuna was a thorn lodged deep into the side of the missionary establishment and the reformist state. Sellers of 'awa, usually white shopkeepers, violated a paternalist prohibition that applied only to Native Hawaiians.

It is important to note that the emphasis of criminality in these cases was on the sale and not the purchase of 'awa, and the practice rather than the receipt of customary care, from which the native people, the state contended, required protection. Even, or perhaps especially, in the case of medico-moral crimes, Native Hawaiians were denied accountability for their own selves by the protocolonial state, a move that further reified their status as wards. Because opium smoking was never construed as an indigenous vice like the consumption of 'awa or the patronage of kahuna, its enjoyment was cast as a foreign imposition, a case of Hawaiians under the influence of a Chinese menace. Undoubtedly, Hawaiian users were ensnared by the nets of law enforcement, but they were recruited into unique and intermediary positions, which will be discussed later.

Though a dubious freedom, to take opium was to exercise a kind of bodily sovereignty against the logic of paternalism and the regime of public health that sought to construct Native Hawaiians as unfit for self-governance down to the level of the body. Speaking in defense of a proposed bill to regulate the importation of opium, Representative Kaunamano stated that "opium had been generally used among native Hawaiians as far back as 1856. . . . He (the speaker) had used opium himself and could speak from experience after giving it a fair trial."[55] Kaunamano's argument defied the paternalistic logic invoked throughout the debate that cast Native Hawaiians as easy victims of opium, doomed to be destroyed by it. His admission of having personally used the substance was more than a cheeky interjection. It was a defiant claim that he, as a Native Hawaiian, had exercised a form of self-possession and self-control that haole ministers actively sought to deny racialized, indigenous Others.[56] Countless numbers of Native Hawaiians could have delivered the same testimony. In dens and homes across the country, countless numbers continued, despite the penalties, to enact an embodied autonomy against the oppressive logics of paternalism and hygiene, hidden from the gaze of the regulatory state.

The moral, racial, and sexual panics of opium, Chinese migration, and interracial intimacy are best framed through the concept of opium's interiors. These hidden enclosures antagonized reformers and undermined protocolonial governance precisely because they delineated those domains of migrant Chinese and indigenous Hawaiian life that could be neither exposed nor regulated in full. In his sinophobic manifesto, Squires complained: "This once innocent Hawaiian people are now the victors of John Chinaman. They are enticed into dens of debauchery, dens of deception, dens of corruption, dens of infamy, dens of gambling, dens of contagion, dens of opium, dens within dens, dens adjoining dens,

dens encircling dens, and lastly dens, the most filthy that the human power can conceive of."[57] The dens, opera houses, dead bodies, and closed fists of opium culture taunted the protocolonial governmental gaze, revealing the deceptive exterior of a social world impenetrable to elite haole observers.

Opium's transits mapped that which was unknowable, and yet urgently important, to regimes of governance. Its exact effects within the bodies and minds of smokers—themselves closed cavities of crucial information—were not even fully understood by contemporary reformers. Castle cited a mere eleven deaths directly caused by opium over a period of four years.[58] Throughout his treatise he lamented the general dearth of statistical information available to model social realities for the purposes of biopolitical governance. "What its effects have been," he admitted, "can never be known in the absence, not of reliable, but of *any* vital statistics in most parts of the Kingdom."[59] Nevertheless, he and other activists and officials continued to decry the "extinction of the Hawaiian race" that would surely result from the licensed traffic of opium and the circulation of opiated Chinese.

The frequent refrain that Chinese were literally killing off Native Hawaiians was deceptive and instrumental. In reality, evidence suggested that Chinese migrants revitalized Hawaiian communities by improving their financial viability and extending their economic citizenship beyond the confines of the haole plantation. As conjugal partners they provided for mixed and extended families, a fact that impressed even the most sinophobic of observers. As petty traders willing to barter, they collaborated with Native Hawaiians resistant to the capitalist market of wage labor and cash exchange. As rice farmers, they served a similar function, renting native land parcels (*kuleana*) through a system of tenancy and land use that, like bartering, was indigenous to both Hawaiian and southern Chinese economic cultures. For many Hawaiian families, then, social and economic intercourse with Chinese migrants staved off their dispossession from the land and allowed them to sustain domestic life despite constant sieges by colonial political economy.[60]

In truth, the Hawaiian body that haole reformers accused the Chinese of killing was a sign for the Hawaiian nation itself. It was not, however, the sovereign indigenous nation that the figure of the Native Hawaiian body might imply, but the special domain of white colonial prerogative whose resources—land, people, and wealth—were being poached by the Chinese. The myth of the Hawaiian-killing Chinaman was instrumental to the maintenance of protocolonial sovereignty, as it allowed haole politicians and propagandists to scapegoat the migrants for their own administrative ineptitude. When Castle quoted a policeman as saying that during the licensing years "it was a common thing . . . to find a person on the floor dead from the effects of using opium, and sometimes it was a native," he was inviting his readers to picture the Chinese seller who had killed him.[61]

Politics of the Pipe: Illicit Commerce and Intoxicated Counterpublics

But was it opium that left the corpses? And was it opium that would kill off the remainder of the declining indigenous population? Haole authorities entrusted with the life of the nation were engaged in an experiment of protocolonial governance with devastating results. Despite implementing the kinds of liberal, scientific, and humanitarian reforms that came to characterize the technocratic and humanistic regimes of late imperialism, they found themselves conducting racial autopsies, speculating and studying the causes of native death. "You, Hawaiians," Gibson apostrophized in his hygienic treatise, "need a great physician . . . who would explore Hawaiian diseases in their vilest haunts."[62] With a major vested interest in the colonial capitalist future of the islands, haole authorities could not afford to consider that the great dying of native people had been caused by the implementation of policies so antithetical to indigenous lifeways and livelihoods as to destroy both altogether.

But the natives knew this. Those who lingered on *kalo* (taro) patches and leisured in opium dens sought alternatives to the future offered by colonial capitalist modernity. So did many Chinese, particularly those from the coolie classes whose cooperative impulses mediated the manifold abuses of the colonial political economy. And these groups that refused to assimilate to the imperatives of the global marketplace or accept haole hegemony shared a social world of opium that was covert, subversive, and autonomous. The historian Nayan Shah writes that "the common method of smoking opium encouraged a special intimacy."[63] He describes men lying face-to-face on bunks, sharing pipes of opium. The scholar (and opium enthusiast) Peter Lee describes the socially cohesive practice of smoking around a shared lamp. Seasoned smokers speak of initiation and tutelage, for opium was a difficult drug to prepare, and novices almost always enlisted the help of willing experts. Opium was a social substance and a socializing experience.[64] Beneath the salacious and sensationalist myths, the panicked claims that opium induced smokers to criminal and sexual deviance, lay an embodied experience that may afford insights into indigenous and migrant life irretrievable from the colonial archive.

Claims that Chinese cruelly peddled a deadly drug to natives are difficult to maintain, considering the commonality of opium's consumption among migrants and its hallowed place within their epistemology of care. Practitioners of Taoist medicine extolled the benefits of the drug for centuries. They innovated the method of "smoking" opium to maximize its beneficent properties. Sap harvested from the ripe pods of poppies and processed into opium, when vaporized (not incinerated), released into the lungs of the inhaler a multitude of powerful alkaloids. Coursing together through the bloodstream, these compounds relieved joint and muscle pain, bronchial congestion and asthma, insomnia, gastrointestinal disorders like diarrhea and dysentery, tropical fevers like cholera and malaria, and depression.[65]

Opium's threatening properties, the rapid addiction and gradual emaciation of its users, were offset by special diets, exercises, and periods of detoxification. The notion of "addiction" itself must be complicated by Taoist beliefs that the opium habit could be healthfully sustained by conscientious users.[66] Despite the general lack of vital statistics, it is clear that the vast majority of opium users in late nineteenth-century Hawai'i did not drop dead from the habit. Those who did waste away from addiction were likely predisposed to substance abuse; ignorant of the preventative measures taken by chronic smokers to maintain bodily equilibrium; or, for reasons of financial hardship, unable to secure decent quality opium and adequate stores of food to replenish body fat lost by drug use.[67] Accordingly, colonial conditions of poverty, deprivation, and stress likely exacerbated the toxicity of the drug. Certainly plantation workers consumed the drug to help their bodies conform to the demands of capitalist agriculture. But we must think beyond the rigid political economy of plantations if we are to understand better these smoking subjects.

Troubling though it may be to our modern, rational, hygienic selves, Chinese and Hawaiian smokers alike risked the bodily perils of opium consumption to enjoy its physical, social, mental, and perhaps, liberatory benefits. Desperate smokers may have even resigned themselves to an opiated grave amid the developments and dislocations of protocolonialism. Considering the routine suicides by plantation workers and the trauma and tragedy of indigenous death, this does not seem so farfetched. Whether fatalistic or deliberate, users experienced a drug more subversive than any other. Rather than facilitating their escape from colonial reality, opium enabled smokers—groups of smokers—to retreat to a shared otherworld, "an alternative world to inhabit, a self-contained world of comfort, contentment, and convivial company, complete with a culture all of its own."[68] This alternative space, organized around cooperation, leisure, pleasure, and care, inverted the codes and demands of the colonial capitalist market. For plantation workers drilled by regimented labor, "time itself dissolve[d], leaving the smoker suspended in an artificial eternity."[69]

Opium first struck users as a stimulant before settling into its soporific effects. Smokers experienced various combinations of disembodiment, detachment, and disengagement, and feelings of satiation and tranquility.[70] Contrary to the moralistic claims that opium increased sexual appetites, the drug gave users the impression of having had all appetites appeased.[71] Opium, then, helped to counter the commodification of people and things, as users ceased to feel the strains of their overworked bodies and the material wants they likely had little means to satisfy.

At the same time, the initial hedonism that encouraged smokers to enjoy a pipe undermined the very notions of temperance and restraint that informed the Protestant ethic of leisure.[72] Lee offers a further insight into the disruption constituted by opium use amidst civilizing missions aimed at ordering Hawaiian society: "The addict's behavior is neither moral nor immoral, but rather entirely amoral and neutral, but from society's point of view, this is the worst behavior of all because it does not conform to accepted standards of right and wrong, good and bad, and therefore it allows no room for reform or redemption by society."[73] More terrifying than the savage whose inherent deficiencies precluded his effective civilization was the addict who chose not to be reconstructed, for the latter had evaluated the offer of proper civilized society and determined he had no use for it.

Chinese intent on eventual repatriation may very well have adopted this position toward the dominant culture and society of the islands. Choosing the pipe over polite white society enabled migrants to reproduce, at least in part, the social world of southern China. The material ritual of opium smoking equipped users with a standard and familiar set of paraphernalia that may have served as visual coordinates forming a grid of home. "No matter where he goes, as long as the smoker has some opium and a smoking kit, he always feels at home."[74] By all accounts, opium seemed a well-suited balm for the exclusions and alienations experienced by abject indigenous and diasporic subjects alike.

Few colonial historians are tempted to interrogate the intoxicated subjectivities of subalterns, perhaps because it defies our relentless quest to impute rationality and agency to subjects long deemed to be lacking both. But perhaps rationality and agency were not the only means toward empowerment. And perhaps empowerment and resistance were not actually the most relevant and immediate concepts subalterns reached for in the daily process of making life bearable. It may be that desire and relief were the categories through which they ordered their lives, the objectives they pursued with all the zeal and tenacity we scout out in loftier projects of resistance and liberation. And it may well be that one cannot engage in either project without the other, for the exhaustions and traumas of marginalization are indeed relieved by self-care and fellowship.

Whether stubbornly refusing to assimilate to the dictates of colonial political economy, or actively seeking remedies to its daily abuses, marginalized Chinese and Hawaiian smokers can be read as engaging in a politics of the pipe, a position that was decidedly oppositional to the dominant order. A politics of the pipe entailed seeking out the margins, shadows, and dens of colonial life and rendering them habitable; it meant mobilizing community networks, and enlisting the aid of available substances, to reproduce social life where dominant logics dictated it could not exist. Gathered together by the centripetal forces of imperialism and capitalism and the intimate allure of opium, Chinese and Hawaiian smokers instantiated counter-publics of care and pleasure every time a bowl of processed poppy sap was prepared.

Toward Colonial Sovereignty

Opium's worlds of interracial sociality and intoxicated defiance were fleeting. In their quest to separate two groups who had come together under circumstances of barest life, protocolonial authorities innovated new strategies of surveillance and policing that turned Chinese dealers and Hawaiian clients against each other. The effectiveness of the strategy attests to the relationships of trust, friendship, and familiarity that had developed between two groups who shared conditions of colonial marginality. At least as early as 1880, police enlisted the services of Hawaiian smokers as informants, offering them half of the fines exacted from perpetrators found guilty of breaching any part of the ponderous body of opium laws. "The Chinaman who would furnish opium to the Hawaiian, well knows that his victim after enjoying the deadly trance caused by its use, will report to the police for the reward promised," Castle smugly announced.[75] Thus incentivized, Hawaiian smokers were co-opted by the protocolonial state and incorporated into the burgeoning regime of Chinese exclusion.

Late in 1892, a report by the Special Committee on Opium, convened in July of that year, was published. The authors resolved to expose the evils of opium, "principally to the native members [of the legislative assembly], who may not [have been] fully cognizant of all its bearings and hideous consequences and need[ed] to be educated on the subject."[76] The report offered a brief history of opium in China, focusing on the hypocrisy of British imperialism, the corruption of Chinese officials, and the eager consumption of the drug by Chinese masses. It rehearsed the familiar concerns with the effect of opium on the productivity of laboring bodies, and determined that "all inclination for exertion [became] gradually lost" by smokers.[77] The authors surveyed the imperial world for proof of the drug's universally deleterious effects on public health and morality, and highlighted regulatory strategies that could be employed by the Hawaiian government. They concluded that prohibition was the only logical option to suppress a trade carried on through corruption and deceit.

Referencing China, whose venal officials sold the health—and ultimately, the sovereignty—of the nation in exchange for foreign bribes, provided not only a historical context, but a case of comparison. Hawaiian officials in the deep pockets of treacherous Chinese merchants had betrayed the nation. The text fixated on smuggling as the most pernicious element of opium trafficking, a practice that explicitly undermined the bordered sovereignty of the kingdom. At the same time, the crisis of smuggling portrayed the nation as incapable of regulating its own affairs. The addict corrupted and "enslaved" by the drug was like the kingdom corrupted and dependent on bribes—and both were unfit for self-governance.

In the final pages of the report, the committee pointed to its own failure to uncover any substantial information on smuggling as further proof that the problem of opium had become absolutely intractable, and the ringleaders of its sale frighteningly powerful.[78] After implicating the royal family in the smuggling ring, the committee made a disturbing recommendation that prefigured the tumultuous events to come: should the Hawaiian government fail to take adequate action to protect the kingdom against the scourge of opium, a "vigilante committee" should be formed to take matters into its own hands.[79]

The vigilante committee that formed some months later, at the start of 1893, did not cite opium smuggling as an explicit pretext for overthrowing the native sovereign, Queen Lili'uokalani. It did, however, substantiate its power according to the same logics of colonial governance outlined in the report. The exigency of opium regulation in a moment of supposed crisis had served as a potent warrant for increased haole authority and oversight of migrant and indigenous life. The discourse around opium helped to elaborate a politics of paternalism toward Native Hawaiians that denied their claims to both bodily sovereignty and collective autonomy, and materialized a regime of exclusion against Chinese migrants by framing their mobility as an explicit threat to the health of the nation. These dual outcomes of the regulation of opium proved indispensable to the extension of American hegemony in Hawai'i, serving as both ideological pretexts and political claims for the islands' eventual annexation to the United States in 1898.

The great debate around opium in the kingdom rehearsed arguments for the protection of Native Hawaiians by white authorities while authoring Chinese as exceptional legal subjects. Furthermore, the policies enacted to regulate the drug's traffic institutionalized the pernicious racial constructions that would prove so crucial to the efforts of haole political usurpers. While the legal exceptionality of Chinese subjects first iterated in the opium licensing laws was preserved and extended by discriminatory immigration laws that worked to rationalize the racial landscape of the islands, the legal vulnerability of indigenous Hawaiians produced by regulatory policies called forth formal colonial management by a foreign empire. Ultimately, both claims of racialist colonial thought were reified by American legislation that barred Chinese from entry to Hawai'i and transferred the sovereignty of the Hawaiian nation to the United States.

NOTES

1. I use the term "protocolonial" in describing the Hawaiian state to draw attention to the political and economic structures built and manipulated by American and European ministers whose imperial intentions, though coded and covert, were nonetheless conspicuous to the general public. George Steinmetz, *The Devil's Handwriting: Precoloniality and the German Colonial State in Qingdao, Samoa, and Southwest Africa* (Chicago:

University of Chicago Press, 2007), 76. Steinmetz explains that "under protocolonial conditions, technologies of foreign rule are elaborated in advance of any claims to sovereignty over a territory." For a thorough account of the colonization of Hawai'i by American agents, see Noenoe K. Silva, *Aloha Betrayed: Native Hawaiian Resistance to American Colonialism* (Durham, N.C.: Duke University Press, 2004) and Jonathan Kay Kamakawiwoʻole Osorio, *Dismembering Lahui: A History of the Hawaiian Nation to 1887* (Honolulu: University of Hawaii Press, 2002).

2. Ralph S. Kuykendall, *The Hawaiian Kingdom*, vol. 3: *1874–1893, The Kalākaua Dynasty* (Honolulu: University of Hawaii Press, 1967), 17–53.
3. Walter Murray Gibson, "Address to the Hawaiian People" (Lahaina, 1879), 4.
4. Ibid., 5.
5. Ibid. For more on the European myth of Polynesian isolation, see Matt Matsuda, *Pacific Worlds: A History of Seas, Peoples, and Cultures* (Cambridge: Cambridge University Press, 2012).
6. See Kuykendall, *The Hawaiian Kingdom*, 116–122, 135–153, for a discussion of the beginnings of Chinese contract migration that emphasizes sugar interests and the state.
7. For sources on opium regulation in colonial Southeast Asia, see James R. Rush, "Social Control and Influence in Nineteenth-Century Indonesia: Opium Farms and the Chinese of Java," *Indonesia* 35 (April 1983): 53–64; Carl Trocki, *Opium, Empire, and the Global Political Economy: A Study of the Asian Opium Trade, 1750–1950* (London: Routledge, 1999); Anne L. Foster, "Models for Governing: Opium and Colonial Policies in Southeast Asia, 1898–1910," in *The American Colonial State in the Philippines: Global Perspectives*, edited by Anne L. Foster and Julian Go (Durham, N.C.: Duke University Press, 2003); Diana L. Ahmad, *The Opium Debate and Chinese Exclusion Laws in the Nineteenth-Century American West* (Reno: University of Nevada Press, 2007). For an account of opium regulation in metropolitan London, see Sascha Auerbach, *Race, Law, and "The Chinese Puzzle" in Imperial Britain* (New York: Palgrave Macmillan, 2009).
8. For a clear overview of the struggles for sovereignty between imperial powers and indigenous polities in the Pacific Islands, see Peter Hempenstall's essay, "Imperial Maneuvers," in *Tides of History: The Pacific Islands in the Twentieth Century*, edited by K. R. Howe, Robert C. Kiste, and Brij V. Lal (Honolulu: University of Hawaii Press, 1994).
9. In *Native Land and Foreign Desires* (Honolulu: Bishop Museum, 1992), Lilikalā Kame'eleihiwa explores the tense negotiations for power between Hawaiian nationalists and haole interlopers that played out in the mid-nineteenth century over land privatization. In private and public correspondence, haole ministers routinely invoked the racialized discourse of civilization to delegitimize indigenous claims to autonomy and authority.
10. Kamanamaikalani Beamer offers an innovative study of indigenous statecraft in nineteenth-century Hawaiʻi, focusing on the strategic incorporation of haole political techniques by Hawaiian leaders. See Kamanamaikalani Beamer, *No Mākou Ka Mana: Liberating the Nation* (Honolulu: Kamehameha Publishing, 2014).
11. Clarence E. Glick, *Sojourners and Settlers: Chinese Migrants in Hawaii* (Honolulu: University of Hawaii Press, 1980), 12, 14.
12. For a full account of this process in the United States, see Erika Lee, *At America's Gates: Chinese Immigration during the Exclusion Era, 1882–1943* (Chapel Hill: University of North Carolina Press, 2004).
13. Godfrey Rhodes, "Thoughts on the Hawaiian Situation, by a Member of the House of Nobles" (Honolulu: Pacific Commercial Advertiser Steam Print, 1881), 9. To clarify, I do not mean to conflate regulation with exclusion, but use the two terms as points on a

continuum of strategies used by states to manage difference. The objective of exclusion was never eradication, but the refined immobilization and marginalization of subjects deemed to be outside of the nation.

14. *The Daily Bulletin* (Honolulu [Hawaii]), March 17, 1884. *Chronicling America: Historic American Newspapers*. Library of Congress, accessed May 22, 2013, http://chroniclingamerica.loc.gov/lccn/sn82016412/1884-03-17/ed-1/seq-2.
15. *Report of the Minister of Foreign Affairs to the Hawaiian Legislature, Session of 1888* (Honolulu: Pacific Commercial Advertiser Steam Print, 1888), Appendix D: xvii.
16. Ibid.,10. This latter act was inferred by government ministers when the 1887 Act to Regulate Chinese Immigration resulted in the virtual halt of Chinese applications for reentry permits (also known as passports).
17. The notion of recreational use of opium by Chinese is somewhat misleading. Opium had been used medicinally in China for centuries, where the technique of vaporizing ("smoking") the substance to optimize its properties was developed and refined. Its status as a substance of both health and pleasure was not contradictory within the epistemological framework of Taoist medicine. For a rich account of the traditional Chinese practice and understanding of opium use, see Peter Lee, *Opium Culture: The Art and Ritual of the Chinese Tradition* (Rochester, Vt.: Park Street Press, 2006), 13–17.
18. William R. Castle, "Shall Opium Be Licensed?: Opium in Hawaii" (Honolulu, 1884), 3.
19. Lily Lim-Chong and Harry V. Ball, "Opium and the Law: Hawai'i, 1856–1900," *Chinese America: History & Perspectives—The Journal of the Chinese Historical Society of America* (San Francisco: Chinese Historical Society of America with UCLA Asian American Studies Center, 2010), 63.
20. For a full discussion of legislative debates, see ibid., 62–67. Castle, "Shall Opium Be Licensed?" 3.
21. For further discussion of race, colonial law, and imperial governance, see Nandini Chatterjee, "Muslim or Christian? Family Quarrels and Religious Diagnosis in a Colonial Court," *American Historical Review* 117, no. 4 (October 2012): 1104.
22. Castle, "Shall Opium Be Licensed?" 3.
23. For a rich discussion of the early Chinese pioneer merchants, see Glick, *Sojourners and Settlers*, 1–11.
24. For work on coolies and contract labor, see Walton Look Lai, *Indentured Labor, Caribbean Sugar: Chinese and Indian Migrants to the British West Indies, 1838–1918* (Baltimore: Johns Hopkins University Press, 1993) and Moon-ho Jung, *Coolies and Cane: Race, Labor, and Sugar in the Age of Emancipation* (Baltimore: Johns Hopkins University Press, 2006).
25. For an excellent study of anti-Asian agitation among white colonial labor activists, see Kornel Chang, "Circulating Race and Empire: Transnational Labor Activism and the Politics of Anti-Asian Agitation in the Anglophone Pacific World, 1880–1910," *Journal of American History* 96, no. 3 (2009): 678–701.
26. Bob Dye, *Merchant Prince of the Sandalwood Mountains: Afong and the Chinese in Hawaii* (Honolulu: University of Hawaii Press, 1997), 4.
27. Z. Y. Squires, "The Planters' Mongolian Pets; or, Human Decoy Act" (Honolulu, 1884), 8.
28. Ibid., 14.
29. Ibid., 18. Activists like Squires promoted a scheme of sugar cultivation that would have encouraged white settlement in the islands. They envisioned sugar grown on homesteads and processed at collectively owned mills. See also Kuykendall, *The Hawaiian Kingdom*, 49–53.
30. Glick, *Sojourners and Settlers*, xi.

31. Ibid., 28–29. Operating through the dual mechanisms of quarantine and deportation, these regulations include an 1881 ordinance requiring all Chinese entering Hawai'i not under contract to furnish proof that they would not become vagrants, resulting in many incoming migrants contracting with recruiters who were stationed at quarantine facilities. In the 1890s labor contracts regularly included clauses stipulating that upon completion of their terms of service, Chinese migrants could not stay in the islands except as domestics or fieldhands.
32. For an authoritative account of Chinese migrant economic activity, see Glick, *Sojourners and Settlers*, 45–101.
33. Ibid., 83.
34. Castle, "Shall Opium Be Licensed?" 4.
35. Ibid., 5.
36. Ibid., 6.
37. Ibid., 5.
38. Ibid., 3.
39. Statistic quoted in Glick, *Sojourners and Settlers*, 162.
40. Walter M. Gibson, "Sanitary Instructions for Hawaiians" (Honolulu: J. H. Black, 1879), 216. The author notes: "It is cheerfully admitted that an industrious Chinaman makes a good husband for an Hawaiian woman; and in some few instances, such a union has produced many healthy offspring," although he himself is doubtful.
41. Castle, "Shall Opium Be Licensed?" 2, emphasis in original.
42. Ibid., 5.
43. E. H. Allen addressing Royal Hawaiian Agricultural Society, 1852, as quoted in Glick, *Sojourners and Settlers*, 8.
44. Warwick Anderson, "Immunization and Hygiene in the Colonial Philippines," *Journal of the History of Medicine and Allied Sciences* 62, no. 1 (2006): 4.
45. Gibson, "Sanitary Instructions," 213.
46. Ibid., 100.
47. When speaking in terms of "race," I mean to invoke the expansive connotations it would have carried for nineteenth-century subjects. Race throughout these texts is used to signify differences of behavior, custom, and morality. In regards to the Chinese, it has particular sexual and religious connotations that I do not wish to neglect.
48. Nearly a decade later, in his 1888 lecture to the Honolulu Social Science Association, the Reverend Sereno Edwards would list "Wifeless Chinese" as number seven in a list of answers to the titular question of his paper, "Why Are the Hawaiians Dying Out?" It must be noted that these arguments were not merely raced but classed, as marriages between Hawaiian and European elites—a proper form of interracial relating—were not uncommon. In fact, these arrangements were one mechanism through which haole entrepreneurs had consolidated their power over the wealth and lands of the kingdom.
49. Gibson, "Sanitary Instructions," xviii.
50. Ibid., xvii, emphasis in original.
51. *The Hawaiian Gazette* (Honolulu [Oahu, Hawaii]), July 16, 1879. *Chronicling America: Historic American Newspapers*, Library of Congress, accessed May 22, 2013, http://chroniclingamerica.loc.gov/lccn/sn83025121/1879-07-16/ed-1/seq-3.
52. *The Hawaiian Gazette* (Honolulu [Oahu, Hawaii]), July 30, 1879. *Chronicling America: Historic American Newspapers*, Library of Congress, accessed May 22, 2013, http://chroniclingamerica.loc.gov/lccn/sn83025121/1879-07-30/ed-1/seq-4.

53. *The Daily Bulletin* (Honolulu [Hawaii]), October 12, 1886. *Chronicling America: Historic American Newspapers*, Library of Congress, accessed May 22, 2013, http://chroniclingamerica.loc.gov/lccn/sn82016412/1886-10-12/ed-1/seq-2.
54. *Report of the Special Committee on Opium to the Legislature of 1892* (Honolulu, 1892), 16.
55. *The Daily Bulletin* (Honolulu [Hawaii]), October 11, 1886. *Chronicling America: Historic American Newspapers*. Library of Congress, accessed May 22, 2013, http://chroniclingamerica.loc.gov/lccn/sn82016412/1886-10-11/ed-1/seq-2.
56. There is, of course, a class dynamic at work here that speaks to the selective blindness of the drug-regulating state. It was no secret that elite members of society partook in the enjoyment of opium. However, it was its consumption by marginal and "irregular" members of society that threatened the social order and summoned state involvement.
57. Squires, "The Planters' Mongolian Pets," 7–8.
58. Castle, "Shall Opium Be Licensed?" 4.
59. Ibid., 3, emphasis in original.
60. Specific examples of Chinese and Hawaiian economic exchange and cooperation beyond the plantation capitalist economy can be found throughout Davianna Pōmaika'i McGregor's ethnographic study of rural Hawaiian localities, *Nā Kua'āina: Living Hawaiian Culture* (Honolulu: University of Hawaii Press, 2007). For further accounts of Chinese-Hawaiian economic cooperation, see for example Jocelyn Linnekin, *Sacred Queens and Women of Consequence: Rank, Gender, and Colonialism in the Hawaiian Islands* (Ann Arbor: University of Michigan Press, 1990); James H. Chun's *The Early Chinese in Punaluu* (Honolulu: Yin Sit Sha, 1983); and Violet K. Lai's *He Was a Ram: Wong Aloiau of Hawaii* (Honolulu: University of Hawaii Press, 1985).
61. Castle, "Shall Opium Be Licensed?" 5.
62. Gibson, "Sanitary Instructions," 185.
63. Nayan Shah, *Contagious Divides: Epidemics and Race in San Francisco's Chinatown* (Berkeley: University of California Press, 2001), 91.
64. Lee, *Opium Culture*, 71–82.
65. For a thorough description of the pharmacology of opium, see ibid., 45–60.
66. Ibid., 13–17.
67. Ibid., 25–26, 83–104.
68. Ibid., 72.
69. Ibid., 77.
70. Ibid., 71, 76, 82.
71. Ibid., 65–67, 82.
72. Ibid., 82.
73. Ibid., 74.
74. Ibid., 76.
75. Castle, "Shall Opium Be Licensed?" 2–3. See also Lim-Chong and Ball, "Opium and the Law," 69–70.
76. *Report of Special Committee on Opium*, 2.
77. Ibid., 6.
78. Ibid., 18.
79. Ibid., 19–20.

PART III

Lives/Representations

Interlude

KATHLEEN LÓPEZ

Alongside the growth in scholarship on Asians in the Americas, the field has witnessed a proliferation of creative work *by* people of Asian descent in the Americas. The contributors to this section explore race, identity, language, poetics, and politics through their own voices and through literary representations. These kinds of texts echo the recent movement known as Coolitude that focuses on the experiences of Asian indentured laborers and their descendants. Rather than a fixed geographic origin or singular ethnicity, they probe the fluidity of culture, language, identity, and belonging in postcolonial societies. The essays also suggest the possibilities of expanding the historical archive to film, poetry, and literature.

Like many artists, filmmaker Ann Kaneko grapples with the question of the role of her own ethnic background and history in her art. She recognizes her family's immigration story, incarceration experience, and connection to Japan as a central force in the questions she has come to ask about identity. However, she rejects the oversimplified label of her films as Japanese American in favor of a broader interpretation of engaging with issues that are common to Nikkei and non-Nikkei alike. Kaneko's work collectively explores how memory, trauma, displacement, and discrimination in repressive settings are expressed through art and transmitted to later generations.

Words and language, like identities, are constantly in flux. Nowhere is this phenomenon more apparent than with the global migrations of people. Scholar and poet Roshni Rustomji-Kerns examines the overlapping and intersecting encounters between the poetics of different cultures. She also translates the Gujarati haiku under discussion into English for the first time. However, rather than merely acknowledging the complexities of translation in a footnote, Rustomji-Kerns makes them central to her reflection on the poetry. In her commentary she invokes her own personal, familial, community, educational, and cultural background in India, Pakistan, Lebanon, Mexico, and the United States. Her translation remains open-ended: she invites readers from diverse cultural traditions to reflect on what they would associate with the images the poems evoke. Rustomji-Kerns also contemplates the universal role of language, food, and art from the homeland in nourishing the collective nostalgia of diasporic communities.

The cultural production by Asians in the Americas and their descendants is significant in bringing their experiences from the margins to the center of national narratives, in the process often dismantling stereotypes and entrenched cultural notions about Asians. For example, the Chinese shopkeeper appears as a fixture in mainstream literary works and the collective imagination. Writers of Chinese descent in Jamaica and Peru, however, resist this trope by evoking the oppressiveness of working behind the counter for the family businesses. Another stubborn stereotype is the presumed political passivity of Asians in the diaspora, who were used as strikebreakers and perceived to be insular and temporary sojourners rather than settlers with a stake in local communities. Yet, the historical record demonstrates Asian immigrants' political engagement with both the homeland and the adopted country. We know, for example, of Chinese coolies' participation in the nineteenth-century Cuban struggles for independence from Spain, Trinidadian-born Chinese Eugene Chen's role in the anti-imperialist and nationalist movement in early twentieth-century China, Indo-Caribbean involvement in Guyanese independence, and the role of youth of Chinese and Japanese descent in radical revolutionary movements in twentieth-century Cuba and Brazil.

The prolific scholar of Hispanic literature Ignacio López-Calvo analyzes the fiction produced by a contemporary Japanese Brazilian writer to bring to light the complexities and nuances of a collective identity characterized by multiple generations and relationships to a distant homeland. Where historical accounts fall short, literature can capture the passion and conflict underlying Japanese Brazilian involvement in political struggles, whether it be the discrimination they faced during World War II or the participation of Nikkei youth in revolutionary struggles against the Brazilian dictatorship during the 1970s. López-Calvo explores a core tension within the greater Japanese Brazilian community between the celebration of a distinct Japanese ethnicity and a claim to Brazilianness—a tension that extends to other Asian communities in the Americas.

The mundane, daily interactions among Asians and locals are often elided by official archives and national literary canons. The expressive approach represented here explores the central question of how people of Asian descent in the Americas relate to their communities, the homeland, and to supposedly inclusive concepts of national identity such as *mestizaje* and Creolization.

6

Musings on Identity and Transgenerational Experiences

ANN KANEKO

As a filmmaker, I often find that programmers and critics categorize either my films or me by my ethnicity. For a minute, I get a sinking feeling in the pit of my stomach . . . "Yes, I'm Japanese American but that's only one aspect of my identity." Perhaps I am overreacting since they are only seeking to define who I am, and they are trying to make sense of the work. Or perhaps it is my awareness of how these kinds of labels can help to cultivate an audience but can also limit the same. Consequently, because of my own contrarian personality, I have always tried to resist these categories that are thrust upon me and maintain my "unique" status, separate from any labels. I know that other artists and writers have also struggled to negotiate this delicate balance of embracing one's identity while rejecting these oversimplifications, and I acknowledge that I am still learning to cope with them.[1]

For all of my desire to resist these groupings, I realize that who I am as a Japanese American *sansei* and my own family's story *has* had a profound impact on the subjects I have selected and the stories that I have chosen to tell.[2] However, it is always from a slightly obtuse angle that I have tackled these stories which are tied to myself and my family—always trying to slightly complicate what the parameters of identity are.

Indeed, my own family background has motivated me to expand my understanding of the Japanese American experience, but not from probing the Nikkei community in the United States, but through focusing on immigrant and Nikkei communities abroad. Hence, I made *Overstay* and *Against the Grain: An Artist's Survival Guide to Perú*. And, finally, in *A Flicker in Eternity*, I turn the lens back on the Japanese American community here and look at the diary of Stanley Hayami, a *Nisei*-born teenager during World War II. Through this last film, I realize how experiences, especially memory and trauma, are passed down from one generation to the next. This last film has deeply resonated with many Nisei, making me realize how profoundly the communal experience of incarceration and displacement has shaped this community and how important the narrative of overcoming this injustice and suffering has also been.

Learning about Immigration through *Overstay*

I had never met three of my grandparents, and I was curious about their journey to the United States. My maternal grandfather died soon after World War II, and my maternal grandmother, whom I did know, lived next door and died when I was ten. My memories of her were as an *oba-chan*, or grandmother, who had an extraordinary collection of potted plants, an impeccable and immaculate house, and a very strict demeanor. My Japanese was never good enough at that age to ask her what her earliest experiences in San Diego were when she arrived in the United States so it is only through photographs and the retelling of this history by my mother that I have any sense of what my grandparents experienced.

My father's parents had returned to Japan before my father married so none of my siblings or myself grew up with any sense of who our paternal grandparents were. These were the days before it was so easy to jet across the ocean; and, in fact, my father never saw his father alive again during the almost twenty years that elapsed after they separated. It is only through later conversations I have had with my father's sister who lived in Japan with my grandparents that I have had a few glimpses of who they were. These holes in the narrative of my own family no doubt prompted me to make *Overstay*, which looks at the immigrant experience of foreign migrant workers in the 1990s and were part of the reverse migration to the country my grandparents departed. Through this film, I definitely got a taste of what it was like to be a new immigrant in a more insular country like Japan. Though the country was different and technology had transformed communication and travel, I found many parallels between my grandparents and these "newcomers" to Japan.[3]

In *Overstay*, I look at the experiences of six undocumented young people in Japan in the mid-1990s. They all came to Japan at the end of the economic bubble. The film reveals why they have come to Japan, the work they do, the discrimination and challenges that they face there, and their relationships with other foreigners as well as with Japanese. The characters come from a range of countries: Pakistan, Iran, the Philippines, and Perú. When I was making this film, I often compared the experiences of the subjects in my film with the stories that I had heard about my *Issei* grandparents. Over and over again, I was reminded of the similarities in their experiences and how the circumstances of being an immigrant shaped their mindset and values. I didn't know the exact details of the networks of friends and relatives that my grandfathers used to settle in the United States, but I knew it must have been through such contacts that they landed their first jobs and places to stay.

Yamaguchi Toshio, who employs Mujahid, one of the Pakistani young men in the film, explains: "First of all, Mujahid, his father first came here. Long ago in Japan, for example, I live here in Tokyo, and you come from the countryside for the first time, you know how your parents used to say, 'If you go to Tokyo, this person lives there so look him up.' That still seems to exist among them. That's why, when he came to Japan, he came here directly."[4] Similarly, through conversations with my own family I learned about the networks my grandparents utilized. Through my aunt, I found out that my paternal grandfather had emigrated with the help of a Christian organization. My mother revealed that her father had followed the footsteps of his half brother to Hawaii and then to the United States. Growing up, I only vaguely understood how my grandparents came to the United States, but now my experiences in Japan and these stories helped me to formulate a more concrete vision of how my grandfathers transitioned to life in America. In turn, my grandmothers came through marriage: my paternal grandmother was a *shashin hanayome* or a "picture bride" and my paternal grandfather went back to Japan to marry my grandmother after his first wife and child had died in a fatal car accident.[5] Both of my grandmothers came from the same region as my grandfathers so this also helped to fortify these ties with their own regional communities.

Maekawa Kazutoshi, Ashraf's employer, originally from Okinawa, can relate to his Pakistani employees' need to immigrate because many Okinawans immigrated to the Americas in the early twentieth century. Okinawans, who were colonized by the Japanese and who are ethnically distinct with their own culture and language, have long been discriminated against in Japan. Hence, Maekawa has an insider's understanding of the situation as someone who left Okinawa for "mainland" Japan a generation or two earlier and no doubt had to overcome prejudice and cultural differences. The poverty caused by Japanese colonization also encouraged many Okinawans to seek out new opportunities abroad, and Maekawa relates the Okinawan immigration experience to that of "newcomers" to Japan: "I think they are challenged by the situation. And I'm not sure I should say this, but it's money. That was the case among Japanese [immigrants]. I'm from Okinawa, and there were many second, third, and fourth sons who went to Brazil. Why? Because there wasn't enough work or money. So it's just a repetition of this."[6]

I found it interesting and perplexing that the Japanese government still valued bloodlines. Although they badly need to supplement their workforce due to a declining birthrate and a rapidly aging population, they have limited who can work in Japan based on blood ties and discriminate against those who cannot prove this lineage. Hikari, the Peruvian woman in my film, resided in Japan using a fake Nikkei identity. In 1990, the Japanese government created the 1990 Immigration Control and Refugee Recognition Act, which created a kind of Nikkei visa for those who could prove Japanese lineage, granting them long-term residency, which would allow them to do unskilled work. This was a kind of back door way for the government to allow for more immigration especially during these boom years; and in this way, many Nikkei Brazilians and Peruvians came to work in Japan. Hikari complains of the unfairness of the Japanese government to grant visas to only those who can trace bloodlines to Japan, based on a *jus sanguinis* notion of immigration policy, as opposed to the *jus soli* approach, which allows birthright citizenship. This kind of Nikkei visa exists in a society that values these blood connections and where birthright citizenship does not exist. This contrasts with Hikari's notion of citizenship because both Perú and the United States, as well as many other countries in the Americas, ascribe to birthright citizenship since these countries have sought out immigrants to settle their lands.

Through her, I am able to explore the complicated legalities of controlling immigration and excluding other people based on ethnic and racial identity. Not being Nikkei is a disadvantage because foreign workers without special skills have no path to legal status apart from marriage to a Japanese national or seeking political asylum status, which is extremely difficult to acquire in Japan. Even though I am Nikkei, I wanted to look at what it meant to not be Nikkei, and I pondered what these bloodlines meant to me. Konishi Makoto of the Mukogawa Union in Nishinomiya where Hikari resided attempts to explain the Japanese government's handling of Nikkei immigration. "On one hand, the government does not want foreign workers. On the other, corporations want cheap labor. So to get around this, they opened the doors to *Nikkeijin* [ethnic Japanese]. Why just Nikkei? I think it's strange, too, but it's because of their ties to Japan they have allowed them to enter. After that, Brazilians and Peruvians, in particular, have been coming to Japan."[7] Hikari voices her opinion about these practices and, of course, her displeasure with these laws since she falls outside of those who are legally allowed to work in Japan:

> With regard to the issue of the Nikkei and that the Japanese government only wants Nikkei to have visas as I said before, it's racist to me. Why not others? Why do you necessarily have to be Nikkei, a person with a Japanese name, when anyone can work the same? This encourages the mafia, selling registered family names and documents in my country and in others. I imagine it's the same in Bolivia, Columbia, and Brazil because I know people from these countries who've also bought their papers. It's

in the newspaper everyday—"Travel to Japan. Work in Japan." They sell everything—any document you need, even a passport with fake names.[8]

Konishi goes on to summarize the situation: "Nikkeijin are viewed as both foreigners and Japanese. Because of the blood relation, Japanese companies oddly feel more at ease. Still only Nikkei are allowed to enter. But everyone has the right to work, not just the Nikkei."[9]

Indeed, as I did research for the film and talked to many other Nikkei Peruvians and Brazilians, I learned how their grandparents had immigrated to South America and how they had come to grow up in these countries. Learning about Japanese immigration policies and how they impacted Nikkei and other non-Nikkei immigrants also taught me how similar American policies like the Immigration Act of 1924 had shaped the flow and settlement of Japanese to the United States in the early twentieth century. This landmark policy, also known as the Johnson-Reed Act, set limits for all immigration and specifically prohibited the immigration of Middle Easterners, East Asians, and Indians. This notoriously racist policy expanded the limits placed on the Chinese by the earlier Chinese Exclusion Act and targeted the Japanese, who were also perceived as part of the "yellow peril." As a result, Japanese immigration halted in 1924, which also impacted the very distinct generation formation in the Japanese American community. Indeed, these kinds of policies and the different approaches to immigration policy continue to mold the way immigrants decide where to settle, find residency, and possibly seek citizenship and is the reason that immigration policy continues to be the hot topic that it is today.

Unpacking Identity in Perú

If *Overstay* was a way for me to answer "what was it like," then *Against the Grain: An Artist's Survival Guide to Perú*, was a way for me to think about "what if?" Having learned from making *Overstay* that deciding on where to immigrate was guided by government immigration policy and by which country offered the most opportunity and possibilities of wealth, I realized the chances of ending up in South America were quite high if circumstances were even slightly different. If one of my grandparents had decided to immigrate after 1924, they would have been denied entry to the United States and been forced to seek another home. If they had relatives in South America, they might have chosen to go where they had support. Or, if they had been convinced that prospects were just as good in Perú or Brazil, for example, they might have opted for one of those countries instead. In fact, this does not seem far-fetched since I recently found out that I have some distant relatives on my mother's side that immigrated to Columbia.

In *Against the Grain: An Artist's Survival Guide to Perú*, I look at four artists who have made work that is politically oriented in response to the repressive government of Alberto Fujimori. This film explores a range of topics, including art, freedom of expression, repression, and corruption, but it also takes a complex look at identity and how it plays into the values and artwork of these artists. I like to think that each of them is a reflection of different facets of myself, too.

Of the four artists, Alfredo Márquez was active in the punk scene during the 1980s, imprisoned for four years as a suspected terrorist. Natalia Iguíñiz is a woman concerned with gender and class issues, and Claudio Jiménez Quispe is a folk artist who makes *retablos*, a kind of portable, wooden Catholic altars. He was displaced and forced to emigrate from his home in the mountains to the big city by the war with the Shining Path. The fourth character is Eduardo Tokeshi, a Japanese Peruvian, actually Okinawan Peruvian, from Lima. Similar to some Nisei and most Sansei, he does not speak Japanese and has trouble communicating with his parents. Through Eduardo, the film looks at the Peruvian Nikkei community and Fujimori's relationship to it. He talks about his reaction to the turmoil that resulted from the war with the Shining Path during the 1980s and 1990s and his personal challenges with language, expression, and choosing a profession that his immigrant parents could accept.

Eduardo's identity as a Japanese Peruvian is complicated by the election of President Fujimori, also known as "El Chino." This complex and ironic namesake is explained in the film. "*Chino*" means "Chinese" or "Chinaman" in Spanish, but in Latin America, this term refers to anyone who looks East Asian, which includes Chinese, Japanese, and even indigenous people whose eyes have a more pronounced epicanthic fold. It can be both somewhat derogatory as well as affectionate, and Fujimori chose to embrace it as a term of endearment, using it to show how he could relate to indigenous and working-class communities, as someone who was a regular guy and a person of color like them. But this nickname also backfired when Fujimori's politics were not favorably viewed, and *Chino* became the symbol of a Peruvian strongman.

In this film, Eduardo's story obviously has parallels to my own background, and like me, "he struggles with his identity as a son of Japanese immigrants."[10] Similar to my grandparents, his started out as entrepreneurs in Lima, owning a small *bodega*, or corner shop, in the central part of Lima. His parents, like my own, were skeptical about his pursuing a career in the arts, just as my parents continue to have their doubts about my film career. In Lima, Japanese are a kind of "model minority," who had been deemed successful due to their reputation for "honesty, hard work, and technology," indeed the campaign slogan of Fujimori. In the film, Eduardo struggles with his association with Fujimori and although he does not agree with El Chino's politics, he finds himself linked to this politician by virtue of his physical appearance, suffering the backlash of these ties.

As I filmed in Lima months after Fujimori had fled the country, I experience what I imagine Eduardo must have encountered repeatedly under Fujimori's administration. In one scene, I am filming in the Plaza of San Martín, which was known at that time in 2001 as a colorful forum for the working-class public to congregate and voice their political views. A gap-toothed man emerges from the crowd and declares to the camera: "I want to send a message to the Japanese." Although I deny that I am Japanese, he roundly disregards me and continues: "That's OK. Anyway, Fujimori has demonstrated what the Japanese really are—that they are miserable thieves. Opportunists and imperialists. We are going to kick out all of the Japanese from our country!"[11] It is clear that this man makes no distinction between Nikkei and Japanese nationals. But somehow he is sending a message to the Japanese in Japan through me, who he appoints as their emissary. However, I could not help but wonder about Japanese Peruvians who lived side-by-side with him, like poet Doris Morimisato, who accompanied me that day and was thoroughly shocked by his prejudicial views.

In the film, I cut to Eduardo who explains his conundrum of being Nikkei—because of physical features, he is identified with another country with whom he has few ties: "Someone tells you, 'Why don't you go back to your country?' I think this is key. Because you say, 'To where?' OK, then. I'll go to my country but where is it? Japan? I couldn't survive for half an hour in a place where I don't speak the language and where I don't have any ties."[12] Perhaps more significantly, Eduardo talks about how his cultural in-between-ness has influenced him in becoming a visual artist since it was one of the ways he felt he could communicate himself: "So you realize that you pass a third of your life, trying to understand what they [his parents] are saying. So this probably creates a hole, which you try to fill with a language, which is much more universal. For this reason, I think one looks for a language that is visual, universal, and doesn't need translation."[13] Hence, through Eduardo, I was able to gain an insight into what it meant to be Nikkei in a country like Perú, navigating language and culture. This had all become even more complicated when Fujimori ascended to power and impacted how all Nikkei Peruvians were viewed.

Although these parallels between Eduardo's and my own experiences are quite obvious, I often explain to my audiences that I believe that each of the main characters in the film represent a different aspect of who I am and my interests that go beyond my Japanese American identity. Of course, in choosing my characters, I was looking for a range of stories that would complement each other and help to tell the larger story of what it was like being an artist living in Perú under Fujimori. However, in retrospect, I also realize that my affinity to each of these individuals is through some aspect of how I also identify as an artist. Natalia, as a woman working in a patriarchal society like Perú's, must deal with gender inequities, restrictions on how women express their sexuality in a Catholic society, and pressures of balancing one's career and motherhood. Although Natalia's middle-class status in Perú affords her access to privileges such as in-home nannies and domestics that are not accessible to me in the United States where the cost of labor is much higher, her lifestyle does make me ponder the state of women in a place like Lima and compare notes as a woman who deals with similar challenges, balancing career and motherhood in the United States.

Alfredo, who was part of the punk scene and imprisoned as a suspected terrorist, appealed to my curiosity regarding what it was like to really be targeted for making work that made waves during these years of strict control under Fujimori. Although my own work has never been particularly controversial, I like to fantasize that my work might be so bold as to entice objection and believe that I would have the courage to stand up to authorities if I were questioned about my views as he had been.

Claudio makes retablos, and was displaced and forced to immigrate to the big city of Lima from Ayacucho, his home in the south, in order to flee from the violence of the Shining Path. This internal war had a devastating effect on the entire country and took its toll on individuals like Claudio. Although his experiences are very different from my own, I suspect there is something about his forced displacement due to the circumstances of war to which I can relate. Although not my own experience, my parents were forced to evacuate their homes due to Executive Order 9066 during World War II, which designated the West Coast as a military zone and rounded up all people of Japanese ancestry in those areas and forced them into camps. There is something about Claudio's demeanor that reminded me of my own family—perhaps the humility that they had cultivated because of the adversity they had experienced. This story has been ingrained in my own personal history and has probably impacted me on a much deeper level than I can acknowledge and, of course, is the basis for *A Flicker in Eternity*.

Reflecting on the Legacy of Incarceration

A Flicker in Eternity is based on the diary of Stanley Hayami, a Nisei teenager, who was an aspiring artist that was incarcerated in Heart Mountain and drafted into the 442nd Regimental Combat Team. Perhaps I had always avoided the internment camp story since so many films had already been made about the experience. However, this film was an opportunity to make something that was closer to my own family's story since my grandparents and my parents had also been incarcerated and their lives abruptly interrupted by World War II. The approach of the film was different since we were telling it from a first-person, teenager's perspective and the prospect of animating his drawings and cartoons to show who he was excited me. He is so much the ordinary teenager obsessed with grades; and, like Eduardo, he grapples with the same conflict that the children of many immigrants face when they want to pursue a creative livelihood. No doubt that the pressure to make a more practical career choice is influenced by his parents: "I've been thinking a lot about my life work lately. My heart tells me to be an Artist-Writer, but I lack confidence. Michelangelo and Leonardo. They were geniuses and I'm not. My mind tells me to be something practical like an architect. . . . I made up my mind. I'm going into the artist-writer field. And I'm going to be the best artist in the world. So the world better watch out. Hayami is going to the top!"[14]

As I have been contemplating how familial history shapes the choices that we make and the work we choose, the investigations of two colleagues, Asiroh Cham and Kristen Smiarowski, have especially prompted me to think about how experiences, memory, and trauma get transferred from one generation to another. I cannot help but think about these questions in the context of my own experiences dealing with the Japanese American community while showing *A Flicker in Eternity*.

Despite my own reservations about choosing such a predictable Japanese American topic, I made *Flicker*, believing that Stanley's first-person perspective was fresh and unique since it was the voice of a young person and not that of an elderly Nisei, recollecting experiences from seventy years ago. Of course, it's not surprising that the biggest supporters of this film have been my parents' generation. The Japanese American community, and especially Nisei, has been *overwhelming* in attending the film, buying it and monetarily supporting our fundraising efforts.

Yet I also find this ironic and curious given my own reticence to broach this topic. Intellectually, I understand why the Japanese American community has come out to support this film, but experiencing firsthand so much support for one of *my* films is new to me. Although I may like to think that the world has finally acknowledged my talents, I realize that it is probably the topic that brings together this amazingly loyal audience.

This experience has prompted me to think about how the legacy, memory, and trauma of an experience is transferred to succeeding generations. Asiroh Cham, a filmmaking colleague and mentee, has researched intergenerational trauma in the Cham American community.[15] The Cham are a minority indigenous group who originally resided in Vietnam, but were pushed out of both Vietnam and Cambodia due to conquest and conflict over the last several centuries. Especially during the Indo-Chinese conflict, over two million Cham fled

Vietnam, Cambodia, and Laos. Consequently, this community has suffered extraordinary injustice, and it has been important within the community to preserve the story of how they have overcome these hardships, struggled for recognition, and survived as a people. I do not pretend to compare the magnitude of these different experiences, weighing hardships against each other, but rather reflect on how these defining narratives are perpetuated.

Recently, I have been doing video documentation for choreographer Kristen Smiarowski of her dance and installation project entitled, "The Key Game Project: Sleep, Staring, Well." In this project, she explores the construction of cultural memory in the context of the Holocaust experience. Working with Smiarowski and her ongoing investigation of how memory is constructed in the Jewish American community, it has made me take pause and contemplate the parallels between the Jewish and Japanese American communities in how they have constructed cultural memory in response to these defining historical experiences.

Having made a number of other films, I do not feel like I risk being "typecast" by this one film, and I am finally willing to acknowledge how I have been deeply influenced by the Japanese American incarceration experience, which I have inherited from my parents. My partners on this project, Sharon Yamato and Joanne Oppenheim, seem even more attached to telling this story than I am. Sharon is a very young Nisei and was an internee as a small child. I suspect the silence in her own family about this episode has prompted her to be so adamant about telling this story.

As for Oppenheim, an older Jewish American, I cannot help but wonder if she was interested in this chapter in Japanese American history because of parallels to the experiences of injustices in her own heritage. In a grant proposal, she referenced *The Diary of Anne Frank*: "As I read Stan's diary, I was reminded of another wartime diary, written by a Jewish girl in Amsterdam, during the same time in history. Since the Holocaust and the incarceration are often studied together, the Hayami story offers teachers an opportunity to examine the similarities as well as the differences between the exclusion of these two ethnic groups."[16]

Although the effects of intergenerational memory and trauma may seem most evident in my exploration of the Japanese American experience of World War II incarceration, the impact of this experience is probably more dramatic because of the singularity and uniqueness of this event as it has affected this community. The legacy and effect of immigration is more commonplace in the spectrum of different ethnic groups throughout the history of the United States so the ability to draw out the significance of these experiences is more nebulous, although apparent in my mind.

Altogether these observations make me realize how deep our own family narratives impact the stories that interest us as artists and scholars. I cannot deny that my identity as a Japanese American has clearly had a huge role in steering me to choose these topics as ways to explore my own family and past. Understanding more of the historical and political context of how these experiences were formed has made me able to draw connections with other communities and events. These projects have also allowed me to expand my own understanding of what it means to be Nikkei, in a variety of countries and a range of historical junctures. It reaffirms that identity is very complex and mutable, depending on circumstances. Perhaps this essay will help others to ponder the relationship between their own personal stories with the larger investigations that they have chosen to pursue.

NOTES

1. Hamid Naficy's chapter "Situating Accented Cinema," in *An Accented Cinema: Exilic and Diasporic Filmmaking* (Princeton: Princeton University Press, 2001), 10–39, does an excellent job in setting up the challenges of "ethnic" filmmakers.
2. *Sansei* literally means "third generation" in Japanese. In the context of the Japanese American community, *Issei* refers to the first generation who immigrated to their adopted country and *Nisei*, to the second generation who were born there. This is different than some immigrant groups that count the first generation born in the new homeland as "first generation."
3. In the lexicon of Japanese immigration, "newcomers" refers to the new foreign immigrants who came to Japan in the late 1980s and 1990s as opposed to the "old comers" who are the *Zainichi* ("residing in Japan") Koreans who are now permanent residents in Japan. Zainichi Koreans were forced to migrate to Japan as laborers during the early twentieth century, when Korea was still a colony of Japan. Despite generations of living in Japan, the Zainichi still do not have citizenship although they have been born and raised in Japan.
4. Ann Kaneko, dir., *Overstay* (1998; Los Angeles: Ann Kaneko, 2005), DVD.
5. *Shashin hanayome* was a practice among early immigrants (chiefly Japanese and Korean) whereby suitors sought out brides using a matchmaker and photographs.
6. Kaneko, dir., *Overstay*.
7. Ibid.
8. Ibid.
9. Ibid.
10. Ann Kaneko, dir., *Against the Grain: An Artist's Survival Guide to Perú* (2008, Los Angeles: Ann Kaneko, 2008), DVD.
11. Ibid.
12. Ibid.
13. Ibid.
14. Ann Kaneko and Sharon Yamato, dir., *A Flicker in Eternity* (2013, Los Angeles: Ann Kaneko/Sharon Yamato, 2013), DVD.
15. See Asiroh Cham, "Negotiating (In)Visibility in the Cham American Diaspora" (M.A. thesis, University of California, Los Angeles, 2012).
16. Joanne Oppenheim, "Project Purpose" (California State Library: California Civil Liberties Public Education Program Grant, 2009/10), 3.

7

Intersecting Words

Haiku in Gujarati

ROSHNI RUSTOMJI-KERNS

Eduardo Galeano in his *Book of Embraces* tells us about a man who had worked in vineyards all his life. As he was dying he revealed what he had learned in his work: It isn't the grape that makes wine, it is the wine that makes the grape. Galeano wonders if we do not make the words, but it is the words "that tell who we are."[1] And words of course have their own geo-histories, their traditions, their specific births, and their specific lives and deaths.

It was November 1947 in Karachi, Pakistan. I listened as a *Bapaiji*, a paternal grandmother, taught her two young granddaughters their first lesson about words, *shabda*, and letters, *akshar*. Two sisters, one nine years old, the other about seven years, were fighting. They had been forbidden to hit, scratch, bite, pinch, or otherwise physically harm one another when they disagreed with one another. The sisters were therefore resorting to words. "*Junglee*!" said one. "Stooopid!" answered the other. "Idiot!" The retort was, "*Gaadi*!" The older sister tried longer words in English, "Lunatic! Absolutely mad." The younger sister didn't miss a beat, "*Gheli. Taddan gheli*!" she said in Gujarati. At this point their Bapaiji, fluent in Gujarati and English with memories of her father's Mandarin, intervened. "*Bas*! Stop!" she said. The sisters were allied in their remonstrations. "But we are not hitting one another. We are just using words." "Gujarati *and* English," said the older sister proudly. It would take her a few more years to absorb her mother's lessons about colonization/decolonization, Independence and Partition.

"Words are never 'just words.' They are who you are," said Bapaiji. "Every word you hear, you say and even every word you read or write becomes a part of you. It enters your brain and from there it travels all through your body. Words make you who you are."

"Thoughts are who you are. They come first. My teacher told us that." The older sister was sure of her school learning.

"No, it is feelings. You feel." The younger sister didn't trust teachers.

The grandmother tried to persuade the two children, "You think in words, you feel in words, you breathe words—in and out." She decided to take the opportunity offered by the discussion to lecture her two grandchildren on their less than satisfactory orthography. She tried to explain that the way they formed their letters, their akshar, in Gujarati and English was sloppy. According to her, "Sloppily written letters make sloppy words." I do not know if the two young girls understood their grandmother's explanation that although they knew akshar as a single letter of the alphabet they wrote or read, it could also be a syllable and a sound.

Whenever the children's Bapaiji spoke about "word," she used the Sanskrit-based noun shabda instead of the more commonly used word in Parsi Gujarati, *bol*. Her use of shabda was deliberate. Shabda, which is "meaning" as well as "sound," also carries the nuances of (linguistic) performance, of creation. Words express not only who we are but also where, when, and why we create and re-create ourselves through our different word-performances such as conversations, arguments, and of course, poetry.

Poetry, which is *kavya* in Sanskrit and *kavita* in many of the contemporary daughter languages of Sanskrit, can be crafted in verse or prose. It was again Bapaiji who reminded the children that *kavi*, a poet, is also a sage. It was many years later when I was thinking about the conversation between the grandmother and the two girls that I realized that the words, the nouns kavita/kavi, arise from the verb root word, *kuu*, "to make a sound." Sound, which according to one of the many South Asian creation narratives, created the universe. Sound translated into substance, into akshar, can become among other substances, a word, a shabda. Bapaiji would have understood what Eduardo Galeano was trying to express when he wrote that it is wine that makes the grape and words that make us.

Returning to Galeano and the man who worked in vineyards, there is always the question about the ability of wine to travel well. What about words, languages, and their specific geographies, histories, rules, and regulations of craftsmanship? Beyond the political debates about the "official" language of a nation-state and the smuggling of languages across invisible or visible borders guarded by laws and walls and fences and well-armed human beings, what happens when languages, words, and the traditions and rules of word performances from different geo-histories encounter, interact with one another in the longstanding geo-historical process we have decided to call "globalization"?[2]

Debbie Lee-DiStefano in her presentation at the Symposium on Asians in the Americas held at Pepperdine University in 2013 challenged students/scholars of Asians in the Americas to explore "the interaction between different cultural productions in the Americas." It is interesting and important that Lee-DiStefano used the word "interaction," not "influence" or "comparison." I would expand "interaction" to include "intersections" as well as "encounters" between different cultural productions in the Americas or anywhere else in the world.

The "interaction between different cultural productions" has of course had a long history and examples of these "productions" can be found across our planet. For example, the lyrical *ghazals* composed in English mainly in the United States by Agha Shahid Ali (1949–2001) have an extended geo-history from Asia to Europe to the Americas. Ghazals have traveled from the Arabic literary form, the *qasidas*, of West Asia to the tenth-century Farsi ghazals of Iran to the Urdu, Bengali, and other languages of South Asia, and to some of the languages of Europe and in the case of Agha Shahid Ali, the English of a Kashmiri American poet in the United States of America.

Briefly, ghazals consist of unrhymed couplets, each line consisting of twelve syllables. The couplets need not be united by a single theme. Ghazals, from the Arabic to mean "discourse" or "talking to a woman," speak and sing mainly of love. Erotic, secular love nearly always unrequited; secular love that very often gets translated into spiritual love. The poet is often metamorphosed—as in most of the ghazals of Agha Shahid Ali—into the persona of a rebel lover seeking justice.

In his statement in the anthology, *Living in America: Poetry and Fiction by South Asian Americans*, Agha Shahid Ali wrote:

> [I am] by virtue of being a subcontinental, the product of three major world civilizations/cultures—the Hindu, the Islamic, and the Western. This very rich situation, the result of various historical "accidents" is further textured by [my] status as an "exile" in the United States. From the point of view of [my] poetry, [I] consider my site a lucky, even a privileged one, for [I feel] that [I], like other writers in English from the subcontinent, [have] the "right" to redefine the language, "discover" it for the "first" time.[3]

Agha Shahid Ali's ghazals, often "sing" of the landscapes, the geo-political histories of home and exile of the peoples of the Americas, India, Pakistan, Kashmir, Palestine, Europe.

The following are some couplets from some of Agha Shahid Ali's ghazals:

> **In Jerusalem a dead phone's dialed by exiles.
> You learn your strange fate: You were exiled by exiles.

**By the Hudson lies Kashmir, brought from Palestine—
It shawls the piano, Bach beguiled by exiles.

**"Even things that are true can be proved." Even they?
Swear not by Art but, dear Oscar Wilde, by exiles.[4]

**And I, Shahid, only am escaped to tell thee—
God sobs in my arms. Call me Ishmael tonight.[5]

In these couplets, we have Herman Melville and Edward Said and Oscar Wilde and Asia, Europe, and the Americas.

There is an echo of Agha Shahid Ali's statement on composing in English when the Indo-United Statesian poet, essayist, and novelist Meena Alexander writes that "The new American poet thinks in many tongues, all of which flow into English she uses: a language that blossoms for her."[6]

Although the "the new American poet" discussed by Alexander may "think in many tongues" s/he does not always compose, write in English. For example, the language that blossoms for the Indo-American writer Panna Naik as she composes poetry and prose in the United States is her mother language, Gujarati. Naik has lived in Philadelphia since 1960 and her first poem, "Snapshot" (the English word title and the poem are written in Gujarati), was published in 1972. Her first collection of poems, *Pravesh*, was published in 1976. Naik is considered by her audience of Gujarati readers and literary critics to be one of the leading Gujarati poets writing today anywhere in the world. She is among the eleven poets discussed in a volume on Gujarati poets published in 2012 by Image Publications (India). The title of the volume is *Gulmahorthi Daffodils: From Gulmahorthi (flame tree flowers) to Daffodils.* The title is borrowed from a line in one of Panna Naik's poems in the volume. A series of volumes on Gujarati writers living and writing in the United States was released at the Gujarati Literary Convention in the United States in September 2012. The first volume in this series is on Naik and her work.

Panna Naik's 2011 collection of poems is titled *Attar-Akshar: Haiku in Gujarati*. The first part of the title is printed in Gujarati, the second part in English. Keeping in mind the above discussion on akshar and shabda, I would title the collection in English as *Perfumed Letters: Haiku/Kavita*. The nuances and different meanings of "letters" in English give the title an appropriate feeling of ambiguity. Especially since the poetic theories and the craft of kavya and kavita honor and appreciate ambiguity in poetry written in verse or prose.

When Panna Naik informed me that she had published a collection of haiku in Gujarati, I remembered reading a paper by Juan Ishikawa regarding haiku written in Latin America by people of Japanese descent. In his paper,

Ishikawa discussed the imagery and symbols derived from the world of nature in Latin America that inform the haiku written in Latin America.[7]

Naik uses imagery and symbols from the world of nature she remembers from India as well as those she has encountered in the United States. What is interesting is how perfectly Naik's word-images of nature from the United States work within the intellectual and emotional word associations in the traditions of Gujarati/Sanskrit poetry. For a reader who is familiar with both Sanskrit and English poetics, Naik's Gujarati haiku with their interaction between Gujarati words and the essence of Japanese word performance, the haiku, presents numerous thought-provoking, fascinating encounters, interactions between multiple cultural perspectives and their literary traditions.

The following is from an introduction that Naik wrote for the Symposium on Asians in the Americas held at Southeast Missouri State University in 2012:

> Let me give you a little background about my upbringing and how I became a poet. I am not the first literary figure in my family. My grandfather wrote a novel back in 1888. My father with his type-setting and press accessories business had a keen interest in literature and knew many major writers of the Gandhi era. I also received a deep appreciation of Sanskrit and Gujarati religious and secular poetry from my mother who would recite these to me as a child.
>
> My undergraduate and graduate degrees are in Gujarati and Sanskrit literature, studying the former with an eminent scholar poet Dr. Jhaveri. In those days, I very much wanted to write, to be a poet, but I did not. I could not.
>
> I came to America after getting married. This new country and new life had plenty to offer—a whole new world. I acquired two more master's from Drexel University and the University of Pennsylvania. It helped me retain my Indianness and imbibe what the West had to offer. While my life in the United States seemed to be full of activity, my life within was terribly lonely. That's when I met and heard Anne Sexton, the famous poet from Boston. She wrote without any inhibitions. The sincerity and transparency in her poems did magic to my inner world. I thought I also have lot to say and why not try writing? She inspired me to write about myself and give a voice to women around me.
>
> Before I started writing poetry, there were poems about women in Gujarati but all of them were written by men. I wanted to write from a woman's point of view and about women's sensitivity and sensibilities. Coming from an Indian background, there were some topics that were sort of taboo. People never talked about sex or menstruation or childlessness or man-woman relationships which had gone sour. I knew a lot of

women and wanted to give voice to those women, not just to me. In that sense I am a feminist.

People want to know what else I write about. I write about how I view India sitting ten thousand miles away. I write about America because I am an insider and I am also an outsider. I write about the abundant nature of this country. Some of these experiences one can never have sitting in India, especially falling snow or daffodils blooming and cherry blossoms. I have also written a lot of poems about my mother after she passed away.

America has given me freedom and flexibility to write whatever I want to write. I have published nine volumes of poetry and one collection of short stories, all in Gujarati. I write in Gujarati—the choice is consciously mine—a language which is neither read nor spoken in the society in which I live. My readers, however few, are not around me. They are thousands of miles away. I do get some feedback from them through reviews, letters, and e-mail. I do not get any linguistic sustenance which a writer, especially a poet, needs from the people around her. My vocabulary is not continually replenished. I have to survive on what I gathered some decades ago when I left India.

There is a double jeopardy here in the United States for me. If I am no longer completely in tune with contemporary Indian society, I am not entirely at home in American society either. I do not have the instinctive understanding of the society in which I live. Nor does the society have a cultural context of what I write. There is a cultural gap here which is hard to fill. It is this gap which tells that I could never be a part of American mainstream.

My latest collection (of poetry) consists of one hundred and twenty six haiku. A lot of poets have tried their hand at haiku but only a few have published them in Gujarati. As we know, it is a Japanese form with seventeen syllables. In Gujarati we have seventeen letters—five, seven, five. It looks very easy but is a very slippery and deceptive form. I was fully aware that it certainly is not a play of seventeen letters. One has to show, not tell, the depth of poetic expression. I like haiku for its brevity and picturesque quality using an image or a metaphor.

As Panna Naik and I worked on English translations of some of her haiku-kavita, I realized that the question was not of keeping strictly to the usually discussed seventeen-syllable form but the question for me was "why has Panna composed these haiku-kavitas?" I asked Panna, "Why and how does haiku speak to you as a poet, as a reader of poetry and as a scholar of literature?"

Panna Naik's response reminded me, once again, of how seldom we bring into our discussions of literary interactions, influences, encounters, the important and basic discussions about the specific literary theories, traditions, belief systems regarding art as it reflects, informs, and relates to specific cultures.

Naik's response centered around the emphasis in haiku on evoking, suggesting feelings, as well as thoughts through traditionally recognized word-imagery. She had recognized this aspect of haiku as reflected in a word that is central to South Asian art—*rasa*. The best translation of *rasa* could be the "essence" of an emotion, a feeling that is given life through word-imagery, word associations, and the nuances that words carry for which we could use the word *dhvani*. Dhvani as the reverberations, the nuances, the ripples of sound, of words. The sound of a drumbeat and the image of a pebble cast in a pool of water are often used to explain dhvani. Rasa/dhvani is what Panna Naik encountered in the haiku she read translated from Japanese into English and also in the works describing/discussing the craft of traditional—as well as not so traditional—haiku.

To paraphrase Roberto Bolaño in an interview titled, "Literature Is Not Made from Words Alone," Panna Naik and I "inhabit" the same mother language, Gujarati, while we continue to live with and within English.[8] The English translations used in this presentation are based on drafts of translations done by the poet herself, by the Indo-American poet Saleem Peeradina and by me. The brief comments at the end of each verse are based on my background—personal, family, community, cultural, as well as on my formal education in different literatures and languages. Panna Naik is familiar with my translations and comments.

1. તડકો સૂતો
ડાળી પર, ફૂલનું
ઓશીકું કરી[9]

[Transliteration]
Tadako suuto
Daali par, phoolnun
Oshikun kari

[Translation]
Making flowers its pillow
Sunshine sleeps
On the branch

[Is love the rasa, the feeling, the sentiment in this haiku? A pillow of flowers raises the South Asian image of Kama, the young god of love with his flowery arrows. Are sunshine and the plant lovers?]

2.તડકો કૂદે
ઘાસઘાસમાં, જાણે
પીળું સસલું[10]

[Transliteration]
Tadako kuude
Ghaasghaasman, jaane
Pilun sasalun

[Translation]
On the tall, tall grass
Sunshine jumps—
A yellow rabbit

[In the Indian fable, it is the rabbit not the chicken that is terrified by the smallest thing. It is *bikkun saslun*, timid rabbit, not Chicken Little. And it is a rabbit in the moon not a man with a lantern. Yellow is a color associated in most of the West with lack of courage or with brightness and sunshine. In South Asia it is often associated with the sacred and secular qualities of turmeric. Is the sunshine-rabbit/rabbit-sunshine supposed to be brave and steadfast or is the sunshine turned to an image of a rabbit jumping because it is timid and fearful?]

3.પીઠી ચોળાવી
બેઠાં છે ડેફોડિલ્સ
ઘાસમંડપે[11]

[Transliteration]
Pithi cholaavi
Bethan chhe deffodils
Ghaasmandape

[Translation]
Turmeric-anointed
Daffodils sit
Under a grass canopy

[Not a cloud of daffodils but turmeric-anointed sages? brides? bridegrooms? sit under an official canopy. Echoes of Japanese haiku and the memory of William Wordsworth are encountered in this South Asian American haiku.]

4.અંધારસ્ટેજે
પવન પખવાજે
સ્નોફ્લેક્સ નૃત્યો[12]

[Transliteration]
Andhaarsteje

Pavan pakhavaje
Snowflakes nartyo

[Translation]
On a dark stage
Snowflakes dance to
the wind's drumbeat

[I see the ash-smeared, whitened figure of Shiva dancing to his drumbeat in one of his abodes, a dark place in the high mountains where snow falls! I wonder what Panna sees. I also wonder what feelings, thoughts, other readers recognize in this haiku.]

5.ડુંગરા ડૂબ્યા
ધોધમાર ધુમ્મસ
વરસાદમાં[13]

[Transliteration]
Dungara duubya
Dhodhmar dhummas
Varasaadman

[Translation]
The hills, flooded
In a downpour of
Torrential fog

[For me, born in South Asia and now living in Northern California, this haiku invokes memories of the monsoons of my motherland and then the reality of fog in the San Francisco Bay Area. The image of monsoons in South Asian poetry is associated with the union of lovers or the separation of lovers or the time when monks do not go out to beg or preach in the world. Wet fog? South Asian word associations from nature encountering reality in the Americas as in the fog-bound city of San Francisco, California.]

6.ચંદ્રપપિપાસુ
દરિયો હાંફે, મોઢે
વળતાં ફીણ[14]

[Transliteration]
Chandrapipasu
Dariyo haanphe, modhe
Valatan feen

[Translation]
Thirsty for the moon

The ocean pants
White foam at its mouth

[The essence and the nuances of foaming at the mouth in the English could be anger, madness. It is different in the Indian tradition. The white foam on top of the waves is an image for either a woman's lovely smile or a king's fame.]

These then are some of the haiku from *Attar-Akshar: Haiku in Gujarati* and my readings of them. What would other readers associate with these images? What cultural traditions would they bring? How would the encounters, the interactions, and intersections between the creation of Gujarati haiku in the United States and the different readings of them play out not only in the Americas but also in South Asia and Japan?

In the classical and still very much alive literary traditions of South Asia that Panna Naik and many other South Asian writers and readers share and carry with them to the Americas and other parts of the world, the creation of art as well as the receiving, the appreciation of art is often explicitly equated with, described as the cooking of as well as the enjoyment of excellently, perfectly prepared food. And it is within this framework of art as sustaining and nourishing us wherever we are and whoever and whatever we encounter, interact with, that I conclude with the following poem.

The poem is a meditation by the poet Panna Naik on the yearning for one's "original" home through the image of a Japanese maple tree. The poem was composed in Philadelphia in Gujarati. The physical presence, substantial image of a tree from Japan, growing in the United States being described by a United Statesian poet from India, offers a response to Lee-DiStefano's challenge regarding exploring "the interactions between different cultural productions in the Americas."

The poem is from Panna Naik's collection *Gulmahorthi Daffodils.*[15]

જાપાનીઝ મેપલ છોડ અને હું

ધરતીમાં
ઊંડાં ફેલાયેલાં
મૂળિયાંવાળો
ઘરઆંગણે વાવેલો
જાપાનીઝ મેપલ છોડ
વધીને
વૃક્ષ થવા માંડયો છે.
હવે એ
દર ઉનાળે
રતુંબડાં પાંદડાં ફરકાવતો
લળી લળીને
પવન સાથે વાતો કરતો

ખડખડ હસશે.
એને
ક્યારેક
જાપાન યાદ આવશે ખરું?
મને મુંબઈ યાદ આવે છે.

[Transliteration]
DHARATIMAN
Uundaan felaayela
Muliyavaalo
Gharaangne vaavelo
Japanese maple chhod
Vadhine
Vruksha thava maandyo chhe.
Have e
dar unaale
ratumbdan paandadaan farakaavato
lali laline
pavan saathe vaato karato
khadkhad hasashe.
ene
kyarek
Japan yaad aavashe kharun?
Mane Mumbai yaad aave chhe.

[Translation]
JAPANESE MAPLE TREE AND ME
The Japanese maple
Is growing into a tree
Its spreading roots reaching deep into the soil.
Now
Every summer
Its ochre leaves will bend
Talk, laugh with the wind.
Will it sometimes
Remember Japan?
I remember Mumbai.

NOTES

1. Eduardo Galeano, *The Book of Embraces*, trans. Cedric Belfrage (New York: W. W. Norton, 1991), 18.

2. Karen Yamashita explores this question through her narrative-essay in the Foreword to *Encounters: People of Asian Descent in the Americas*, edited by Roshni Rustomji-Kerns with Rajini Srikanth and Leny Mendoza Strobel (Boulder, Colo.: Rowman and Littlefield, 1999), xi–xiii.
3. Roshni Rustomji-Kerns, ed., *Living in America: Poetry and Fiction by South Asian American Writers* (Boulder, CO: Westview Press, 1995), 33.
4. Agha Shahid Ali, *The Veiled Suite: The Collected Poems* (New York: W. W. Norton, 2009), 297.
5. Ibid., 193.
6. Meena Alexander, *Poetics of Dislocation* (Ann Arbor: University of Michigan Press, 2009), 3.
7. Juan Ryusuke Ishikawa, "The Brazilian Saijiki: Beyond Agricultural Practices" (Paper presented at the Annual Conference of the Association of Asian American Studies. Austin, Texas, April 2010).
8. Robert Bolaño, *The Last Interview and Other Conversations*, trans. Sybil Perez (Brooklyn, N.Y.: Melville House Publishing, 2009), 49.
9. Panna Naik, *Attar-Akshar: Haikus in Gujarati* (Mumbai: Image Publishing Pvt. Ltd., 2011), 132.
10. Ibid., 119.
11. Ibid., 93.
12. Ibid., 150.
13. Ibid., 164.
14. Ibid., 179.
15. Panna Naik, *Japanese Maple Gulmahorthi Daffodils* (Bombay: Image Publications, 2012), 58.

8

Cultural Celebration, Historical Memory, and Claim to Place in Júlio Miyazawa's *Yawara! A Travessia Nihondin-Brasil* and *Uma Rosa para Yumi*

IGNACIO LÓPEZ-CALVO

> I am aware that in the 1930s, before the War, we were Japanese born in Peru. I believe I'm lucky to belong to the generation of Japanese born in Peru, and then to have become part of that, of Peruvians children of Japanese.
>
> –Japanese Peruvian José Yoshida Yoshida (1935–)[1]

In 2006, the *Nisei* (second-generation) author Júlio Miyazawa (1948–) published, thanks to the economic support of some *dekasegi* (Japanese Brazilian temporary workers in Japan) friends, his first novel, *Yawara! A Travessia Nihondin-Brasil* (Yawara! Crossing Nihondin-Brazil). His declared intention was to pay homage to the centenary of the inception of Japanese immigration to Brazil, which would be commemorated two years later.[2] However, most of the novel, which won, along with two other works, the 2009 Prêmio Literário Nikkei (Nikkei Literary Award), was written between 1978 and 1980. The history of the Nikkei community in Brazil explored in *Yawara!* and in his second novel, *Uma Rosa para Yumi* (A Rose for Yumi, 2013), is precisely the metaphorical "Travessia" mentioned in the subtitle of his first novel. This "crossing" refers to the change of mentality and self-identification, within the Japanese Brazilian community. It also echoes different stages (not always chronological) through which this community has gone: 1) from an initial, pre–World War II period when characters still see themselves as loyal subjects of the Japanese empire and identify either as Japanese immigrants or as Japanese born in Brazil; 2) through a period of identitarian uncertainty for some characters that transverses both the pre- and postwar periods; 3) to the postwar period, in which some characters progressively shift their national affiliation and become patriotic and proud Brazilians.

I consider Miyazawa's *Yawara!* one of the most sophisticated Portuguese-language fictional explorations of identitarian conflicts within the Japanese Brazilian community, which also happen to be a central issue in Nikkei discourse. As the anthropologist Takeyuki Tsuda explains,

> Identity refers to a conscious awareness of who one is in the world based on association with certain sociocultural characteristics or membership in social groups. The individual's identity consists of two components: the self and the social identity. The self (or self-identity) is the aspect of identity that is experienced and developed *internally* through the individual's own subjective perceptions and experience of the social environment. However, an identity is also *externally* defined by others in accordance with standardized cultural norms and social roles, which can be called the individual's social identity.[3]

Yawara! re-creates this traumatic identitarian *tour de force* between Japanese and Nikkei characters' internal self-perceptions and external social influences, coming from both majority Brazilian population and the Nikkei community. I argue that the author's choice of topic—in particular, the passages dealing with Mário Japa's multiple identities—is related to his intention to validate and vindicate symbolically the hard-fought Brazilianness of the Nikkei community. Ultimately, the author presents this psychological journey as a celebration of his ethnic heritage and, more importantly, of his community's contributions to the betterment of Brazil.

In my view, Júlio Miyazawa's *Yawara! A Travessia Nihondin-Brasil* and *Uma Rosa para Yumi* are emblematic works in the Portuguese-language Nikkei literary and cultural corpus, as they explore, mostly from the perspective of Japanese Brazilian self-definition and self-representation, why so many Japanese immigrants decided to emigrate and eventually settle in such a faraway country that, at the time, was deeply committed to a process of whitening the population. Both works draw the sociocultural progress of the Japanese immigrants and their descendants throughout the decades, transforming their public image from a perceived inexpensive and docile labor to a so-called "model minority" and even a key part of Brazilian national identity. Like other works in the collective discourse of the Nikkei community—composed of all genres of literature, film, and documentaries, Miyazawa's writing attempts to celebrate cultural difference, all the while defending the Nikkei community's right to belong within the Brazilian imaginary and national projects and negotiating a common

Brazilian identity. This cultural production, therefore, is reflective of Nikkei public strategies to negotiate their own authentic Brazilianness throughout the decades, which are concomitantly indicative of this community's awareness of perceived notions of the Brazilian national essence, regardless of its mythical or constructed origins. In the process, as will be seen, Nikkei discourse resorts to ethnic assumptions that are equally mythical in nature: in some cases, in the community's goal to narrate conflict and trauma, historical amnesia (trying to erase the dark chapters of anti-Japanese hysteria in Brazil, for example, or considering the Shindo Renmei [meaning League of the Subjects' Path, a terrorist organization founded by Japanese immigrants who injured and killed other Japanese immigrants who accepted that Japan had lost the war] episode a taboo) has been as useful as historical memory. After all, as Homi Bhabha reminds us, "Being obliged to forget becomes the basis for remembering the nation, peopling it anew, imagining the possibility of other contending and liberating forms of cultural identification."[4] In the same way as negative ethnic stereotypes dealing with the "yellow peril" myth were a considerable obstacle to the integration of the Nikkei community, at times positive stereotypes dealing with the perceived fixed nature of racial typology have been embraced in a sort of strategic essentialism that may empower the community. This stance is certainly noticeable in Miyazawa's works.

Both novels explore how Brazil changed Japanese immigrants and their descendants, from an initial collective feeling of "unhomeliness," that is, of being geographically and culturally displaced in a strange and hostile land, or being caught in an undefined cultural identity between the ancestral culture of one's parents and the local culture, or sometimes identifying fully with their native Brazilian culture.[5] This identitarian diversity, however, should not be read as an assimilationist discourse, since the vindication of cultural difference is one of its leitmotifs and different Nikkei characters in these works identify Japanese, Japanese Brazilian, or Brazilian. At the same time, Miyazawa echoes how Japanese immigration (along with the immigration of other disenfranchised ethnic groups that could not easily be considered either black or white) ultimately changed Brazil and challenged elite articulations of Brazilian national identity. In many respects, through this strategic cultural discourse, the Nikkei community presents itself as an economically beneficial component of the Brazilian national body, as a path to modernity, and as a model to imitate by the rest of Brazil. As Jeffrey Lesser argues, proof of the success of their strategies and negotiations is that "by the mid-twentieth century, elite paradigms about who was and was not an acceptable Brazilian changed so markedly that many Europeans were no longer in the 'white' category while some Asians and Middle Easterners were."[6]

Indeed, the fictional Japanese immigrants' strategies for survival and community formation, their progressive integration into mainstream society, and their claim to place all form part of a collective narrative that affects much of Japanese Brazilian cultural production. Readers can often find the tension created between Nikkei writers and filmmakers' celebration of cultural difference and the concomitant claim to Brazilianness and national belonging. However, I argue that they are intimately related: the open celebration of the Nikkei community's achievements in different fields—and particularly of the involvement of its leftist youth in national politics during the 1970s—in *Yawara!* and *Uma Rosa para Yumi* responds to a will to power, and more specifically, to the author's vindication of the true Brazilianness of his ethnic group.

Between Dichotomies: Cultural Isolation/ Adaptation and Oppression/ Resistance

Since *Yawara!* is not a widely read novel, I will provide, in the next few pages, a summary of its plot, concentrating on the key issues of cultural isolation and adaptation as well as oppression and resistance. Miyazawa's exploration of the "crossing" in the subtitle of the novel begins with the inception of the immigration process, focusing, from a sentimental—at times bordering on the melodramatic—perspective, on the reasons for emigration, the immigrants' nostalgia for Japan, and the identitarian uncertainties they tried to overcome. *Yawara!* addresses the different steps of the immigration process, including the "pull" and "push" factors. It echoes, for instance, how the Japanese government and the emperor encouraged emigration as a way to alleviate the social tensions produced by an acute economic crisis and how, out of patriotism, many Japanese peasants obeyed the emperor's wishes; others naïvely believed the official declaration assuring prospective emigrants that it would not take long for them to become wealthy in Brazil before returning to Japan triumphantly in a few years. Yet, as the novel reflects, the first wave of immigrants soon realized that living and working conditions in the adoptive country would be much harsher than advertised. Increasingly feeling deceived, their disappointment was further fueled by the racism they had to withstand, particularly during World War II (Brazil joined the Allied forces in August of 1942).

The structure of *Yawara!* intertwines three different stories that are linked by kinship and friendship. The novel re-creates the lives of three Japanese immigrant families who arrived in Brazil in 1936 with the help of the Associação Nipônica no Brasil (Japanese Association of Brazil). In December of 1945, after the end of World War II, they founded a small village in the region of Atibaia, in the state of São Paulo. Although these characters are fictional, the author claims to have found inspiration in people he met in the region of Jabaquara; the action, however, takes place in real Brazilian locations and includes historical facts. The characters from the original community of Atibaia and their descendants—a synecdoche of the Nikkei community in Brazil—choose very different paths, ranging from cultural isolation within the Japanese immigrant community to full cultural integration into mainstream Brazilian society. For instance, Kenhiti and his wife Akemi, one of the three original Japanese families who arrived in 1936, never manage to adapt to the host country. In fact, Kenhiti, a humble peasant from Hiroshima's countryside and a judo expert, worries more about the preservation of Japanese culture than about learning the customs of Brazilian society. Making things even harder, he is unjustly imprisoned for two years after defending his nephew Goro from the physical attack of the Brazilian landowner's son. After being freed, the psychological trauma has been so severe that Kenhiti ends up committing suicide, along with his wife, Akemi:

> The brightness of the sun bothered the eyes of Kenhiti, who, in his feverish imagination, believed he was contemplating Japanese land. For this reason, he looked at it scared and full of happiness, and screamed:
>
> "*Fuji-San*! Mount Fuji . . . *Fuji-San*! Beloved fatherland!"
>
> . . . Screaming and running through a seemingly shorter path yet leading directly to the cliff, Kenhiti extended his hand to Akemi, who grabbed it. That way, united by the same idea, both jumped to eternity![7]

The delusional vision of the iconic Mount Fuji—one of the main symbols of the Japanese nation—in the Brazilian countryside suggests their inability to grasp the new reality in a strange culture and a foreign land. After spending a year depressed because they cannot have children, Akemi finally gets pregnant but the baby eventually dies. Then, Kenhiti finds out that his relatives died when the atomic bomb was dropped on Hiroshima. The novel implies that Kenhiti's failure to adapt to the new culture, customs, and language, added to the death of his relatives, contributed to his eventual demise.

The feeling of *saudade* (roughly meaning "longing, nostalgia, homesickness") is omnipresent in this novel as well as in much of Japanese Brazilian literature and film. At the onset of the narrative, the *Issei* (first-generation) Koiti Furukawa, head of another of the first three Japanese families that arrived aboard the *Argentina Maru* in 1936, is described nostalgically singing sad Okinawan songs, waiting for letters from his relatives in Japan, and writing a book he plans to publish in Japan. Yet, in contrast with his friend Kenhiti, who is always longing to return to Japan, Koiti's early ability to integrate himself into the new environment saves him from a similar outcome. Koiti easily meets and befriends Brazilian people during his trips to baseball championships and even participates in Carnival parades, seemingly the ultimate proof of his integration into Brazilian culture. At one point, thanks to his diplomatic and emotional management skills, Koiti manages to postpone Kenhiti's arrest by reminding a Brazilian politician who had earlier sought Japanese votes that he once thanked him with a flower bouquet for his wife. Another Issei character that makes a successful attempt at adapting to Brazilian society and culture is Goro, the older son of Toshiro and Noriko (the third Japanese couple of the small group of Issei that founded the small village in Atibaia). His extroverted personality and natural ability to speak Portuguese allow him to befriend his Brazilian neighbors and classmates. Goro finds motivation to learn the language quickly in his infatuation with his Brazilian teacher, Antônia, as well as in his determination to avoid his classmates' mockery. *Yawara!* also reflects how immigrant children had an easier path to cultural adaptation and how later, Nisei and *Sansei* (including mestizos) born after 1940 did not speak Japanese or observe Japanese customs, which created a significant cultural gap with their elders. Another source of discrepancies, as seen in the novel, is the opposition of Japanese parents to mixed marriages.

Yawara! provides numerous examples of the oppression that the Japanese had to withstand, particularly during World War II. For instance, Goro and his younger brother Kootaro have to interrupt their studies as a result of the increased discrimination against the Japanese community during this period; later, Kootaro is beaten by local boys for calling his horse Burajiru ("Brazil" pronounced with a Japanese accent). The novel reminds us that during the ensuing years, Japanese immigrants would be considered internal enemies: their actions were seen with suspicion, they were forbidden to speak Japanese in public, and Japanese social gatherings were strictly forbidden. More importantly, the omniscient narrator explains that Japanese immigrants were concerned with "the continued incarceration of members of the Japanese community—in many cases, without formal accusations, without right to legal defense, and without knowing the time of confinement."[8]

Along with these scenes of oppression, *Yawara!* re-creates Japanese resistance during World War II. Thus, when the local oligarch orders Koiti's arrest for purchasing a hunting rifle, Sensei (teacher), a cultured pioneer who helps new arrivals, uses his influence to prevent his imprisonment. Likewise, as a reaction to the oligarch's appropriation of Japanese-owned land and to the constant harassment carried out by his son, the community decides to move to the state of Paraná, where they will eventually find success growing and commercializing cotton. Miyazawa also presents solidarity as another form of resistance when the Japanese community offers emotional support and leaves money for the imprisoned Kenhiti, whose act of self-defense (he broke the landowner's son's arm using his judo skills) also suggests that the Japanese community in Brazil did not withstand oppression passively. Curiously, although the title, *Yawara!*, makes reference to a 1964 song about struggling and hope, sung by the cultural icon Misora Hibari, it can also refer to judo or jujutsu. In fact, the book cover includes the kanji for "Yawara," 柔, which is also a Japanese weapon used in various martial arts. The narrator also mentions that, for some time, the Japanese gained a reputation for being unable to adapt to work in coffee plantations, which reflects their refusal to comply with the landowners' exploitative schemes.

In spite of all these cases of discrimination and oppression, *Yawara!* does not fall into manichaean conclusions. In fact, it includes scenes of interethnic solidarity, as several Afro-Brazilian characters help the Japanese or Nikkei. Thus, an Afro-Brazilian neighbor named Zefa (Josefa) feeds Akemi (Kenhiti's wife) when she is weak, breastfeeds her baby upon noticing his malnourishment, and invites the Japanese couple for dinner at her house on Christmas Eve. Years later, in 1975, another Afro-Brazilian, Alberto, helps Mariano Goro Harikawa (Akemi and Kenhiti's offspring) overcome his psychological imbalance and later weeps upon hearing Mariano's sad life story. They eventually become close friends: "I would only allow Alberto to call me 'Japa' when no one was around. He, a black guy of all people, would come up with such cheap racism."[9] These alliances between Japanese immigrants and Afro-Brazilians, two marginalized groups at the time, are not uncommon in Japanese Brazilian literature. In some cases, these Afro-Brazilian characters come close to Hollywood cinema's stock character of the selfless "magical negro," a black person with a special insight or power who suddenly comes to the aid of the white protagonist, even at the risk of sacrificing his or her life.

Some white characters also help the Japanese immigrants. For instance, Tonho, the old warden, teaches Portuguese to Kenhiti and even sets him free for one day on the Christmas Eve of 1946. But the Japanese community's most faithful ally during the early years is the schoolteacher Antônia, who protests: "The war is not the colonists' fault and they have done nothing to deserve hate."[10] Later, her marriage to Goro becomes a national allegory for peaceful miscegenation and transculturation between the local population and Japanese immigrants. Their marriage symbolizes the birth of a new Brazil, where the Japanese immigrant community has finally found a home. Antônia has overcome her father's anti-Japanese prejudice to embody her generation's greater tolerance toward these immigrants and their descendants. Antônia and Goro's relationship is, on the other hand, a window to a different reality: anti-Brazilian and anti-black racism among Japanese immigrants. Thus, Goro prudishly tells Antônia, "My mother said that a wedding between a Japanese man and a Brazilian woman is not right."[11] Likewise, when Zefa takes Akemi's undernourished baby and breastfeeds her, the Japanese immigrant is first in shock and then, despite being grateful, hides it from her husband Kenhiti: "She feared being despised by her husband, even more if he knew that Goro was being breastfed by a black woman."[12]

Through a prolepsis that takes us to the São Paulo of the 1970s, Part II of *Yawara!* reads almost like a different novel. It focuses on the descendants of Japanese immigrants and, particularly, on Kenhiti and Akemi's son, the Nisei Mariano Goro, who, suffering from dissociative identity disorder, ends up becoming a notorious member of an armed group that is fighting against the dictatorship. The sociocultural and psychological dilemmas caused by both Mariano Goro's own identitarian confusion and mainstream society's discrimination have dire consequences for him. With the help of a psychiatrist, he realizes at one point that he suffers from dissociative identity disorder and that he is actually the political fugitive known as Mário Japa. This mental disorder has led him to adopt two distinct identities or personalities that, at different times, take control over his behavior. At least once a month, Mariano Goro/Mário Japa suffers from attacks during which he speaks to an alter ego in his mind, calling him Caro Mano (Dear Brother). Then, he tries to relieve his anxiety by running until he feels exhausted. In one of these "dialogues," Mariano Goro admits to his alter ego that learning about the existence of Nisei revolutionaries made him question his own role in society. He also confesses that the first time he saw a "Wanted" sign with his own photograph on it, he pretended not to see it, just like other members of his community, who felt embarrassed by the participation of Nissei in the armed struggle. Therefore, through a sort of double vision, he is able to see himself through the eyes of more conservative members of his ethnic community. Mariano's first reaction was to think: "Damn! Even the Japanese are robbing banks!"[13] This use of the word "even" also suggests a case of double consciousness in which a Nikkei man sees his own ethnic group, through the eyes of majority Brazilians, at the border of the Brazilian nation or as a human national border. Yet he later adds that integration was bound to happen because by the 1970s, many Nikkei had become more involved in Brazilian mainstream society. Mariano Goro himself is an example of this process, as he became politicized almost by accident: he reluctantly won a union election and then became a sort of hero among his co-workers. Noticing that this new facet of his life helped him overcome his personal crisis, he soon began to enjoy union struggles.

Mariano Goro, who narrates Part II, explains that the bicultural Nisei's efforts at integration into mainstream society peaked during the 1960s and 1970s: "Many of us wanted to look Brazilian and act Brazilian in the way we were, ate, and dressed."[14] He also recalls how his adopted father scolded him during a match between boxers from Japan and Brazil for cheering for the latter. Along these lines, after seeing his innocent son imitate his classmates' mockery of slanted eyes, Mariano Goro feels compelled to educate him about racial tensions in Brazil: "For Brazilian children, we are different. For us, they are different. Nothing else. You don't need to do that. You don't need to care about that. We belong to another race. You were born here. You country is here."[15] As seen, although, in real life, there were often other issues involved in these clashes, including immigrant and socioeconomic status, only ethnic differences are mentioned in these passages.

Closing the circle, Part III, whose protagonist is the sixty-six-year-old Koiti Furukawa, one of the co-founders of the original Japanese community in Atibaia, returns to the homesickness and nostalgia that characterized the first chapters: he bemoans the suicide of his friend Kenhiti and cries upon hearing a little girl dressed in a kimono thank him in Japanese: "Thank you, grandfather."[16] Koiti loses control of his emotions in public again, thus going against the emotional self-control and restraint that is one of the traditional teachings of Japanese culture. The trauma of the journey has therefore not been overcome: even in the case of the well-adapted Koiti, uprootedness takes its toll.

Identitarian Formations and Nikkei Pride

In contrast with the rural atmosphere and the sometimes melodramatic tone of Part I of *Yawara!*, in the rest of the novel the tone radically changes, showing fully integrated, urban Japanese Brazilian characters who have become involved in local politics and use colloquial, sometimes coarse language: "The bitch is fooling everybody," states Mariano Goro, referring to a woman he finds screaming in the street.[17] Therefore, as is common in literature by and about Asians in Latin America, while the original Asian worldview tends to be romanticized and exoticized through a refined atmosphere enriched by sophisticated poetry, music, and amorous feelings, the Latin American *criollo* worldview is conceived of in opposite terms: unrefined, coarse, and sexually crude.

In the second part of the novel, Mariano Goro's identitarian problems and difficult integration into mainstream Brazilian society synecdochically embody the trials and tribulations of his ethnic community. The uncertainty about whether he is Japanese, Brazilian, or something else consumes him. As stated, this may be another source of meaning for the word "travessia" (journey) in the novel's subtitle. It may allude not only to the Japanese community's spatial travel from Japan to Brazil (and, for many descendants, "back" to Japan), but also to the Japanese community's temporal journey from Issei, to Nisei, Sansei, Yonsei, Gosei (first, second, third, fourth, fifth generation), which involves a psychological travel from holding a Japanese identity to a number of different outcomes, including a Japanese Brazilian identity, an unhyphenated Brazilian identity in which the cultural or sentimental links to the ancestral land have been more or less erased, or holding multiple identities unproblematically.

Along with this identitarian diversity, the novel also re-creates the progressive shifts in national allegiance within several generations of these families, as well as the hostile path to full Brazilian citizenship.

In texts that re-create Japanese immigration to Latin America, the "colonists" (as the first immigrants were called at the time) often make it clear that their goal is to earn enough money to return to their homeland as soon as possible and start a new life. Life goals change, however, among their descendants. Thus, in *Yawara!*, Mariano Goro and other Nisei characters that grow up in Brazil no longer dream about "returning" to Japan once they have become wealthy; in fact, they have never visited their ancestral fatherland. Yet their phenotype, a constant source of mockery and insults coming from majority Brazilians, continues to be a seemingly insurmountable obstacle in their dream of feeling like they truly belong in Brazil. Thus, in one of the central episodes in *Yawara!*, Mariano Goro/Mário Japa develops two conflicting selves as a result of the discrepancies between his self-identity (the cultural categories the character uses to define himself) and a competing social identity (the cultural categories that society imposes on him). Ultimately, the novel implies that the protagonist's fragmented experience of identity and resulting pathological dissociative disorder (a metaphor for the in-between, hybrid life of the Japanese community in Brazil) are an outcome of the trauma and stress suffered throughout a life marked by discrimination and racist prejudice. For Nikkei like Mariano Goro, it is frustrating to be treated as foreigners or mocked because of their phenotype in their own country. This exclusion from the Brazilian body politic becomes apparent during his arrest, when Mariano Goro is convinced that the police have confused him with someone else. Although the cultural construct of his self-identity tells him that he is a Brazilian because of the place where he was born, the policemen impose a competing societal cultural construct by repeatedly asking him: "'What are you doing here in Brazil, Jap? Do you have to get involved in the things of the country? Couldn't you stay quietly in your country?'"[18] These traumatic situations throughout his life are the sources of the conflict between what Mariano Goro experiences internally and what is externally defined by society.

In *Yawara!*, therefore, identitarian conflicts and existential dilemmas arise when Nikkei characters believe that they have to choose between Japanese ethnicity and Brazilian nationality. Mariano Goro, perhaps the author's alter ego, embodies this dilemma to the point of suffering from dissociative identity disorder. Although he feels attracted to the richer, multiethnic life surrounding him and would love to "act Brazilian," he claims that his Japanese ethnic roots will not allow it. Paradoxically, one of the main sources of the protagonist's existential angst and debilitated mental health is his inability to understand the reason behind the existence of Nisei guerrillas, as he feels that Nisei people are stateless: "we have a race but we don't have a fatherland. That one, Japan, was not our homeland. This one, Brazil, we rejected it."[19] Specifically, he cannot fathom how revolutionary Nisei youths have been able to overcome their identitarian uncertainties to the point of becoming involved in the revolutionary struggle against the dictatorial government, "in spite of their skin and their neatly Oriental features."[20] He also resents Japan for its aggressive colonialism, consumerism, loss of traditions, and for abandoning the Nikkei in Brazil during and after World War II. He eventually solves the quandary by realizing that the question of whether he is Brazilian or Japanese is flawed:

> If many Nisei born in Brazil more or less during those two decades, who had gone through that false dilemma, had understood what was happening, they would have had a different approach to life and people. It was a false dilemma because in order to be Japanese, it was not necessary to renounce one's fatherland, and to be Brazilian, it was not necessary to renounce one's race. Each person's experiences, his social and economic circumstances, were reflected in different ways in personality swerves caused by that false dilemma.[21]

This statement summarizes the main thrust in Miyazawa's two novels: that there is no need to reject one's ethnocultural heritage because there are different ways of being Brazilian.

Although *Yawara!* includes the chapter of Shindo Renmei's terrorism and the minor negative episode of the fights between Nikkei and Korean youth (who had not forgotten the horrors of World War II by the time they began to move to Brazil in the late 1960s), Miyazawa does not shy away from expressing his ethnic pride in several passages. In the first chapters, for instance, we are told that the Brazilian landowner was jealous of the productivity of the lands he rented to Japanese settlers. The novel also celebrates the fact that by the 1950s, some Japanese immigrants already owned large estates and that some years later, members of the Nikkei community became prominent in Brazilian politics. This economic and political success, we are reminded, would not have been possible without the pioneers' efforts. Another significant milestone is the appearance of the first Japanese homeless people, who are a source of shame for the community (one of them, however, is known for his mastery of mathematics). This fact also suggests an increased diversity in socioeconomic status within the Japanese Brazilian community.

But beyond celebrating Nikkei achievements, the novel also suggests a certain pan-Asian pride, perhaps strategically reifying positive stereotypes and the "model minority" myth, as it is called in the United States. The narrator points out, for instance, that besides having a reputation for being honest and serious workers, Nikkei students had the best grades and were determined to keep that reputation, even though it could also be a stigma: "After all, the Japanese and the other Orientals were the 'brainiacs.' They had to keep the fame of the race."[22] Close behind students of Japanese and Chinese descent, Koreans are also said to be among the best students. The same pan-Asian awareness is also evident in the epigraph taken from a Chinese legend that opens the novel and is later quoted in the plot.

Mariano Goro, however, does not share this widespread ethnic pride, plausibly questioning the "model minority" myth: "I did not feel the same as those who obtained the first positions in the SATs, singing their own praises for being Oriental, Japanese. Thereafter, there was an identity crisis, which, I imagine, many offspring of Japanese born between the 1940s and 1960s also suffered."[23] Although this disidentification with pan-Asian pride could be interpreted as a reflection of his identitarian uncertainties, it is probably a sign of his deeper integration into mainstream Brazilian society. It also proves that the character (an alter ego of his author) is critical of both positive and negative stereotypes about his ethnic group.

Overall, Miyazawa traces the psychological evolution of his characters as well as the diversity of their experiences and identities, leading some to join samba parades during the Carnival while others succumb to melancholia and identitarian uncertainties. In Koiti's case, it is clear that, a century after the inception of Japanese immigration to Brazil, the sojourner mentality has not disappeared. Even in the cases of Nisei or immigrant characters that learn Portuguese and adapt to the new Brazilian customs, the limits of national belonging are exposed once their subconscious betrays them with identitarian dilemmas or majority Brazilians exclude them from the national discourse.

From Survival to Social Commitment

Although the narrator mentions that some characters in *Yawara!* are from the Ryukyu Islands (the official name for Okinawa), the intersectionality and double oppression resulting from belonging to an ethnic (or subethnic) group that was, at the time, marginalized in both Japan and Brazil, is never addressed. The novel denounces, instead, the racism and marginalization that Japanese immigrants had to withstand in rural areas of the state of São Paulo mostly before and during World War II, but also, at a lower intensity, during the postwar period. On the other hand, it reflects the Nikkei community's reverse racism against Brazilians and other immigrants they considered *gaijin* (outsider, foreigner, non-Japanese).

Yawara! also underscores the sociopolitical and cultural heterogeneity of the Nikkei community. The author points out, for example, the differences between Okinawan and *Naichi* ("mainland" Japanese) cultural traditions. He describes Japanese customs (particularly those from Okinawa) that immigrants brought to Brazil, including their food, clothing, religious beliefs, hierarchical societal structure, and love for martial arts such as judo and kendo, or sports such as baseball. The novel includes terms in the Japanese and Okinawan languages, adding their translation to Portuguese in either footnotes or the text itself. Interestingly, toward the end of the novel the author begins to leave Japanese and Okinawan words untranslated, as if they had at last lost their subordinated status in relation to the Portuguese language. This choice gives the impression that these untranslated terms open the door to the presentation of an also untranslated culture for the reader, challenging her to accept it as is.

Miyazawa highlights the different paths taken by immigrants. This is particularly evident in the chapters that address the brief history of the Shindo Renmei, a terrorist organization composed of Japanese immigrants mostly from the state of São Paulo who, during the second half of the 1940s, refused to believe that World War II had ended and that Japan had surrendered: "a conflict that arose among the Japanese themselves: the dispute between the *kachigumi* (winning faction) and the *makegumi* (losing faction). He had heard about the *Shindo Renmei*, whose followers threatened and attacked their countrymen who admitted Japan's defeat, thus causing thousands of incarcerations in the State of São Paulo."[24] Kachigumi were members of the Japanese community who believed that Japan had been victorious in World War II and makegumi, those who believed their country had surrendered. From 1946 to early 1947, Shindo Renmei's assassins, popularly known as *tokkotai* (a synonym for *kamikaze*), killed with firearms or *katanas* (traditional Japanese swords) at least twenty-three Japanese Brazilians and wounded 147 others who believed the news about Japan's defeat. The terrorists, who considered their victims *corações sujos* (dirty hearts) and referred to them as Makegumi or "defeatists," accused them of betraying the Japanese emperor. Highlighting a socioeconomic schism within the community, the "defeatists" were usually the most informed, wealthy, and adapted to mainstream Brazilian culture. Indeed, according to Jhony Arai and Cesar Hirasaki, "Most Japanese not only believed that Japan had been victorious, but also paid dues to the sect. There were more than 120,000 sympathizers who paid monthly fees and nearly 20,000 associates in sixty branches scattered throughout São Paulo."[25] Accordingly, a footnote in the novel explains that 80 percent of the Japanese community sided with the kachigumi or "victorists" of the Shindo Renmei. Yet among the members of the original community in *Yawara!* only the *jichan* (grandfather) Ryutaro seems to support them openly. By contrast, Kenhiti, Goro, and Koiti (who also denies the Japanese emperor's divine nature), believe that Japan has been defeated. The rest of the community simply avoids the topic.

As stated, in *Yawara!* the ultimate proof of Nikkei youth's Brazilianness is the active engagement of some of them in national politics and in revolutionary groups that fought against the dictatorial government that reached power after a coup d'état in 1964. Yet, according to Lesser, their strategy backfired as it unexpectedly reinforced the Nikkei's minority status: "Ethnic militancy was supposed to lead to Brazilianness. Ironically, it did the opposite."[26] Moreover, at the time most members of the Nikkei community, convinced that it was wiser to continue keeping a low profile, rejected these revolutionary activities. As depicted in the novel, the existence of Nisei revolutionaries became an embarrassment for the community and a taboo that was avoided in conversations. Yet Miyazawa proudly presents Mário Japa as a Japanese Brazilian hero.

His protagonist is based on a real-life person. In his study *A Discontented Diaspora* (2007), Lesser summarized the biography of the Nisei Mário Japa (1948–), whose given name was Shizuo Osawa (it has also been spelled Chizuo Osava). Now a journalist in Rio de Janeiro, Osawa was a former member of the Vanguardia Popular Revolucionária (Revolutionary Popular Avant-Garde; VPR), the same Marxist organization in which the now president of Brazil, Dilma Rousseff, was a militant:

> When Shizuo Osawa became Mário Japa in the late 1967 this was unknown to the state. Authorities only began to learn that Mário Japa was Shizuo Osawa on the rainy night of 27 February 1970. Having gone twenty-four sleepless hours, he decided to drive a load of weapons and revolutionary pamphlets from one hide-out to another when the person assigned to the task did not appear. Driving along the Estrada das Lágrimas (Road of Tears) in greater São Paulo, Osawa fell asleep at the wheel and crashed. In the wrecked car the police found an unconscious Japanese-Brazilian whose documents said he was Shizuo Osawa. To their surprise, they also discovered weapons and VPR propaganda in the trunk. Osawa, now awake, was taken first to the emergency room, then to the local police station and finally to DEOPS headquarters "for treatment."[27]

After the accident, Osawa was imprisoned and tortured. For some time, the Brazilian government considered him the right-hand man of Carlos Lamarca, the leader of the VPR and a former army captain. In March 1970, Lamarca, fearing that Osawa would reveal the secret location of a guerrilla training camp, abducted Nobuo Okuchi, the Japanese consul in São Paulo, to exchange him for Osawa, four other revolutionary prisoners, and three children. Incidentally, although not directly suggested in the novel, Lamarca's decision to kidnap the Japanese consul—rather than the consul of a different nationality—is in itself indicative that he saw the Nikkei Osawa as a foreign, Japanese national rather than the Brazilian citizen he was, as it implies that he demanded an exchange of "Japanese" prisoners from the government.

Lesser's study also reveals that the historical Osawa's concerns about his ethnic group's cultural identity were similar to those of Mariano Goro in the novel: while Osawa was working as a banker in Curitiba, he published, in the magazine *Panorama*, an essay titled "They Want to Be Brazilians," where, using a psychological approach to ethnicity and identity, he insisted "that ethnic integration was not a minority 'problem' but a majority one."[28] Osawa's desire to prove his own *brasilidade* (Brazilianness) and that of his ethnic group, therefore, precedes his revolutionary activities. Lesser also discloses the ethnic prejudice that guided the DEOPS's investigations: instead of creating a file for his birth name, there was only one for his code name "Mário Japa." Likewise, Osawa's fellow revolutionaries refused to stop calling him "The Jap," even though this represented a serious danger for his security.[29] But the most racist reaction to the realization that there were Nikkei revolutionaries involved in the armed struggle against the dictatorship came from the Brazilian press: "The revelation that a Japanese Brazilian was among those to be traded for the Japanese consul shocked the public." The *Jornal da Tarde* took the most aggressive approach, publishing an article headlined, "Pay Close Attention: The Japanese Terror."[30] It is evident, therefore, that both the fictional character and the real-life Osawa had to cope with majority Brazilians' inability to concede full Brazilian citizenship to a Nikkei, even though he was fighting courageously for his country's freedom. Interestingly, in an interview with Guto Silveira, Osawa admits that he took advantage of the positive stereotype of the Japanese as honest people in Brazil: "It was difficult to keep all the clandestine people hidden. It was always necessary to rent houses. And for that, it was useful to be Japanese and to have credibility. I rented many houses without even giving my name."[31] It seems, therefore, that while Osawa rejected the essentialization of his ethnic group and the social identity or cultural categories imposed by mainstream society, he also knew how to take advantage of positive stereotypes.

Besides Mário Japa, Miyazawa proudly mentions in *Yawara!* other Nisei men and women who participated in the armed struggle, a topic that is further developed in his second novel, *Uma Rosa para Yumi*. The author praises the self-sacrifice of these brave, young Nikkei and laments the lack of recognition they have received: "These episodes, which became part of Brazil's recent history, ended up not being registered in the annals of the Japanese Brazilian community and the memory of the engagement of these Nisei youths and of others not mentioned here is still waiting for the acknowledgment of their own community."[32] Several of them, we learn in *Yawara!*, were tortured and killed by the military dictatorship, including Hiroaki Torigoe, Yoshitane Fujimori, and Suely Yumiko Kanayama. Kanayama (1948–1974), a short, thin, and timid Nikkei born in the small town of Coronel Macedo, in the State of São Paulo, was a member of the Brazilian Communist Party (Partido Comunista de Brasil; PCdoB) and the Araguaia guerrilla, a revolutionary movement created in the Amazonia to mobilize local peasants, fight the military dictatorship, and impose a socialist government in the country. Kanayama's disappearance in Araguaia in 1974 was investigated by the Truth Commission dealing with deaths and disappearances during this period. The novel points out that in real life Kanayama refused to surrender when surrounded by soldiers in the jungle and was shot over one hundred times, after injuring one of them. She was later honored with street names in Campo Grande, Rio de Janeiro, and Campinas, São Paulo. According to Lesser, there are different accounts of her death, mostly tied to her bravery and the typical connection of Nikkei ethnicity to violence, but also including one with a "quasi-mystical interpretation that Kamayana [*sic*], like a European Catholic saint, remained alive even in death."[33]

Yawara!, therefore, acquires testimonial traits in these passages that highlight the Nikkei's sacrifice for justice in Brazil and respond to the urge to reclaim the past. Perhaps its epigraph is a reference to these lesser-known heroes: "A Chinese legend says that warriors who live great emotions do not die. Climbing great mountains you will perhaps be able to see them flying softly through great valleys."[34] These "warriors" in the epigraph may refer to either the Nikkei guerrillas or the first trailblazing Issei to arrive in Brazil, who set the ground for the success of future generations. Tellingly, Miyazawa declared, in the website "Projeto incorporado ao Museu Histórico da Imigração Japonesa no Brasil" (Project Incorporated to the Historical Museum of Japanese Immigration to Brazil), that the main motivation to write *Yawara!* was his desire to leave a testimony of the Japanese Brazilian community's painful attempt at becoming fully Brazilian: "For a long time during our youth, we tried to become Brazilian, hiding our eyes behind sunglasses. But it didn't work. They kept calling us Japanese, asking us to return to our land! How could we return to our land if our land was here, in Brazil? We suffered a lot trying to become Brazilians, we lost our origins and our personality. We claimed another one, which was difficult to justify, but possible . . ."[35] From this perspective, the entire Nikkei community in Brazil could be identified—perhaps falling into a self-orientalizing cliché—with the warrior metaphor in the epigraph.

Uma Rosa para Yumi: The Recovery of Historical Memory

Miyazawa continues with the exploration of some of these same topics in *Uma Rosa para Yumi*, but this time with an explicit emphasis on a historical memory reconstruction—a foundational aspect of social identities—that may not be welcome by everyone in the Nikkei community. Whereas *Yawara!* has a wider focus on the history of Japanese immigration, *Uma Rosa para Yumi* emphasizes, with apparent cathartic results for the narrator, the remembrance of political violence during the military dictatorship and its current affective and traumatic consequences on the Nikkei community. Dedicated "to male and female freedom and equality fighters, especially to revolutionary Nisei," it pays a nostalgic homage to their idealism and contribution to the political struggle against dictatorship during the 1970s by rescuing their historical legacy from oblivion and dignifying their memories.[36] In this second novel, the author leaves aside the psychological approach of Part II of *Yawara!*, resorting instead to real-life names and individual stories in order to memorialize and celebrate their sacrifice. For the author, this sacrifice for a more just society, which he sees as heroic, is the undeniable proof of their community's patriotism and right to full Brazilian citizenship: some of its younger members ran the risk of being ostracized by their own ethnic community or imprisoned, tortured, and killed by governmental forces, and others gave their life altogether for their country's freedom.

The novel, resorting again to social memory, also documents a shift of mentality in the Nikkei community: in spite of the identitarian ambivalence of some Nikkei characters, many now identify mostly as Brazilian, speak only Portuguese, and even fight heroically for their native country's freedom, a synecdoche of the patriotism of the entire Nikkei community. Therefore, by including his memoirs of revolutionary activity, Miyazawa takes *Uma Rosa para Yumi* closer to the testimonial genre: truth telling and the clarification of recent Nikkei minority histories take center stage.

In contrast with the realistic approach and mostly chronological development of the plot in *Yawara!*, *Uma Rosa para Yumi* uses numerous analepses and prolepses, as well as metaliterary techniques that often prevent the reader from suspending disbelief in the plotline. It adds, for example, the perspectives and experiences of other survivors and former participants in the revolutionary struggle, including that of the author's alter ego, called Itizó by his family and friends in the neighborhood of Liberdade, and Ricardo by his classmates at the Universidade de São Paulo. Itizó/Ricardo, whose double name is reflective of a seemingly comfortable double identity as a Nikkei *and* a Brazilian man, recalls the grief that his own political involvement caused within his family. Thus, after losing part of his index finger while trying to throw a tear gas bomb back at the police, his older brother, Tadao, scolds him for all the suffering he is causing to their mother. In response, Ricardo/Itizó (toward the end of *Uma Rosa para Yumi*, the omniscient narrator, who had been referring to Ricardo/Itizó in the third person throughout the plot, suggests that he is none other than Ricardo himself) criticizes his brother for being alienated by a military dictatorship that is supported by selfish people like him. At one point, the argument suddenly veers from politics to race:

> You are not solving anything with this political thing. In fact, that is not a problem of our race!
>
> —What race? What race are you talking about?
>
> . . .
>
> —I am talking about us, the Japanese. You ought to look at our people, who live here in Brazil. No one is involved in those things. With that thing you're doing, you're hurting everyone, all of us. You're a bad example for the Japanese!
>
> —And you're a traitor to the homeland. You don't even know the National Anthem. . . .[37]

This aggressive exchange illustrates the political divisions not only within the Nikkei community but also within its families, which had been briefly addressed in *Yawara!* While the more conservative Tadao sees no reason for Nikkei youth to get involved in local politics, his younger brother considers his oppositional stance a patriotic duty.

Interestingly, Lesser maintains that besides the struggle for freedom, there were additional motivations behind Nikkei participation in revolutionary activities: "Activists, in contrast, usually considered themselves to be outsiders from the formally organized 'colony' of community organizations, newspapers, and festivals. Militancy was not only a challenge to the dictatorship; it was a challenge to the politically and culturally conservative generation of their parents."[38] Indeed, the open challenge to his relatives is obvious in the arguments used by Ricardo/Itizó, who is convinced that Tadao's passive demeanor is "serving the system" and feels contempt for his cousins, whose only obsession is the symbolic capital provided by material possessions.[39] From his revolutionary perspective, Ricardo/Itizó argues that his relatives are easily manipulated by the censored political news provided by the national television network, because they are out of touch with the sociopolitical reality of Brazil. A few years later, however, Ricardo/Itizó forgives his brother Tadao after finding out that the latter was actually proud of his involvement in the political struggle. In any case, it is apparent that even though it represented a minority position within the Nikkei community, the author applauds the bravery and generosity of the young revolutionaries during those years.

Another real-life revolutionary whose courageous effort and sacrifice is commemorated in the novel with the goal of helping the Nikkei community to come to terms with its past is Gushiken, who was a militant of Libelu, a Trotskyite organization that fought the dictatorship. The narrator also recalls his beautiful Nisei friend Suzana, who fell into a depression after realizing (erroneously) that her love for Ricardo/Itizó was unrequited; in reality, we learn, his deep involvement in the political movement at the university forced him, in

November 1973, to go clandestine for two years, which separated them forever. As the narrator recalls, "Among the leftist militants, no one was anybody's. All of them belonged to the revolutionary struggle."[40]

Jumping more than thirty years forward to 2007, Ricardo/Itizó pays visits to several of his former revolutionary friends, thus opening the door to the incorporation of their experiences into the plot. One of them is the lawyer Regina Alexsandra Nogueira, a leader of the Communist Party of Brazil and former fellow humanities student, who was forced to go clandestine and, unbeknown to Ricardo/Itizó, was also in love with him for some time. Now, Ricardo/Itizó and Regina nostalgically recall their common friend Suely Yumiko Kanayama (Lesser spells her name "Kamayana"), also a member of the Communist Party of Brazil and a Nisei revolutionary whom everyone called "A Japonesinha" (the Little Japanese Woman), who was shot over one hundred times by government soldiers while fighting for the guerrillas in Araguaia. Later, "Yumi," as her friends used to call her, had a small street in Campinas named after her, which becomes a source of pride and vindication for Ricardo/Itizó and Regina. The title of the novel, therefore, suggests that the entire plot is a nostalgic letter of thankfulness to the late revolutionary and others like her, dead and alive, who sacrificed their youth fighting against the dictatorship. The novel itself, with all its collective memories, is a metaphoric monument, a material memorial to their hitherto silenced heroism and bravery, aimed at interrogating institutionalized versions of the recent past.

In a sudden temporary and thematic jump, *Uma Rosa para Yumi* incorporates the history of the Nikkei community in Brazil, including dekasegi experience, into the plot. Surprisingly, the chapters dealing with this topic provide an alternative story for Suely Yumiko "Yumi" Kanayama. It is, therefore, up to the reader to decide which one is true. In this version, rather than being shot by government soldiers, Yumi has become a nun in a Japanese convent, after having a daughter named Bete (Elizabete) with her own brother, Akira. Using a creationist approach in the epilogue, the first-person narrator struggles mentally with his own characters, Itizó and Akira (Yumi's brother), who protest their author's intention of getting rid of them. Whereas the author insists that Akira must continue to be fictional, the character complains that his return to Brazil and some episodes of Yumi's life have not been narrated yet. As to Itizó, the author's alter ego, he declares his mission after claiming to be real: to recover Yumiko's true story. In this alternative story, Itizó is a dekasegi who manages to save some money only to spend it all during the months he remained unemployed upon his return to Brazil, a common experience among Brazilian dekasegi.

If one considers a possible allegorical interpretation of this unexpected plot twist, it would not be too far-fetched to read it as a commentary on ethnocultural and racial identity in Brazil. The revolutionary Yumi, who ends up being shot during a confrontation with the Brazilian army, represents the fully integrated Nikkei who conceives of social freedom in her native country as a patriotic duty. Her heroic martyrdom becomes the ultimate proof of her deep-seated Brazilianness and symbolizes the birth of the new, multicultural, and tolerant Brazil. By contrast, the alternative Yumi as a nun back in Japan who ends up being impregnated by her own brother, Akira, embodies a silenced and isolated Nikkei whose relative ruins her life forever. This episode of incest could be read as a commentary on the long-held isolationist stance and sojourner mentality of remote rural communities in the states of São Paulo and Paraná. Yumi's joining a Catholic convent in Japan, on the other hand, also elicits colonialist connotations. The veiled message of the implicit author, therefore, suggests the need for further integration into mainstream Brazilian society. This should not be confused, however, with assimilationist propaganda, as Miyazawa repeatedly celebrates cultural difference in both novels.

In other words, whereas Ricardo/Itizó's double (Nikkei and majority Brazilian) identity is portrayed as an unproblematic life choice, Yumi's alternative story of incest and convent reads as a warning against the perils of the survival of a cloistered and isolationist mentality within the Nikkei community.

The Birth of Liberdade

As proof of the author's anti-assimilationist stance, *Yawara!* proudly describes daily life and local customs in the predominantly Japanese neighborhood of Liberdade, in São Paulo, whose neighbors no longer have to defend themselves from racial slurs. Among other historic landmarks, Miyazawa highlights the creation of the Banco América do Sul and the success of Japanese restaurants, publications, movie theaters, different types of Japanese stores (which now contribute to the Carnival), and even a casino, all of which helped strengthen, according to him, Japanese identity in the city.

Uma Rosa para Yumi also presents, from a nostalgic perspective, the history of Liberdade, the (formerly) Japanese neighborhood of São Paulo, conceived of as a symbol of universal unity among the different ethnicities: "Here, one can find Japanese, Koreans, Chinese, Vietnamese, Asians in general, their descendants, and Brazilians. In that small area thousands of people move around, a live demonstration of miscegenation, the natural mixture of culture and races. . . . The stores, persons, and typical things of each country that are present there are proof that the universal unity of peoples is possible."[41] Resorting to a metanarrative approach, the narrator incorporates other narrations about the neighborhood from his friends and former freedom fighters' perspectives. The author's interpretation of the social reality around him, including that of the neighborhood of Liberdade, is often filtered through a Marxist outlook:

"As can be observed, with this friend's account, a fellow partner of the social struggles in the next decades, it was possible to have different races and cultures living together, if the economic conditions allowed this just and harmonic development. However, as is known, the black community was expelled from its space, mainly for economic reasons, where capitalist gain is implacable."[42] Miyazawa laments, therefore, the fact that the socioeconomic success of his own ethnocultural community (which he openly celebrates in his literature) indirectly contributed to further marginalize and displace another historically disadvantaged group: the Afro-Brazilian community. As seen, throughout his works, Miyazawa attempts to connect the struggle of Japanese immigrants with that of the marginalized Afro-Brazilian community, an aspect that is reminiscent of other authors' attempts, in both Brazil and in Peru, to link Japanese history and culture with those of local indigenous communities. As Lesser argues, these tactics that foment a social memory of mythical origins are often times aimed at highlighting the "natural" capacity of the Japanese for adaptation to the local customs or their rightful belonging to the country.

In the context of Miyazawa's aforementioned attempts to connect the Nikkei community's history with that of Afro-Brazilians, we learn that in the early 1950s, the Galvão Bueno street in the Liberdade neighborhood was inhabited by Afro-Brazilians and had almost no businesses, but it gradually became populated by Japanese denizens: "Brazilians began to go away. Although they were not expelled, whenever they went into a bar, Brazilians felt bad because there were only Japanese."[43] The narrator also mentions the presence of Chinese and Korean immigrants in Liberdade. Initially, we learn, the small Japanese community lived in a different area of the neighborhood, where they sold Japanese products made both in Japan and Brazil. According to the memories of the narrator's cousin, it was the construction of the Niterói movie theater that caused the rapid growth of the Japanese community in Liberdade during the 1950s, as it soon attracted other businesses, including one with geishas brought directly from Japan. The first Japanese in Liberdade, he recalls, were humble families that sold their lands in rural areas of the state of São Paulo and moved to the city, opening a business there so that their children could continue their studies. Incidentally, this emphasis on education is often highlighted in Japanese Brazilian literature as one of the engines behind the material and social progress of Japanese immigrants and their Nikkei descendants. The narrator's cousin also recalls how one day he stopped going out with his majority Brazilian friends to join a group of Nisei friends, with whom he felt a greater affinity. Another landmark achievement of the Japanese community in Monte Alto, as presented in the text, is their first daily radio program, known as the "Nipponese Hour."

During the 1950s, Japanese emigration to Brazil was renovated as a result of the "U.S. ban on Japanese entry and its occupation of Okinawa," which displaced local inhabitants to build military bases.[44] When almost 55,000 Issei immigrants (the so-called Japão Novo) arrived, their relationship with local Nikkei, including the narrator and his relatives, became increasingly hostile. As a result, during the following decade, there were legendary fights between both groups in Liberdade, which ended up being exaggerated by *São Paulo Shimbun* and *Paulista Shimbun*, the local Japanese Brazilian press, to the delight of some Nikkei youth: "when the new Japanese, the Issei, arrived, they would arrive to Galvão Bueno street wanting to take over and tease the girls disrespectfully. They were used to that type of provocation in Japan. There were many fights because of this. Nisei youth, who were organized, responded accordingly."[45] In the end, there were complaints from the Japanese consulate, which sought the intermediation of two Nisei politicians. These fights between Nikkei youth and new arrivals evidence the appearance of a Nikkei cultural identity that is separate and different from that of Japan. In the same way that Nikkei youth's worldview is different from that of their parents, who often tried to keep a low profile, they cannot identify with the demeanor and culture of Japanese newcomers either. While this type of infighting is relatively common in the case layered migrations, as established communities often condemn the behavior of newcomers of their own ethnic background, it is interesting to note that the anecdote is inserted immediately after highlighting the admirable coexistence of people from different ethnic backgrounds in Liberdade.

Lesser has briefly studied these incidents between Japão Novo new immigrants and the rest of the Nikkei community: "Longtime residents were often shocked by the attitudes of young Japanese toward everything, from the emperor to sexual relations. The newcomers were equally confused: They had trouble understanding old dialects filled with Japanized Portuguese words and wondered if earlier immigrants had become *Brasil-bokê* ('made senile in Brazil')."[46]

Conclusion

Yawara! A Travessia Nihondin-Brasil and *Uma Rosa para Yumi* offer a panoramic view of the history of the Nikkei community in Brazil. They bring to the fore identitarian conflicts that affect the community as well as uplifting historical episodes that may contribute to emancipate its collective consciousness. At the same time, these two novels serve a didactic mission: like much of Japanese Brazilian cultural production, they educate readers about the formation and status quo of a hybrid culture that has successfully blended two very different national cultures into a liminal third space from which Brazilian national identity has been challenged and transformed. From this "in-between" space, Miyazawa's writing (and, by extension, Nikkei collective discourse) contests the fixity, purity, or homogeneity of both Japanese and Brazilian cultures. These two novels, part of the social articulation of a Nikkei minority perspective, become sites of contestation of the very idea of national culture and the Brazilian nation, as both negative and positive ethnic stereotypes are revisited and questioned. "Received" cultural traditions and presumably fixed ethnic traits are ultimately transformed in the very site of the interstices between the purportedly monolithic Japanese and the Brazilian cultures. In this ongoing process of hybridization portrayed in Miyazawa's novels, his characters strategically move in and out of Japaneseness according to the circumstances or their author's intention to emphasize either cultural difference or belonging within the Brazilian nation. In the end, Miyazawa, like the other Japanese Brazilian authors and filmmakers, exercises his right to self-representation, to articulate an alternative national history, to present a differential knowledge coming from a minority group, and to elaborate an empowering Nikkei minority discourse from the periphery of mainstream Brazilian society.

Overall, *Uma Rosa para Yumi* reads as a continuation of the Japanese Brazilian "crossing" (i.e., the spatial, temporal, cultural, and psychological transition of the Japanese and Nikkei community in Brazil) mentioned in the title of his first novel, by adding information on three different, albeit interrelated, topics: the Nisei's political struggle during the 1970s, the dekasegi experience, and the history of the Liberdade neighborhood, which can be read as an exploration of the formation of a Japanese community in São Paulo and, by extension, in Brazil. In his second novel, Miyazawa tries to offer a more experimental text, adding the polyphony of multiple perspectives and creationist dialogues among the implicit author and two of his main characters. Along with these metanarrative techniques, there is a blend fiction, testimonial, and memoirs, where one can find not only a direct message but a plausibly allegorical one. In any case, both *Uma Rosa para Yumi* and *Yawara!* serve the same purpose: to celebrate the economic, sociocultural, and political achievements of the Japanese and Nikkei community in Brazil, particularly the active involvement of Nikkei youth in revolutionary activities during the dictatorship of the 1970s, thus claiming a place in the national project. In the process, they reveal the Nikkei community's resistance tactics during the first decades, its cultural strategies for community formation, and its progressive integration into mainstream Brazilian society, which, as stated, finds a point of inflection during the 1970s through the sociopolitical commitment of leftist Nikkei youth, of which Miyazawa was part. Both texts, therefore, become indirect tools to negotiate the place of the Nikkei community in Brazil always within national borders, without resorting to assimilationist discourses. The post-national approaches present in the works of several Sino-Peruvian and Japanese Peruvian authors are also absent from Miyazawa's narratives.[47]

In the author's note at the end of *Uma Rosa para Yumi*, Miyazawa offers a disclaimer: he feels no shame or regret for not having fully acquired Japanese culture during his childhood. As he explains, those were different times and circumstances: "Since I did not enjoy the circumstances to live two lives at the same time, I see today that I did not have the opportunity to have the valuable experience of a people and a civilization whence we originated, which forged its history through sacrifices, sweat, tears and happiness, with their mistakes and achievements, also forging their identity, which brought an immeasurable contribution to the construction of a new world for everyone."[48] The author, therefore, suggests that since now the times have changed and it is socially acceptable to express pride in one's ethnic heritage without running the risk of being accused of an anti-Brazilian stance, he is attempting, through his literature, to challenge obsolete notions of a traditional, fixed, and homogenous Brazilian identity. This is precisely why in the "Author's note" included in *Uma Rosa para Yumi*, he describes *Yawara!* as a "settling of scores and a reconciliation."[49] Instead of recommending an assimilationist "melting pot" message, *Uma Rosa para Yumi* provides, like many other Japanese Brazilian literary texts, a proud re-creation of the customs and traditions of the Japanese community in Brazil, including *yaitô* (burning a certain area of the body to cure rheumatism) or *miai* (the Japanese tradition of introducing a single man to a single woman to consider the possibility of marriage). It also describes how Nikkei culture is an ongoing project (rather than a set of fixed cultural traits), as these traditions have evolved or were lost in the new, hybrid Nikkei cultural third space: "—Times are changing. If it were as in the past, you could marry one of Kurô-san's daughters through miai. Now, women are the ones who are choosing men. It is not as in the time of old anymore—said Fusako."[50]

Through these two novels, Miyazawa also celebrates a new way of being Brazilian: by articulating, from the periphery of Brazilian mainstream society, his ethnic roots and cultural difference, all the while claiming a place in the Brazilian national project. At the same time, Miyazawa's appeal to the collective and historical memories of his community is an attempt to foster group identity and self-recognition: through his literature, he reminds Brazilian Nikkei about their past, which may guide them to conceptualize their present, contemplate the future, and encourage them to pass on this representation of their "shared past" to future generations. Finally, the writing of these two novels has cathartic overtones, as they fill a vacuum for recognition both within the Nikkei community and in the historical narratives of the country.

NOTES

1. José Yoshida Yoshida, e-mail message to author, February 24, 2015.
2. Júlio Miyazawa was born in Guararema, in the state of São Paulo. His father, an Issei named Kurô Miyazawa born in Niigata, Japan, migrated to Brazil in 1938. His mother, a Nisei named Cisuco Miyazawa, was born in Marília, Brazil. At the age of thirteen, Miyazawa moved to São Paulo, where he witnessed the development of both the Japanese community and the neighborhood of Liberdade.
3. Takeyuki Tsuda, *Strangers in the Ethnic Homeland: Japanese Brazilian Return Migration in Transnational Perspective* (New York: Columbia University Press, 2003), 9–10.
4. Homi Bhabha, *The Location of Culture* (London: Routledge, 1994) 161.
5. "Unhomeliness" is Homi Bhabha's term to define the sense of being culturally displaced, caught between two cultures, and not "at home" in either of them. It is often felt by those who lack a clearly defined cultural identity. Ibid., 13.
6. Jeffrey Lesser, "Ethnic Myths as National Identity in Brazil," in *National Myths: Constructed Pasts, Contested Presents*, edited by Gérard Bouchard (New York: Routledge, 2013), 68.
7. Júlio Miyazawa, *Yawara! A Travessia Nihondin-Brasil* (Saõ Paulo: self-published, 2006), 98–99.
8. Ibid., 45.
9. Ibid., 151.
10. Ibid., 26.
11. Ibid., 32.
12. Ibid., 77.
13. Ibid., 117.
14. Ibid., 129.
15. Ibid., 144.
16. Ibid., 252.
17. Ibid., 107.
18. Ibid., 163.
19. Ibid., 127.
20. Ibid.
21. Ibid., 125.
22. Ibid., 145.
23. Ibid., 124.
24. Ibid., 41–42.
25. Ibid., 134.
26. Jeffrey Lesser, *A Discontented Diaspora: Japanese Brazilians and the Meanings of Ethnic Militancy, 1960–1980* (Durham, N.C.: Duke University Press, 2007), xxx.
27. The Departamento de Ordem Política e Social (Department of Political and Social Order) was a governmental police department created in 1924 to repress sociopolitical movements who fought against the dictatorship during the Estado Novo and the military regime of 1964. Lesser, *A Discontented Diaspora*, 132.
28. Ibid., 128.
29. Ibid., 130–131.
30. Ibid., 142.
31. Guto Silveira, "Ex-guerrilheiro retorna a Ribeirão Preto após 60 anos," *Revista Epoca*, February 27, 2011, accessed July 12, 2014, http://portal.rac.com.br/noticias/index_teste

.php?tp=brasil&id=/76565&ano=/2011&mes=/02&dia=/27&titulo=/ex-guerrilheiro-retorna-a-ribeirao-preto-apos-60-anos.

32. Miyazawa, *Yawara!*, 228–229.
33. Lesser, *A Discontented Diaspora*, 110.
34. Miyazawa, *Yawara!*, n.p.
35. Júlio Miyazawa, "Sem a sua história a minha . . ." *Centenário da Imigração Japonesa: Projeto incorporado ao Museu Histórico da Imigração Japonesa no Brasil*, accessed June 25, 2014, http://www.japao100.com.br/perfil/383.
36. Júlio Miyazawa, *Uma Rosa para Yumi* (São Paulo: self-published, 2014), 9.
37. Ibid., 131.
38. Lesser, *A Discontented Diaspora*, 76.
39. Miyazawa, *Uma Rosa para Yumi*, 135.
40. Ibid., 126.
41. Ibid., 15.
42. Ibid., 58.
43. Ibid., 51.
44. Jeffrey Lesser, *Immigration, Ethnicity, and National Identity in Brazil, 1908 to the Present* (New York: Cambridge University Press, 2013), 182.
45. Miyazawa, *Uma Rosa para Yumi*, 52.
46. Lesser, *Immigration*, 182.
47. For more information on this topic, see Ignacio López-Calvo, *Dragons in the Land of the Condor: Writing Tusán in Peru* (Tucson: University of Arizona Press, 2014) and Ignacio López-Calvo, *The Affinity of the Eye: Writing Nikkei in Peru* (Tucson: University of Arizona Press, 2013).
48. Miyazawa, *Uma Rosa para Yumi*, 159.
49. Ibid.
50. Ibid., 34.

BIBLIOGRAPHY

Against the Grain: An Artist's Survival Guide to Perú. Directed by Ann Kaneko. Los Angeles, Calif.: Ann Kaneko, 2008. DVD.

Ahmad, Diana L. *The Opium Debate and Chinese Exclusion Laws in the Nineteenth-Century American West.* Reno: University of Nevada Press, 2007.

Alexander, Meena. *Poetics of Dislocation.* Ann Arbor: University of Michigan Press, 2009.

Ali, Agha Shahid. *The Veiled Suite: The Collected Poems.* New York: W. W. Norton and Company, 2009.

Alonso, Manuel F., and T. Valero Martínez, eds. *Cuba before the World at the Panama-Pacific Exposition.* New York: Souvenir Guide of Cuba Co., 1915.

Alvarado, Rocio González. "Acusan a China de competencia desleal." *La Prensa*, January 30, 2005.

———. "Piratería China de artesanías amenaza subsistencia del mercado de la ciudadela." *La Jornada*, July 14, 2008.

Alvarez, Sonia E. *Engendering Democracy in Brazil: Women's Movements in Transition Politics.* Princeton: Princeton University Press, 1990.

Alvarez, Sonia E., Evelina Dagnino, and Arturo Escobar, eds. *Cultures of Politics, Politics of Cultures: Re-envisioning Latin American Social Movements.* Boulder, Colo.: Westview Press, 1998.

Álvarez Ríos, Baldomero. *La Inmigración China en la Cuba colonial: El Barrio Chino de La Habana.* Havana: Publicigraf, 1995.

Amador, José. *Medicine and Nation Building in the Americas.* Nashville: Vanderbilt University Press, 2014.

Anderson, Benedict. *Imagined Communities: Reflections on the Origin and Spread of Nationalism.* New York: Verso, 1991. Revised edition, London: Verso, 2006.

———. "The New World Disorder." *New Left Review* 193 (1992): 13.

Anderson, Warwick. "Immunization and Hygiene in the Colonial Philippines." *Journal of the History of Medicine and Allied Sciences* 62, no. 1 (2006): 1–20.

Andrews, George Reid. *The Afro-Argentines of Buenos Aires, 1800–1900.* Madison: University of Wisconsin Press, 1980.

Apter, Andrew. "Herskovits's Heritage: Rethinking Syncretism in the African Diaspora." *Diaspora: A Journal of Transnational Studies* 1, no. 3 (1991): 235–260.

Arai, Jhony, and Cesar Hirasaki. *100 anos da imigração Japonesa no Brasil.* São Paulo: Bunkyo, Imprensa Oficial, 2008.

Armony, Ariel C. *The Dubious Link: Civic Engagement and Democratization.* Stanford, Calif.: Stanford University Press, 2004.

Auerbach, Sascha. *Race, Law, and "The Chinese Puzzle" in Imperial Britain.* New York: Palgrave Macmillan, 2009.

Ayorinde, Christine. *Afro-Cuban Religiosity, Revolution, and National Identity.* Gainesville: University Press of Florida, 2004.

Balibar, Etienne. "Is There a Neo-Racism?" In *Race, Nation, Class: Ambiguous Identities*, edited by Etienne Balibar and Immanuel Wallerstein, 17–28. London/New York: Verso, 1991.

Bannerjee, Sukanya, Aims McGuinness, and Steven C. McKay, eds. *New Routes for Diaspora Studies.* Bloomington: Indiana University Press, 2012.

Barabantseva, Elena. "Trans-Nationalising Chineseness: Overseas Chinese Policies of the PRC's Central Government." *ASIEN* 96 (July 2005): 7–28.

Barcia, María del Carmen. "Un modelo de inmigración 'favorecida': el traslado masivo de españoles a Cuba, 1880–1930." *Catauro* 2, no. 4 (2001): 36–59.

Beamer, Kamanamaikalani. *No Mākou Ka Mana: Liberating the Nation.* Honolulu: Kamehameha Publishing, 2014.

Benavides, G. "Power, Intelligibility, and the Boundaries of Religions." *Historical Reflections* 27 (2001): 481–498.

Benhabib, Seyla, and Judith Resnick. "Introduction: Citizenship and Migration Theory Engendered." In *Migrations and Mobilities: Citizenship, Borders, and Gender*, edited by Seyla Benhabib and Judith Resnick, 1–46. New York: New York University Press, 2009.

Benton, Gregor, ed. *The Chinese in Cuba: 1847–Now.* Lanham, Md.: Lexington Books, 2009.

———. "San Fancón and the Goddess of Mercy: Two Chinese Folk Gods in Cuban Transfiguration." *Cultural and Social History* 10, no. 1 (2013): 93–108.

Bhabha, Homi. *The Location of Culture.* London: Routledge, 1994.

Bialogorski, Mirta, and Daniel Bargman. "The Gaze of the Other: Koreans and Bolivians in Buenos Aires." *Patterns of Prejudice* 30, no. 4 (1996): 17–26.

Bolaño, Robert. *The Last Interview and Other Conversations.* Translated by Sybil Perez. Brooklyn, N.Y.: Melville House Publishing, 2009.

Bronfman, Alejandra. *Measures of Equality: Social Science, Citizenship, and Race in Cuba, 1902–1940.* Chapel Hill: University of North Carolina Press, 2004.

———. "The Allure of Technology: Photographs, Statistics, and the Elusive Female Criminal in 1930s Cuba." *Gender and History* 15, no. 2 (2007): 60–77.

Butler, Kim. "Multilayered Politics in the African Diaspora: The Metadiaspora and the Minidiaspora Realities." In *Opportunity Structures in Diaspora Relations: Comparisons in Contemporary Multilevel Politics of Diaspora and Transnational Identity*, edited by Gloria Totoricagüena, 19–51. Reno: Center for Basque Studies, University of Nevada, 2007.

Cabrera, Lydia. *El Monte: Igbo, Finda, Ewe Orisha, Vititi Nfinda: notas sobre las religiones, la magia, las supersticiones y el folklore de los Negros Criollos y del pueblo de Cuba.* Miami: Ediciones Universal, 1974.

Caggiano, Sergio. *Lo que no entra en el crisol: inmigración boliviana, comunicación intercultural y procesos identitarios.* Buenos Aires: Prometeo, 2005.

Carr, Barry. "'Omnipotent and Omnipresent'? Labor Shortages, Worker Mobility, and Employer Control in the Cuban Sugar Industry." In *Identity and Struggle at the Margins of the Nation-State: The Laboring People of the Central America and the Hispanic Caribbean*, edited by Aviva Chomsky and Aldo Lauria Santiago, 260–291. Durham, N.C.: Duke University Press, 1998.

Castellanos, Israel. "Anomalia Atávica en el Occipital de un criminal." *Vida Nueva* 6 (1914): 222–225.

———. "Los Chinos en Cuba: su criminalidad." *Gaceta Médica del Sur* 33, no. 4 (1915): 74.

———. "La forma geométrica de la cara en los delincuentes Cubanos." *Gaceta Médica del Sur* 22 (1915): 217–219.

———. "Los músculos faciales y la fisonomía de un delincuente." *Vida Nueva* 34 (1916): 30–33.

———. *La brujería y el Ñañiguismo Bajo el punto de vista medico-legal.* Havana: Imp. Del Lloredo, 1916.

———. "Confidencias de Israel Castellanos, de la Habana." *Higia* 2 (1917): 307–316.

Castle, William R. "Shall Opium Be Licensed? Opium in Hawaii." In *Kalakaua's Hawaii, 1874–1891 [microform]: A Collection of Pamphlets Dealing with the Political, Social, and Economic History of Hawaii during the Reign of King Kalakaua and the Many Controversies of the Period.* Honolulu: Hawaiian Historical Society, 1968.

Castles, Stephen, and Alastair Davidson. *Citizenship and Migration: Globalisation and the Politics of Belonging.* London: Macmillan, 2000.

Cham, Asiroh. "Negotiating (In)Visibility in the Cham American Diaspora." Master's thesis, University of California, 2012.

Chang, David W. "Current Status of Chinese Minorities in Southeast Asia." *Asia Survey* 13, no. 6 (1973): 587–603.

Chang, Kornel. "Circulating Race and Empire: Transnational Labor Activism and the Politics of Anti-Asian Agitation in the Anglophone Pacific World, 1880–1910." *Journal of American History* 96, no. 3 (2009): 678–701.

Chatterjee, Nandini. "Muslim or Christian? Family Quarrels and Religious Diagnosis in a Colonial Court." *American Historical Review* 117, no. 4 (2012): 1101–1122.

Cheng, Christopher David. "Japanese Cubans: Past, Present, and Future." Directed M.A. Study submitted to the Monterey Institute of International Studies in partial fulfillment of the requirements for the degree of International Policy Studies, Graduate School of International Policy Studies, December 19, 2006.

Chomsky, Aviva. "'Barbados or Canada?' Race, Immigration, and Nation in Early Twentieth-Century Cuba." *Hispanic American Historical Review* 80 (2000): 415–462.

Chun, James H. *The Early Chinese in Punaluu.* Honolulu: Yin Sit Sha, 1983.

Clemens, Elisabeth S. "Securing Political Returns to Social Capital: Women's Associations in the United States, 1880s–1920s." In *Patterns of Social Capital: Stability and Change in Historical Perspective*, edited by Robert I. Rotberg, 247–272. Cambridge: Cambridge University Press, 2001.

Corbitt, Duvon C. "Chinese Immigrants in Cuba." *Far Eastern Survey* 13, no. 14 (1944): 130–132.

Córdova y Quesada, Federico. "Clase y procedencia de la inmigración que debe proteger el estado." In *Memoria oficial. Quinta conferencia nacional de beneficencia y corrección de la isla de Cuba, celebrada en Santiago de Cuba del 14 al 16 de abril de 1906*, edited by Jorge Dehogues, 385–392. Havana: Librería "La Moderna Poesia," 1906.

Coyula, Mario, Miguel Coyula, and Rosa Oliveras. *Towards a New Kind of Community in Havana: The Workshops for Integrated Neighborhood Transformation.* Havana: GDIC, 2001.

Delgado, Kevin M. "Spiritual Capital: Foreign Patronage and the Trafficking of Santería." In *Cuba in the Special Period: Culture and Ideology in the 1990s*, edited by Ariana Hernández-Reguant, 51–66. New York: Palgrave Macmillan, 2009.

Duara, Prasenjit. "Between Sovereignty and Capitalism: The Historical Experiences of Migrant Chinese." In *Diasporic Histories: Cultural Archives of Chinese Transnationalism*, edited by Andrea Riemenschnitter and Deborah L. Madsen, 95–110. Aberdeen, Hong Kong: Hong Kong University Press, 2009.

Dye, Bob. *Merchant Prince of the Sandalwood Mountains: Afong and the Chinese in Hawaii.* Honolulu: University of Hawaii Press, 1997.

Eng Herrera, Pedro, and Mauro G. García. *Martí en los chinos, los chinos en Martí*. Havana: Grupo Promotor del Barrio Chino de la Habana, 2003.

Erel, Umut. "Migrating Cultural Capital: Bourdieu in Migration Studies." *Sociology* 44, no. 4 (August 2010): 642–660.

Espinosa, Mariola. *Epidemic Invasions: Yellow Fever and the Limits of Cuban Independence, 1878–1930*. Chicago: University of Chicago Press, 2009.

Espinosa Luis, Mitzi. "Si tú pleguntá, a mi me gusta hacer cuento: Felipe Luis narrates his story." In *The Chinese in the Caribbean*, edited by Andrew R. Wilson, 129–142. Princeton: Markus Wiener, 2004.

Estévez, Rolando Álvarez. *Presencia Japonesa en Cuba: centenario del inicia de las relaciones entre Cuba y Japón*. Havana: Ediciones GEO/Fundación Fernando Ortiz, 2003.

Fedderke, Johannes, Raphael de Kadt, and John Luiz. "Economic Growth and Social Capital: A Critical Reflection." *Theory and Society* 28, no. 5 (October 1999): 709–745.

Fernández, Juan Santos. "Clase y procedencia del inmigrante que debe proteger el estado." In *Memoria oficial. Quinta conferencia nacional de beneficencia y corrección de la isla de Cuba, celebrada en Santiago de Cuba del 14 al 16 de abril de 1906*, edited by Jorge Dehogues, 367–384. Havana: Librería "La Moderna Poesia," 1906.

———. "La Inmigración." *Anales de la Academia de las Ciencias de la Habana* 43 (1906): 4–25.

A Flicker in Eternity. Directed by Ann Kaneko and Sharon Yamato. Los Angeles: Ann Kaneko/Sharon Yamato, 2013. DVD.

Foster, Anne L. "Models for Governing: Opium and Colonial Policies in Southeast Asia, 1898–1910." In *The American Colonial State in the Philippines: Global Perspectives*, edited by Anne L. Foster and Julian Go, 92–117. Durham, N.C.: Duke University Press, 2003.

Fox, Jonathan. "How Does Civil Society Thicken? The Political Construction of Social Capital in Rural Mexico." *World Development* 24 (1996): 1089–1103.

Friedman, May, and Silvia Schultermandl, eds. *Growing up Transnational: Identity and Kinship in a Global Era*. Toronto: University of Toronto Press, 2011.

Fuentes, Leonardo Padura. *El viaje más largo*. Havana: Ediciones Unión, 1994.

Fung, Archon, David Weil, Mary Graham, and Elena Fagotto. *The Political Economy of Transparency: What Makes Disclosure Policies Effective?* Harvard University, John F. Kennedy School of Government, 2004.

Galeano, Eduardo. *The Book of Embraces*. Translated by Cedric Belfrage. New York: W. W. Norton and Company, 1991.

Gibson, Walter Murray. "Address to the Hawaiian People." In *Kalakaua's Hawaii, 1874–1891: A Collection of Pamphlets Dealing with the Political, Social and Economic History of Hawaii during the Reign of King Kalakaua and the Many Controversies of the Period*. Honolulu: Hawaiian Historical Society, 1968.

———. *Sanitary Instructions for Hawaiians*. Honolulu: J. H. Black, 1879.

Glick, Clarence E. *Sojourners and Settlers: Chinese Migrants in Hawaii*. Honolulu: University of Hawaii Press, 1980.

Gómez, Andrés Galera. "El resurgir de una nueva escuela: Israel Castellanos y el atavismo del delito." *Asclepio* 15, no. 2 (1988): 81–97.

Goossaert, V. "1898: The Beginning of the End for Chinese Religion?" *Journal of Asian Studies, Ann Arbor* 65, no. 2 (2006): 307–336.

Graham, Mary. *Information as Risk Regulation: Lessons from Experience*. Harvard University, John F. Kennedy School of Government, 2001.

Grimson, Alejandro. *Relatos de la diferencia y la igualdad*. Buenos Aires: Eudeba, 1999.

Grupo para el Desarrollo Integral de la Capital. *La maqueta de La Habana*. Havana: GDIC, 2001.

Guerra, Lillian. *The Myth of José Martí: Conflicting Nationalisms in Early Twentieth-Century Cuba*. Chapel Hill: University of North Carolina Press, 2005.

Guiteras, Juan. "La imigración china y el Canal de Panama." *Reforma social: revista mensual de cuestiones sociales, económicas, políticas, parlamentarias, estadísticas y de higiene pública* 1, no. 1 (1914): 1–6. First published as "La inmigración china" in *Anales de la Academia de Ciencias Médicas, Físicas, y Naturales de la Habana* 50 (1913): 558.

Hall, Stuart. "Cultural Identity and Diaspora." *Framework: The Journal of Cinema and Media* 36 (1989): 222–237.

———. "New Ethnicities." In *Colonial Discourse and Postcolonial Theory*, edited by Patrick Williams and Laura Chrisman, 223–227. New York: Columbia University Press, 1994.

Halpern, Gerardo. *Etnicidad, inmigración y política: representaciones y cultura política de exiliados Paraguayos en Argentina*. Buenos Aires: Prometeo, 2009.

Hearn, Adrian H. *Cuba: Religion, Social Capital, and Development*. Durham, N.C.: Duke University Press, 2008.

———. "Harnessing the Dragon: Overseas Entrepreneurs in Mexico and Cuba." *China Quarterly* 209 (2012): 111–133.

———. "Transformation: Transcendence or Transculturation? The Many Faces of Cuban Santería." *Humanities Research* 10, no. 1 (2003): 56–62.

Helg, Aline. *Our Rightful Share: The Afro-Cuban Struggle for Equality, 1886–1912*. Chapel Hill: University of North Carolina Press, 1995.

Hempenstall, Peter. "Imperial Maneuvers." In *Tides of History: The Pacific Islands in the Twentieth Century*, edited by K. R. Howe, Robert C. Kiste, and Brij V. Lal, 29–39. Honolulu: University of Hawaii Press, 1994.

Higa, Marcelo G. "The Emigration of Argentines of Japanese Descent to Japan." In *New Worlds, New Lives: Globalization and People of Japanese Descent in the Americas and from Latin America in Japan*, edited by Lane Ryo Hirabayashi, Akemi Kikumura-Yano, and James A. Hirabayashi, 261–278. Stanford, CA: Stanford University Press, 2002.

Hilgers, Tina. "Recentering Informality on the Research Agenda: Grassroots Action, Political Parties, and Democratic Governance." *Latin American Research Review* 43, no. 2 (2008): 272–281.

Hira, Anil. *An East Asian Model for Latin American Success*. London: Ashgate, 2007.

Hirabayashi, Lane Ryo. *The Politics of Fieldwork: Research in an American Concentration Camp*. Tucson: University of Arizona Press, 1999.

Hirabayashi, Lane Ryo, Akemi Kikumura-Yano, and James A. Hirabayashi, eds. *New Worlds, New Lives: Globalization and People of Japanese Descent in the Americas and from Latin America in Japan*. Stanford, Calif.: Stanford University Press, 2002.

Hoeg, Jerry. "Cultural Counterpoint: Antonio Benítez Rojo's Postmodern Transculturation." *Journal of Latin American Cultural Studies* 6, no. 1 (1997): 65–75.

Hu-Dehart, Evelyn. *Across the Pacific: Asian Americans and Globalization*. Philadelphia: Temple University Press, 1999.

———. "Latin America in Asia-Pacific Perspective." In *Asian Diasporas: New Formations, New Conceptions*, edited by Rhacel S. Parreñas and Lok C. D. Siu, 29–62. Stanford, Calif.: Stanford University Press, 2007.

———. "Indispensable Enemy or Convenient Scapegoat? A Critical Examination of Sinophobia in Latin America and the Caribbean, 1870s to 1930s." In *The Chinese in Latin America and the Caribbean*, edited by Walton Look Lai and Tan Chee-Beng, 67–109. Leiden: Brill, 2010.

Iglesia, Cristina, and Julio Schvartzman. *Cautivas y misioneros: mitos blancos de la conquista.* Buenos Aires: Catálogos, 1987.

Instituto Nacional de Estadísticas y Geografía (INEGI). "Censo de población y vivienda 2010." Accessed October 11, 2011. www.inegi.org.mx.

Ishikawa, Juan Ryusuke. "The Brazilian Saijiki: Beyond Agricultural Practices." Paper presented at the Annual Conference of the Association of Asian American Studies, Austin, Texas, April 2010.

Jerez, Miriam Herrera, and Mario Castillo Santana. *De la memoria a la vida pública: identidades, espacios, y jerarquía de los Chinos en la Habana Republicana, 1902–1968.* Havana: Centro de Investigación y Desarrollo de la Cultura Cubana Juan Marinello, 2003.

"Jia Qinglin Voices Five-Point Hope for Overseas Chinese." *Xinhua*, September 15, 2007. Accessed June 19, 2011. http://news.xinhuanet.com/english/2007-09/15/content_6729877.htm.

Jordan, David K. *Gods, Ghosts, and Ancestors: The Folk Religion of a Taiwanese Village.* Berkeley: University of California Press, 1972.

Jung, Moon-ho. *Coolies and Cane: Race, Labor, and Sugar in the Age of Emancipation.* Baltimore: Johns Hopkins University Press, 2006.

Kalakaua's Hawaii, 1874–1891 [microform]: a collection of pamphlets dealing with the political, social and economic history of Hawaii during the reign of King Kalakaua and the many controversies of the period. Honolulu: Hawaiian Historical Society, 1968.

Kame'eleihiwa, Lilikalā. *Native Land and Foreign Desires.* Honolulu: Bishop Museum, 1992.

Kuykendall, Ralph S. *The Hawaiian Kingdom*, Volume 3: *1874–1893, The Kalakaua Dynasty.* Honolulu: University of Hawaii Press, 1967.

Lai, Violet K. *He Was a Ram: Wong Aloiau of Hawaii.* Honolulu: University of Hawaii Press, 1985.

Lai, Walton Look. *Indentured Labor, Caribbean Sugar: Chinese and Indian Migrants to the British West Indies, 1838–1918.* Baltimore: Johns Hopkins University Press, 1993.

Lee, Erika. "The Chinese Exclusion Example: Race, Immigration, and American Gatekeeping, 1882–1924." *Journal of American Ethnic History* 21, no. 2 (2002): 36–62.

———. *At America's Gates: Chinese Immigration during the Exclusion Era, 1882–1943.* Chapel Hill: University of North Carolina Press, 2004.

Lee, Kyo Bum. *Hanin imin 25 nyeonsa.* Seoul: Sunyoungsa, 1992.

Lee, Peter. *Opium Culture: The Art and Ritual of the Chinese Tradition.* Rochester, Vt.: Park Street Press, 2006.

Lee-DiStefano, Debra. "Siu Kam Wen and the Subjectification of Chinese Peruvians in 'El tramo final.'" In *Orientalism and Identity in Latin America: Fashioning Self and Other from the (Post)Colonial Margin*, edited by Erik Camayd-Freixas, 188–199. Tucson: University of Arizona Press, 2013.

Lesser, Jeffrey. *Negotiating National Identity: Immigrants, Minorities, and the Struggle for Ethnicity in Brazil.* Durham, N.C.: Duke University Press, 1999.

———, ed. *Searching for Home Abroad: Japanese Brazilians and Transnationalism.* Durham: Duke University Press, 2003.

———. *A Discontented Diaspora: Japanese Brazilians and the Meanings of Ethnic Militancy, 1960–1980.* Durham, N.C.: Duke University Press, 2007.

———. "Ethnic Myths as National Identity in Brazil." In *National Myths: Constructed Pasts, Contested Presents*, edited by Gérard Bouchard, 65–75. New York: Routledge, 2013.

———. *Immigration, Ethnicity, and National Identity in Brazil, 1808 to the Present.* New York: Cambridge University Press, 2013.

Lim-Chong, Lily, and Harry V. Ball. "Opium and the Law: Hawai'i, 1856–1900." *Chinese America: History & Perspectives—The Journal of the Chinese Historical Society of America* (2010): 61–74.

Lin, Nan. *Social Capital: A Theory of Social Structure and Action.* Cambridge: Cambridge University Press, 2001.

Linnekin, Jocelyn. *Sacred Queens and Women of Consequence: Rank, Gender, and Colonialism in the Hawaiian Islands.* Ann Arbor: University of Michigan Press, 1990.

Long, Carolyn Morrow. *Spiritual Merchants: Religion, Magic, and Commerce.* Knoxville: University of Tennessee Press, 2001.

Look Lai, Walton. *Indentured Labor, Caribbean Sugar: Chinese and Indian Migrants to the British West Indies, 1838–1918.* Baltimore: Johns Hopkins University Press, 1993.

Look Lai, Walton, and Tan Chee-Beng. *The Chinese in Latin America and the Caribbean.* Leiden, The Netherlands: Brill, 2010.

López, Guadalupe. "Expanden cultura China." *Frontera*, February 12, 2009.

López, Johnny. "El Chinito Pichilón." Musical recording, New York: Decca [format: 78–10, publish # 21266–1], 1942.

López, Kathleen. "'One Brings Another': The Formation of Early-Twentieth-Century Chinese Migrant Communities in Cuba." In *The Chinese in the Caribbean*, edited by Andrew R. Wilson, 93–127. Princeton, NJ: Markus Wiener, 2004.

———. "The Revitalization of Havana's Chinatown: Invoking Chinese Cuban History." *Journal of Chinese Overseas* 5, no. 1 (2009): 177–200.

———. *Chinese Cubans: A Transnational History.* Chapel Hill: University of North Carolina Press, 2013.

López, Mario. "Cambian giros de comercios a bodegas." *Reforma* (June 5, 2006): 6.

López-Calvo, Ignacio, ed. *Alternative Orientalisms in Latin America and Beyond.* Newcastle: Cambridge Scholars Pub., 2007.

———. *Imagining the Chinese in Cuban Literature and Culture.* Gainesville: University Press of Florida, 2008.

———, ed. *Peripheral Transmodernities: South-to-South Intercultural Dialogues between the Luso-Hispanic World and 'The Orient.'* Newcastle upon Tyne: Cambridge Scholars Pub., 2012.

———. *The Affinity of the Eye: Writing Nikkei in Peru.* Tucson: University of Arizona Press, 2013.

———. *Dragons in the Land of the Condor: Writing Tusán in Peru.* Tucson: University of Arizona Press, 2014.

López del Valle, José. "Biografía del Dr. Juan Guiteras Gener." In *Papeles del Dr. Juan Guiteras*, 7–26. Havana: Consejo Científico, Ministerio de Salud Pública, 1962.

Lopez-Levy, Arturo. *Change in Post-Fidel Cuba: Political Liberalization, Economic Reform and Lessons for U.S. Policy.* Washington, DC: New America Foundation, 2011.

Lowe, Lisa. *Immigrant Acts: On Asian American Cultural Politics.* Durham, N.C.: Duke University Press, 1996.

Mariátegui, José Carlos. *Seven Interpretive Essays on Peruvian Reality.* [1928]. Trans. Marjory Uriquidi. Austin: University of Texas Press, 1971.

Martín, Juan Luis. *De dónde vinieron los Chinos de Cuba: Los Jaca, los Joló, los Puntí y los Amoyanos, en la vida Cubana.* Havana: Editorial Atalaya, 1939.

Martínez-Alier, Verena. *Marriage, Class, and Colour in Nineteenth-Century Cuba: A Study of Racial Attitudes and Sexual Values in a Slave Society.* 2nd ed. London: Cambridge University Press, 1989.

Masterson, Daniel M., and Sayaka Funada-Classen. *The Japanese in Latin America.* Chicago: University of Illinois Press, 2004.

Matsuda, Matt. *Pacific Worlds: A History of Seas, Peoples, and Cultures*. Cambridge: Cambridge University Press, 2012.

McGregor, Davianna Pōmaika'i. *Nā Kua'āina: Living Hawaiian Culture*. Honolulu: University of Hawaii Press, 2007.

McKeown, Adam M. *Chinese Migrant Networks and Cultural Change: Peru, Chicago, and Hawaii, 1900–1938*. Chicago: University of Chicago Press, 2001.

McLeod, Marc. "Undesirable Aliens: Race, Ethnicity, and Nationalism in the Comparison of Haitian and British West Indian Immigrant Workers in Cuba, 1912–1939." *Journal of Social History* 31 (1998): 599–623.

———. "'We Cubans Are Obligated Like Cats to Have a Straight Face': Malaria, Quarantine, and Race in Neocolonial Cuba, 1898–1940." *The Americas* 67, no. 1 (2010): 57–81.

Mejía, Javier. "Festejó Asociación China la 'Semana de Migración.'" *La Voz de la Frontera*, October 24, 2008. Accessed February 15, 2015. http://www.oem.com.mx/esto/notas/n904413.htm.

———. "Prometen a Chinos traer a sus familias." *La Crónica*, October 24, 2008.

Meulenbeld, Mark. "Chinese Religion in the Ming and Qing Dynasties." In *The Wiley-Blackwell Companion to Chinese Religions*, edited by Randall L. Nadeau, 125–144. Chichester: Blackwell Publishing, 2012.

Minor, Milthon. "Abren en Mexicali cámara de empresarios Chinos del noroeste." *Frontera*, March 6, 2010.

Miyazawa, Júlio. *Yawara! A travessia Nihondin-Brasil*. São Paulo: self-published, 2006.

———. Uma Rosa para Yumi. São Paulo: self-published, 2014.

———. "Sem a Sua História a Minha . . ." Centenário da Imigração Japonesa: Projeto incorporado ao Museu Histórico da Imigração Japonesa no Brasil. June 25, 2014.

Mondragón, Santos. "Ambulantes invaden el Centro Histórico." *Noticieros Televisa*, December 25, 2006, http://www.esmas.com/noticierostelevisa/mexico/591949.html.

Montes de Oca Choy, María Teresa. *Las sociedades Chinas en Cuba: pasado y presente*. La Habana: Universidad de La Habana, 2007.

Morales, Catalina Velázquez. *Los inmigrantes Chinos en Baja California 1920–1937*. Mexicali: Universidad Autónoma de Baja California, 2001.

Murphy, Joseph M. "Objects That Speak Creole: Juxtapositions of Shrine Devotions at Botánicas in Washington, DC." *Material Religion: The Journal of Objects, Art, and Belief* 6, no. 1 (2010): 86–108.

———. *Botánicas: Sacred Spaces of Healing and Devotion in Urban America*. Jackson: University Press of Mississippi, 2015.

Naficy, Hamid. *An Accented Cinema: Exilic and Diasporic Filmmaking*. Princeton: Princeton University Press, 2001.

Naik, Panna. *Attar-Akshar: Haikus in Gujarati*. Mumbai: Image Publishing Pvt. Ltd., 2011.

———. *Japanese Maple Gulmahorthi Daffodils*. Bombay: Image Publications, 2012.

Nakasato, Oscar. *Nihonjin*. São Paulo: Benvirá, 2011.

Navejas, Francisco Haro. "El dominio de las emociones: percepciones Mexicanas sobre China." In *China y México: implicaciones de una nueva relación*, edited by Enrique Dussel Peters and Yolanda Trápaga Delfín, 455–471. Mexico City: La Jornada Publishers, 2007.

———. "China's Relations with Central America and the Caribbean States: Reshaping the Region." In *China Engages Latin America: Tracing the Trajectory*, edited by Adrian H. Hearn and José Luis León Manríquez, 209–210. Boulder, Colo.: Lynne Rienner Publishers, 2011.

Ngai, Mae. "Legacies of Exclusion: Illegal Chinese Immigration during the Cold War Years." *Journal of American Ethnic History* 18, no. 1 (1998): 3–35.

Nitobe, Inazo. *Bushido: The Soul of Japan*. N.p.: The Floating Press, 2008. Digital file. Web. June 25, 2014.

Nonini, Donald M., and Aiwha Ong. "Chinese Transnationality as an Alternative Modernity." In *The Chinese Overseas: Routledge Library of Modern China*, Vol. 1: *Conceptualizing and Historicizing Chinese International Migration*, ed. Hong Liu. London: Routledge, 2006.

O'Donnell, Guillermo. "Informal Institutions, Once Again." In *Informal Institutions and Democracy: Lessons from Latin America*, edited by Gretchen Helmke and Steven Levitsky, 285–290. Baltimore: Johns Hopkins University Press, 2006.

Okihiro, Gary Y. *Cane Fires: The Anti-Japanese Movement in Hawaii, 1865–1945*. Philadelphia: Temple University Press, 1991.

———. *Common Ground: Reimagining American History*. Princeton: Princeton University Press, 2001.

———. *Pineapple Culture: A History of the Tropical and Temperate Zones*. Berkeley: University of California Press, 2009.

Oppenheim, Joanne. "Project Purpose." California State Library: California Civil Liberties Public Education Program Grant, 2009/10.

Oppenheimer, Andrés. "La gran esperanza de México: Lograr tener 5 millones de Norteamericanos retirados." *Excelsior*, April 30, 2010.

Oréfiche, Armando. "Chino Li-Wong." Musical recording (with Billo's Caracas Boys), Venezuela: Billo's [format: 78–10, publish # 4056–1], 1953.

Ortiz, Fernando. "Consideraciones criminológicas positivistas acerca de la inmigración en Cuba." In *Memoria oficial: quinta conferencia de beneficencia y corrección de la isla de Cuba*, edited by Jorge Dehogues. Havana: La Moderna Poesía, 1906, 343–344. Reprinted as "La inmigración desde el punto de vista criminológico," in *Derecho y sociología* 1, no. 5 (1906): 54–64.

———.*Hampa afro-cubana: los negros brujos (apuntes para un estudio de etnología criminal)*. Miami: Ediciones Universal, 1973 [1906].

———. "El peligro amarillo." *Cuba y América* 25, no. 15 (January 22, 1908).

———. *La identificación dactiloscópica. Informe de policiologia y de derecho public*. Havana: Imprenta la Universal, 1913.

Ortiz, Fernando, and Harriet De Onis, *Cuban Counterpoint: Tobacco and Sugar*. New York: A. A. Knopf, 1947.

Osorio, Consuelo Naranjo, and Armando García Martínez, eds. *Medicina y racismo en Cuba: la Ciencia ante la Immigración Canaria en el Siglo XX*. La Laguna: Taller de Historia, 1996.

Osorio, Jonathan Kay Kamakawiwo'ole. *Dismembering Lahui: A History of the Hawaiian Nation to 1887*. Honolulu: University of Hawaii Press, 2002.

Overstay. Directed by Ann Kaneko. 1998. Los Angeles: Ann Kaneko, 2005. DVD.

Palmié, Stephan. "Against Syncretism: 'Africanizing' and 'Cubanizing' Discourses in North American Òrìsà Worship." In *Counterworks: Managing the Diversity of Knowledge*, edited by R. Fardon, 80–104. London: Routledge, 1995.

———. *Wizards and Scientists: Explorations in Afro-Cuban Modernity and Tradition*. Durham, N.C.: Duke University Press, 2002.

———. *The Cooking of History: How Not to Study Afro-Cuban Religion*. Chicago: University of Chicago Press, 2013.

Pan, Lynn. *Sons of the Yellow Emperor: A History of the Chinese Diaspora*. Boston: Little, Brown, 1990.

Park, Kyeyoung. *The Korean American Dream: Immigrants and Small Business in New York City*. Ithaca, N.Y.: Cornell University Press, 1997.

Pavez Ojeda, Jorge. *Cartas Mapuche: Siglo XIX*. Vol. 2. Santiago de Chile: CoLibris & Ocholibros & Fondo de Publicaciones Americanistas & Laboratorio de Desclasificación Comparada, Colección de Documentos para la Historia Mapuche, 2008.

Peel, J.D.Y. *Religious Encounter and the Making of the Yoruba*. Bloomington: Indiana University Press, 2000.

Pérez, Louis A. *Cuba under the Platt Amendment, 1902–1934*. Pittsburgh: University of Pittsburgh Press, 1986.

Pérez, Pelayo. "El peligro amarillo y el peligro negro." *Cuba contemporánea* 9, no. 3 (1915): 257.

Pérez, Ricardo Torres. "La actualización del modelo económico cubano: continuidad y ruptura." *Temas* (2011). Accessed June 17, 2011. http://www.temas.cult.cu/catalejo/economia/Ricardo_Torres.pdf.

Pérez de la Riva, Juan, ed. *La républica neocolonial: anuario de estudios Cubanos*. Havana: Instituto Cubano del Libro, Editorial de Ciencias Sociales, 1975.

Pichardo, Hortencia, ed. *Documentos para la historia de Cuba*. Havana: Editorial de Ciencias Sociales, 1969.

Portes, Alejandro. "Social Capital: Its Origins and Applications in Modern Sociology." *Annual Review of Sociology* 24 (1998): 1–24.

Portes, Alejandro, and Julia Sensenbrenner. "Embeddedness and Immigration: Notes on the Social Determinants of Economic Action." *American Journal of Sociology* 98, no. 6 (1993): 1320–1350.

Putnam, Robert D. *Bowling Alone: The Collapse and Revival of American Community*. New York: Simon and Schuster, 2000.

———. "E Pluribus Unum: Diversity and Community in the Twenty-first Century." *Scandinavian Political Studies* 30, no. 2 (2007): 138.

Report of the Minister of Foreign Affairs to the Hawaiian Legislature, Session of 1888. Honolulu: Pacific Commercial Advertiser Steam Print, 1888.

Report of the Special Committee on Opium to the Legislature of 1892. Honolulu, 1892.

"Retiring Americans: Go South, Old Man." *The Economist*, November 24, 2005. Accessed October 10, 2011. www.economist.com/node/5214922.

Rhodes, Godfrey. *Thoughts on the Hawaiian Situation, by a Member of the House of Nobles*. Honolulu: Pacific Commercial Advertiser Steam Print, 1881.

Robinson, St. John. "The Chinese of Central America: Diverse Beginnings, Common Achievements." In *The Chinese in Latin America and the Caribbean*, edited by Walton Look Lai and Tan Chee-Beng, 103–128. Leiden: Brill, 2010.

Román, Reinaldo. *Governing Spirits: Religion, Miracles, and Spectacles in Cuba and Puerto Rico, 1898–1956*. Chapel Hill: University of North Carolina Press, 2007.

Ross, Andrew. *No Sweat: Fashion, Free Trade, and the Rights of Garment Workers*. New York: Verso, 1997.

Rotker, Susana. *Cautivas: olvidos y memoria en la Argentina*. Buenos Aires: Ariel, 1999.

Rush, James R. "Social Control and Influence in Nineteenth-Century Indonesia: Opium Farms and the Chinese of Java." *Indonesia* 35 (1983): 53–64.

Rustomji-Kerns, Roshni, ed. *Living in America: Poetry and Fiction by South Asian American Writers*. Boulder, Colo.: Westview Press, 1995.

Rustomji-Kerns, Roshni, Rajini Srikanth, and Leny Mendoza Strobel, eds. *Encounters: People of Asian Descent in the Americas*. Lanham, Md.: Rowman & Littlefield, 1999.

Salinas, Daniel. "Buscan crear barrio chino en la 'Revu,'" *Frontera*, March 1, 2008.

Salvatore, Ricardo, and Carlos Aguirre, eds. *The Birth of the Penitentiary in Latin America: Essays on Criminology, Prison Reform, and Social Control, 1830–1940*. Austin: University of Texas Press, 1996.

Salvatore, Ricardo, Carlos Aguirre, and Gilbert Joseph, eds. *Crime and Punishment in Latin America: Law and Society since Late Colonial Times.* Durham, N.C.: Duke University Press, 2001.

Salyer, Lucy. *Laws Harsh as Tigers: Chinese Immigrants and the Shaping of Modern Immigration Law.* Chapel Hill: University of North Carolina Press, 1995.

Sánchez, Luz María Fornieles. "El Barrio Chino." *Contrapunto* 3, no. 27 (1993): 25–26.

Sangren, Paul Steven. *History and Magical Power in a Chinese Community.* Stanford, Calif.: Stanford University Press, 1987.

Sarmiento, Domingo Faustino. *Obras*, Vol. 23. Buenos Aires: Luz del día, 1951.

Sassen, Saskia. *Globalization and Its Discontents: Essays on the New Mobility of People and Money.* New York: The New Press, 1998.

Scherer, Frank F. "Sanfancón: Orientalism, Self-Orientalization, and 'Chinese Religion' in Cuba." In *Nation Dance: Religion, Identity, and Cultural Difference in the Caribbean*, edited by P. Taylor, 153–170. Bloomington: Indiana University Press, 2001.

Segato, Rita Laura. *La nación y sus otros: Raza, etnicidad y diversidad religiosa en tiempos de políticas de la identidad.* Buenos Aires: Prometeo, 2007.

Shah, Nayan. *Contagious Divides: Epidemics and Race in San Francisco's Chinatown.* Berkeley: University of California Press, 2001.

Shixue, Jiang. *Cuba's Economic Reforms in Chinese Perspective.* Beijing: Chinese Academy of Social Sciences, 2009.

Silva, Noenoe K. *Aloha Betrayed: Native Hawaiian Resistance to American Colonialism.* Durham, N.C.: Duke University Press, 2004.

Silveira, Guto. "Ex-guerrilheiro retorna a Ribeirão Preto após 60 anos." *Revista Epoca*, February 27, 2011. Accessed July 12, 2014. http://portal.rac.com.br/noticias/index_teste.php?tp=brasil&id=/76565&ano=/2011&mes=/02&dia=/27&titulo=/ex-guerrilheiro-retorna-a-ribeirao-preto-apos-60-anos.

Sing-Wu, Wang. *The Organization of Chinese Emigration 1848–88.* San Francisco: Chinese Materials Center Inc., 1978.

Smart, Alan, and Jinn Yuh Hsu. "The Chinese Diaspora, Foreign Investment, and Economic Development in China." *Review of International Affairs* 3, no. 4 (2004): 544–566.

Smart, Ninian. "The Importance of Diasporas." In *Migration, Diasporas, and Transnationalism*, edited by Steven Vertovec and Robin Cohen, 420–429. Cheltenham: Edward Elgar, 1999.

Squires, Z. Y. "The Planter's Mongolian Pets; or, Human Decoy Act." Honolulu, 1884.

Steele, James W. *Cuban Sketches.* New York: G. P. Putnam's Sons, 1881.

Steinmetz, George. *The Devil's Handwriting: Precoloniality and the German Colonial State in Qingdao, Samoa, and Southwest Africa.* Chicago: University of Chicago Press, 2007.

Stewart, Charles. "Relocating Syncretism in Social Science Discourse." In *Syncretism and the Commerce of Symbols*, ed. Göran Ajimer, 13–37. Göteborg: Institute for Advanced Studies in Social Anthropology (IASSA), 1995.

Strauss, Julia C., and Martha Saavedra, eds. "China and Africa: Emerging Patterns in Globalization and Development." *China Quarterly* 199 (2009).

Tamayo, Diego. "Necesidad de asociaciones particulares de carácter filantrópico que protejan a determinados inmigrantes." In *Memoria oficial: quinta conferencia de beneficencia y corrección de la isla de Cuba*, edited by Jorge Dehogues, 337–338. Havana: La Moderna Poesía, 1906.

Torriente, Cosme de la. *Cuarenta años de mi vida, 1898–1938.* Havana: Imprenta El Siglo, 1939.

Trocki, Carl. *Opium, Empire, and the Global Political Economy: A Study of the Asian Opium Trade, 1750–1950.* London: Routledge, 1999.

Tsuda, Takeyuki. *Strangers in the Ethnic Homeland: Japanese Brazilian Return Migration in Transnational Perspective*. New York: Columbia University Press, 2003.

United Nations Development Programme. *Human Development Index 2010*. New York: Palgrave Macmillan, 2010.

Vasconcelos, José. *The Cosmic Race/La raza cósmica*. [1925]. Trans. Didier T. Jaén. Baltimore and London: The Johns Hopkins University Press, 1979.

Viñas, David. *Indios, ejército y frontera*. [1982]. Buenos Aires: Santiago Arcos, 2003.

Weil, David. *The Benefits and Costs of Transparency: A Model of Disclosure Based Regulation*. Harvard University, John F. Kennedy School of Government, 2002.

Whitten, Norman E., and Rachel Corr. "Indigenous Constructions of 'Blackness." In *Histories of the Present: People and Power in Ecuador*, edited by Norman E. Whitten Jr. and Dorothea Scott Whitten, 45–64. Urbana: University of Illinois Press, 2011.

Yahuda, Michael. *Towards the End of Isolationism: China's Foreign Policy after Mao*. New York: Palgrave Macmillan, 1985.

Yale University. "Environmental Performance Index 2010." Accessed June 16, 2011. http://epi.yale.edu.

Yan, Yunxiang. *The Individualization of Chinese Society*. New York: Berg, 2009.

Yelvington, Kevin A. "The Invention of Africa in Latin America and the Caribbean: Political Discourse and Anthropological Praxis, 1920–1940." In *Afro-Atlantic Dialogues: Anthropology in the Diaspora*, edited by Kevin Yelvington, 35–82. Oxford: James Currey, 2006.

Yinghong, Cheng. "Fidel Castro and 'China's Lessons for Cuba': A Chinese Perspective." *China Quarterly* 189 (2007): 40.

Yúdice, George. *El recurso de la cultura: usos de la cultura en la era global*. Barcelona: Gedisa, 2002.

Yun, Lisa. "An Afro-Chinese Caribbean: Cultural Cartographies of Contrariness in the Work of Antonio Chuffat Latour, Margaret Cezair-Thompson, and Patricia Powell." *Caribbean Quarterly* 50, no. 2 (2004): 26–43.

———. *The Coolie Speaks Chinese Indentured Laborers and African Slaves in Cuba*. Philadelphia: Temple University Press, 2008.

Zhan, Lisheng. "Event Lauds Role of Overseas Chinese." *China Daily*, December 4, 2002. Accessed June 19, 2011. www.highbeam.com/doc/1P2-8797193.html.

NOTES ON CONTRIBUTORS

JOSÉ AMADOR is an associate professor of Latin American, Latino/a, and Caribbean studies at Miami University, Ohio. He specializes in the history of race, gender, and public health in Latin America, with an emphasis on imperial and transnational histories. He is the author of *Medicine and Nation Building in the Americas, 1890–1940* (2015), which received the Norman L. and Roselea J. Goldberg Prize for best book in the area of medicine. He is the coeditor of *Historia y memoria: sociedad, cultura y vida cotidiana en Cuba* (2003), with Fernando Coronil. He has received fellowships from the Ford Foundation, the Rockefeller Archive Center, and the Caribbean Exchange Program at CUNY. His current book-length study focuses on health rights and transgender activism in Brazil.

Associate Professor **ADRIAN H. HEARN** (University of Melbourne) is an anthropologist who examines international relations from the ground up. His work explores China's relations with Latin America and Australia through emerging small business initiatives in Cuba, Chinatowns in Mexico, and agriculture projects in Australia and Brazil. In 2008 Hearn was awarded a Kiriyama Fellowship from the University of San Francisco for his work on China's relations with Mexico, and the Díaz-Ayala Award from Florida International University for his study of China's historical ties with Cuba. Since 2010 he has chaired or co-chaired the Latin American Studies Association (LASA) Section for Asia and the Americas. He is currently undertaking a comparative study of urban agriculture in Beijing, Havana, Melbourne, and São Paulo with funding from the São Paulo Research Support Foundation (FAPESP). His books include *Diaspora and Trust: Cuba, Mexico, and the Rise of China* (2016), *China Engages Latin America: Tracing the Trajectory* (2011), and *Cuba: Religion, Social Capital, and Development* (2008).

Independent filmmaker **ANN KANEKO** is known for her personal films that weave her intimate aesthetic with the complex intricacies of political reality. Often involving subjects in other parts of the world, Kaneko poetically probes the intersection where power impacts the personal. Her films have screened internationally at numerous festivals, and she has been commissioned by the

National Endowment for the Arts and the Getty Center. Her films include *A Flicker in Eternity; Against the Grain: An Artist's Survival Guide to Perú*; *Overstay*; and *100% Human Hair*. Kaneko has been a Fulbright and Japan Foundation Artist fellow and graduated with an MFA in film directing from UCLA. She is the artist mentor for Visual Communications' Armed with a Camera fellowship and currently teaches media studies at Pitzer College.

JULIA KATZ is a graduate student in the Department of History at Rutgers University, New Brunswick. Her research examines Chinese migration to the Hawaiian Islands around the turn of the twentieth century, when American annexation and the extension of Chinese exclusion laws changed the stakes of migrant society, enterprise, mobility, and claims to belonging. She is particularly interested in histories of interracial economic intimacies between migrant Chinese and Native Hawaiians, which offered alternative visions to both white settler colonialism and plantation capitalism. Her work engages questions of American empire, critiques of Asian settler colonialism, and critical indigenous theory.

JUNYOUNG VERÓNICA KIM is an assistant professor of Visual Culture/Media and Latin American Cultural Studies and Literature in the Department of Hispanic Languages and Literatures at the University of Pittsburgh. She received a Ph.D. in Latin American literature with a minor in comparative literature and Asian studies from Cornell University. Both transnational and interdisciplinary in scope, her field of research includes modern and contemporary Latin American literature, Latin American and Korean cinema, cultural studies, critical race and gender studies, and immigration history. She has published articles on Latin American literary studies, Korean immigration in Argentina, as well as on the impact of globalization on New Wave Latin American cinema. Her book in progress, *Asia/Latin America: The Politics of Area Studies*, explores the cultural and migratory flows between Latin America and Asia by looking at literature, cinema, and Asian immigration history in Latin America.

DEBBIE LEE-DISTEFANO is a professor of Spanish at Southeast Missouri State. Her manuscript *Three Asian-Hispanic Writers from Perú* (2008) brings to the forefront the literature of writers of Asian descent. She has many articles published that touch on the themes of cultural production, focusing on individual writers, *mestizaje*, and orientalism, all in the context of interrogating what it means to be Asian in the Americas. She started the Asians in the Americas symposium in 2012 and is coediting a collection *Historical and Cultural Interconnections between Latin America and Asia* with Ignacio López Calvo and Kathleen López. She is also coediting the new *Journal of Asians in the Americas* with Drs. Hsiao Ping Biehl and Luisa Ossa. She and Dr. Biehl have also cofounded the Asians in the Americas Association.

KATHLEEN LÓPEZ is an associate professor with a joint appointment in the Department of Latino and Hispanic Caribbean Studies and the Department of History at Rutgers University, New Brunswick. Her research and teaching focus on the historical intersections between Asia and Latin America and the Caribbean, postemancipation Caribbean societies, race and ethnicity in the Americas, and international migration. She is the author of *Chinese Cubans: A Transnational History* (2013), which examines Chinese migrants in Cuba from the mid-nineteenth century to the present through archival and ethnographic research in Cuba, China, and the United States. She is also an editor, with Ignacio López-Calvo and Debbie DiStefano, of the new book series Historical and Cultural Interconnections between Latin America and Asia (Palgrave Macmillan).

IGNACIO LÓPEZ-CALVO is a professor of Latin American literature at the University of California, Merced. He is the author of *Dragons in the Land of the Condor: Tusán Literature and Knowledge in Peru* (2014); *The Affinity of the Eye: Writing Nikkei in Peru* (2013); *Latino Los Angeles in Film and Fiction: The Cultural Production of Social Anxiety* (2011); *Imaging the Chinese in Cuban Literature and Culture* (2007); *"Trujillo and God": Literary and Cultural Representations of the Dominican Dictator* (2005); *Religión y militarismo en la obra de Marcos Aguinis 1963–2000* (2002); and *Written in Exile: Chilean Fiction from 1973–Present* (2001). He has edited eight volumes of essays and is co-executive director of the academic journal *Transmodernity* and coeditor of the Palgrave Macmillan Book Series Historical and Cultural Interconnections between Latin America and Asia.

ZELIDETH MARÍA RIVAS is an assistant professor of Japanese at Marshall University. Her research focuses on the conception of race through literature written by Asian immigrants in the Americas, as well as the representation of race in Japan in post–World War II literature and film. She has received fellowships and awards from the Ford Foundation, Fulbright-Hays, West Virginia Humanities Council, and National Endowment for the Humanities. Her work has appeared in *Comparative Literature Studies, Journal of Intercultural Studies, Journal of Asian American Studies*, and *Asian American Literary Review*. She is currently completing a book manuscript, *Caught In Between: Interstitial Identities in Japanese Brazilian Cultural Productions*, which uses an interdisciplinary approach to examine historical documents alongside novels, television dramas, poetry, memoirs, and films that depict Japanese immigrants to Brazil and Japanese Brazilian returnees in Japan, spanning 1908 to the present.

ROSHNI RUSTOMJI-KERNS has lived, studied and worked in India, Pakistan, Lebanon, Mexico, and the United States of America. She is a professor emerita from Sonoma State University. She is the coeditor of *Blood into Ink: South Asian and Middle Eastern Women Write War* and the editor of *Living in America: Poetry and Fiction by South Asian Americans*, and *Encounters: People of Asian Descent* *in the Americas.* Her short stories and essays have appeared in journals and anthologies in the United States of America, Canada, Pakistan, India, and Mexico. Her novel *The Braided Tongue* was published in 2003. Her novella *The Great American Movie Script* is scheduled to be published in 2015.

MARTIN A. TSANG is an anthropologist and received his Ph.D. from Florida International University. His doctoral research focused on Chinese influence in Afro-Cuban religions. Tsang has undertaken fieldwork on Afro-Atlantic religions and Chinese diasporas in Cuba and in other countries of the Caribbean and Latin America. He has also worked on applied anthropological projects investigating the syndemics of HIV, intravenous drug use, and tourism in the Dominican Republic. Tsang is a Council on Library and Information Resources (CLIR) postdoctoral fellow at the University of Miami.

INDEX